D1504554

BORN TO HATE
REBORN TO LOVE

Klaus Kenneth

Born to Hate
Reborn to Love

A SPIRITUAL ODYSSEY FROM HEAD TO HEART

MOUNT THABOR PUBLISHING

2012

BORN TO HATE, REBORN TO LOVE
A SPIRITUAL ODYSSEY FROM HEAD TO HEART
Copyright © 2012 by Klaus Kenneth

First American edition 2012

Mount Thabor Publishing
106 Hilltop Road
Dalton, PA 18414 USA

www.thaborian.com

Printed in the United States of America

*All rights reserved. No part of this publication may be reproduced,
stored in a retrieval system, or transmitted, in any form or by any means,
electronic, mechanical, photocopying, recording, or otherwise, without
the prior permission of Mount Thabor Publishing.*

Original edition

Zwei Millionen Kilometer auf der Suche
Paulusverlag, Freiburg, Switzerland 2001

Library of Congress Cataloging-in-Publication Data

Kenneth, Klaus, 1945-
[Zwei Millionen Kilometer auf der Suche. English]
Born to hate, reborn to love : a spiritual odyssey from head to heart /
Klaus Kenneth. -- 1st American ed.
  p. cm.
ISBN 978-0-9774983-9-0 (alk. paper)
1. Kenneth, Klaus, 1945- 2. Orthodox Eastern converts--United States-
-Biography. 3. Spiritual biography. I. Title.
BX739.K46A3 2012
281.9092--dc23
[B]
                    2012021953

This Work is Respecfully Dedicated to
Ursula (now Sr. I.)

Contents

Foreword *by Christopher Veniamin* ix

Preface xi

CHAPTER ONE: *Childhood and Adolescence* 1

CHAPTER TWO: *Running Away* 19

CHAPTER THREE: *Dark Arts, New World* 30

CHAPTER FOUR: *Seeking the Light in India* 42

CHAPTER FIVE: *Riding on through Asia* 57

CHAPTER SIX: *Regaining "Real" Life* 74

CHAPTER SEVEN: *Moving West* 85

CHAPTER EIGHT: *The Lands of the Puma* 101

CHAPTER NINE: *Return to the Old Continent* 113

CHAPTER TEN: *Entering the Cathedral* 135

CHAPTER ELEVEN: *A New Manner of Life* 155

CHAPTER TWELVE: *Gifts* 187

CHAPTER THIRTEEN: *Money and Other Matters* 205

CHAPTER FOURTEEN: *The Hill of Difficulty* 232

CHAPTER FIFTEEN: *A New Door Opens* 244

CHAPTER SIXTEEN: *Have Mercy on Me, a Sinner* 257

Foreword

BORN TO HATE, REBORN TO LOVE is a story for our generation, a story that brings comfort, reassurance and hope to a world immersed in confusion, rejection and despair.

Repelled and repulsed by those who ostensibly represented the Christian faith in his juvenescence, Klaus Kenneth naturally looked elsewhere for the solution to his lonely and tortured existence.

In his sincere search for escape from rejection and abuse, Klaus found himself on an odyssey that took him around the world several times, lured him into a vortex of pleasure and power, and initiated him into the great philosophies and religious traditions of our times.

Having tried it all, and reaching the very brink of the abyss of despair and the desire for nonexistence, Klaus encounters the One whom he had never thought to look for, the One that he had always discounted: the great I AM, the God of Love and healing, the God of regeneration and eternal life.

Dr. Christopher Veniamin, D.Phil. (Oxon.)
PROFESSOR OF PATRISTICS
SAINT TIKHON'S ORTHODOX THEOLOGICAL SEMINARY
FEAST OF THE NATIVITY OF OUR LORD, 2011

Preface

MORE THAN HALF OF MY LIFE has been spent searching for love and truth, and the physical distance covered during my spiritual quest involved travelling around the globe many times over. I have passed through India, Tibet and Thailand, and the Muslim countries of Persia (Iran), Afghanistan, Morocco and Malaysia. I have been to Alaska, Mexico and Brazil, trying out different philosophies, including Communism, atheism and hippie culture. For several years I investigated the Eastern religions of Hinduism, Buddhism, Islam and American Indian spirituality. At other times, I was involved in the underworld of drugs and took mind-blowing steps into Esotericism and the Occult. Nothing however could fill the emptiness in my soul, until the day I found myself facing seven guns. Only then did I have a dramatic and personal encounter with the Unknown God and was saved in quite a miraculous way.

I had always run away from God, from people, and from myself. This was a journey through hell, full of hatred and death, until I could face the truth of who I really was.

I heard the name of Jesus mentioned many times and just as many times I rejected and denied Him. I had no need of Him...or so I thought. Now, loved of a certainty by this very same God and surrounded by His grace, I find myself relating and singing of the love of Jesus, incredible and wondrous.

There may be a reluctance to read this story for some, when they hear the name of Christ, considering things of this kind as but an "illness of the mind". But one who is genuinely striving to discover the truth will read these pages with close attention and joy, and see how alive God is, and with how much love He protects each one of us, day by day, as we make our way through life.

How the English Edition Came About

THE AGE-OLD EXPERIENCE OF THE CHURCH tells us that if you want to serve Christ, you can be sure the enemy will turn up rather quickly; and this is no less true with regard to the coming into existence of the English edition of this book.

While about a dozen translations of this book have been published so far, and have even become best sellers in certain countries, the English version seems to have been given special attention by God. Since the time I had signed a contract for its publication in English, and had already been paid for it, lots of people were eager to obtain a copy. But obviously God had other plans – and the resulting turn of events was due, as I firmly believe, to the prayers of Elder Sophrony. This "miracle" can be read about in the final chapter of my story, so I shall not burden this preamble by repeating it here. But the simple fact is that I did not honour the contract I signed in London in 1983. So, allow me to explain the peculiar chain of events.

To begin with, I learned that Alexandra Noika-Wilson – the sister of Father Rafael, a disciple of Father Sophrony – had made an English translation from a rather old edition of my book in Romanian. I was of course much surprised and very happy about this good news. There were a number of parts, though, which I had to revise and double-check, in order to make sure that everything corresponded to the facts. I was more than grateful for her work and wish to thank Alexandra at this juncture. She set the ball rolling!

Some time later, Milun and Mila, friends from Colchester in England, suggested that parts of my work would need to be "polished" by a professional writer. Milun knew such a man, who agreed to re-write one chapter, so I could see the difference – but in the end, his price was beyond my financial means, and so I gave up the idea.

At that time, at the Monastery of St John the Baptist, I became acquainted with Elizabeth Hookway, from Tiptree in Essex, England, and this wonderful and quite professional lady suggested she would take a look at the text, and was prepared to make improvements to it, if I so wished. After working on it with her for days and months, each time I would visit England, I understood that the text was in need of even more work, so that it would be acceptable to native readers of English. What a wonderful experience and time of friendship it was with Elizabeth Hookway, and also with her daughters, Becky and Esther, who occasionally gave of their knowledge, too. As a result of this collaboration, the text underwent significant modifications over a period of about three years. My thanks, therefore, go out to Elizabeth for all her help! And later, when certain other parts of the book had been double-checked by Ursula (now Sr. I.) – the other main character in the story – we felt the time was right to find a publisher.

I was convinced that this would be the easiest thing in the world, because the book was not only translated in one country after another, but even turned out to be a best seller. But obviously the English-speaking world – like its cuisine – is quite different. My assumption turned out to be wrong. Unfortunately, my first publisher, in London, didn't exist any more, as I found out. Other publishers, in the USA, said they were "too small" for such an enormous story and that it needed a more widespread circulation. They advised me to offer the manuscript to "Random House", in New York. But meanwhile "Random" belonged to "Bertelsmann" in Germany and there was no way to get through to them without an agent. Every time I approached a publisher, I would hear the same stubborn refrain: "You need a book agent." Where could I possibly find such a person? I contacted several persons at the "Bertelsmann" offices in New York, but all my efforts eventually came to nothing. After all, it wasn't their story. ...

Little by little it dawned on me that behind this constant refusal there had to be God's plan and also Father Sophrony's prayers. Consequently, I didn't worry any longer. Meanwhile, via the Internet, an increasing number of people from all around the world were attempting to order the as yet nonexistent English version. But I trusted Father Sophrony's prayers – until I met a world-famous author and publisher – again at the Monastery of St John the Baptist. Anthony Grey asked me, if I would agree to have him publish the book with "Tagman Press". From that moment on the floodgates opened. Alexander Press in Canada, St. Herman Press in California, my brother in Christ, Tony Anthony (*Taming the Tiger*), said he was ready to suggest it to his own publisher – the biggest Christian publisher in Australia – and so on. But this time it was me who was hesitating and trying to discover God's will.

My hesitation obviously had been God-inspired, because – again at the monastery – I met a person who was ready to execute what seemed to be the will and plan of God, namely, to re-write the whole story from A to Z, from cover to cover. Bruce, himself an author and journalist with a well-known magazine, kindly took a look at the typescript, liked the story, and offered to work on it. As the time he could devote to this project was very limited, I had to fly several times to Northern Ireland. And what I experienced during our time together made me feel like a little schoolboy with regard to my knowledge of the English language. I couldn't believe how gifted Bruce was, and not only am I profoundly grateful to him for his work on the book as such, but I am also thankful for receiving a good lesson in humility. Bruce gave the book an entirely new shape, reducing the original 30 relatively brief chapters to ten, and certain sections or passages disappeared completely.

But again, the enemy of God intervened, and during our collaboration in Ireland we were twice forced to abandon the project, owing to unforeseeable circumstances. It looked like it would simply never end. Bruce himself was in a terrible state.

I am at a loss to speak of God's wisdom. I cannot but thank Him, His servant, Father Sophrony, and, last but not least, my spiritual father, Archimandrite Zacharias, for all their common spiritual intervention.

It was Father Zacharias, who mentioned some time ago that it would be good to concentrate my efforts chiefly on the Orthodox world; and – why am I no longer surprised! – just after doing so, I met Christopher Veniamin at St. Tikhon's Monastery in Pennsylvania, and felt that he was the person God had appointed. What a long way from 1983 to this day!

By the prayers of the Mother of God, and of all our beloved saints, Lord Jesus Christ, have mercy on me, and on each and every reader of this book.

Klaus Kenneth
CHRISTMASTIDE, 2011

CHAPTER ONE

CHILDHOOD AND ADOLESCENCE

"ADMIT that you stole that apple!"

"No!"

Whack! A heavy blow from the eighteen year-old boy strikes my face.

"Now admit it. You stole it, didn't you?"

"No!" I continued shouting in despair, and I was hit again and again.

"I saw you, so just admit it!"

"No, no!" the five year-old protested.

I was black and blue from the beating, everything was spinning round and I nearly blacked out.

Again the hard blows rained down. The more I received, the more hardened I became, hating the big boy for hitting me, a small child.

"No never, no!" I shouted. "I haven't taken any apples!"

The adults intervened at that moment, fortunately for me, and our parents, looking very shocked, forcibly separated us.

In my helpless state I won their compassion and none of them paid any attention to the question of guilt. I had in fact stolen an apple from our landlord's tree. But my pride, and the hatred I felt for people in general, prevented me from acknowledging this fact, which I would have died rather than be forced to admit to.

I was bad and hated the world, and in return the world hated me. In the years that followed I survived death more than twenty times: by fire, gas, bullets, water, knife, snakes, drugs, war, suicide, accidents, demons, lynching – only God knows how! Over the course of time, I became convinced that God really knew everything. His grace, which seeks us out and knows us thoroughly, had always been my salvation through the horrors and the hell that I lived through. I had always been a dreamer, and my dream was always beautiful. Sadly, time and time again I fell into the net of the world, because I made the mistake of trusting people. It didn't take me long to discover that the world was in reality such a bad place that "it couldn't possibly be true". However, my only hope was to keep on trusting in people.

The whole sad story began even before conception. My mother never seemed to have accepted me; she couldn't accept life itself. How can this be understood? Today, by the grace of the Holy Spirit, I can recognize and distinguish how the demons, the powers and principalities of darkness and other (unseen) occult forces, direct a person's life, without their being fully aware of why they made this or that choice – at least, so long as their manner of life keeps them outside the power of God's grace.

The powers of darkness are at enmity with life. Scripture tells us that occult influences can be inherited and be active as far back as the fourth generation (Exod. 20:5). In this way, I can explain my mother's attitude and inability to love, even though she wanted children. This is either due to her involvement with the spirits or to what she had inherited from her own mother, or it may be that she herself was never the object of parental love either. I believe that her longing to possess something that would outlive her – between the two world wars everything had been taken away from her – was the reason for her fatal, possessive love. From the moment of my birth I was undoubtedly under the influence of these destructive forces, and before her death she often related to me her experiences with the spirit world and things about her own mother. It was because of these experiences that my mother was unable to accept a new life – in other words, me. I am not now speaking of a conscious decision, but of the state of her soul.

One day I was in deep inner meditation, when I lived through this rejection of my mother. My soul existed from the moment of conception, and by the power of an unknown spirit I could feel, very clearly indeed, that I was, that I existed. I knew that I was living. But this lasted only a fraction of a second, when the "other spirit", the enemy of Love, through the heart and soul of my mother, attacked the new life. This produced a very powerful inner explosion: I burst like a soap bubble.

My "being", having just appeared, writhed in the pain of this deadly experience, while my immortal soul knew that I was no longer alive. I experienced this state in full consciousness.

Biologically speaking, though, my development ran its normal course and when, nine months later, I was born, I did not see "light", but only the "darkness" of the world, and this in a twofold way.

I was born in May 1945, in a tiny village, west of Prague. But my parents had no particular connection with the place. My mother's labour pains came on as our family was making a desperate journey southwards, fleeing the Allied bombing of Berlin, where my parents had, until a few months earlier, enjoyed quite a glamorous existence. She was a famous opera singer; he was a conductor. As the Allied armies closed in, they set out with my two older brothers – aged two and one at the time – hoping to reach a southern region of Germany where relatives might shelter them. Initially they travelled on a hay-cart.

As they made their way through the present-day Czech Republic, they were surrounded by grisly reminders of the hatred that Nazi Germany had inspired among all its adversaries. Towns and villages were bombed and burned, massacred bodies of German soldiers hung from lampposts. But they pressed on, determined to escape the Red Army as it advanced from the east. Only my imminent arrival forced them to stop. My mother needed to lie down somewhere as her labour pains grew worse. The midwife my father found was dead drunk on arrival, and so he had to help as best he could. A little later I was placed in the feeding-trough of a cold stable where a high wind was blowing. But that was not for long, as the soldiers were approaching. My parents picked up their three children and set out on a goods train travelling southwest.

The journey came to an abrupt end, when a harsh voice, coming from inside the train shouted, "Get out!". All the refugees woke up and huddled together fearfully. Before they had time to obey, somebody started raking the passengers with machine-gun fire. My parents could not tell the nationality of the attackers. But miraculously, our family was saved by the furious shooting of an American soldier, who intervened to stop the massacre. It was only forty years later that my father told me about my first narrow escape.

I was later to have a second survival experience, somewhere on the road to southern Germany. There was no food to be found anywhere and I was on the point of starving to death. In despair, my mother went to all the nearby hospitals to beg for food. In a pitiful state, she would show me to the doctor and nurses in charge. But their answers were cold and clear: "Think yourself lucky if you have your child with you for one or two more days – he will not survive. There's not a scrap of food to be had." But then a kind American soldier turned up and gave my mother two cans of condensed milk and some other food needed for survival. Once again, a sign of divine love, which showed that God held his protecting hand over the newly born Klaus and he was not going to die.

Further torments awaited my mother, a young and attractive woman. On arriving in the southern city of Augsburg, she was dragged out from the cattle train in which we had all been travelling in hiding and pulled along to the stationmaster's house. A little later she was pushed back into the wagon, pale and with a disfigured face and torn clothes. With tears in her eyes she told me, shortly before she died, what she had had to endure then so as not to be killed by the soldiers.

When we finally settled down in the town of Biberach, conditions were still very harsh, and there was a terrible shortage of food. But I was physically robust. Despite the famine, I continued to grow. The lack of food was far less frightening than the lack of love.

Our house, where I grew up –
in war-torn Biberach, southern Germany, 1945

Both because of her terrible material circumstances, and also for deeper reasons which concerned her own personal history, my mother was incapable of showing me real maternal love. Nor was my father – a charming but ineffective character – strong enough to guide a young family through those desperately difficult years. Soon after we arrived in our new home, he left my mother. The result was that I never knew what it was like to have the guidance and protection of a father.

Life as a refugee had not appealed to my father; he obviously thought that he deserved something better to eat than the potato peelings which were often the only available food. In our new town, things were not much better. My mother made soup from dry bread that she had collected from neighbours, but he threw it straight out of the window. Given his rude and unfeeling behaviour, perhaps it would have been better to have had no father.

As for my mother, she was so fiercely possessive that she was unable to offer real, unconditional love to my brothers or me. Perhaps one reason for this was that she had lost so much. At the height of her opera career, she was earning huge sums of money and enjoying the adulation of the public. Her home city of Berlin was now in ruins, and the theatres where she used to perform had been bombed to rubble. But her problems were not just material ones. When I looked into her eyes, I saw no maternal tenderness but something very frightening and dark, which made me want to run away.

Thus I had no sense of security and so became a stranger in my own home. From an early age, I would run away, sometimes for days at a time. Often, I would wait in the street for the American tanks to go by, hoping that the soldiers would throw me some dry bread or biscuits. On lucky days, they obliged.

Out of a perverse childish curiosity, I would drink the rainwater from the puddles and sometimes swallow the worms that floated on the surface. At nights, even at the age of five or six, I would often climb on to the roof and try to escape via the gutter. If I was caught, it would end in a beating. Over time, I became more cunning and I would leave the house unobserved, when my mother thought I was in bed.

Even at that very young age, I was curiously attracted by graveyards and anything that had to do with death. On my night-time escapades, I would pass the time by walking slowly through the cemetery and sometimes by sleeping on the graves. I was testing the limits of my courage, and also trying to hide from an unfriendly world. Perhaps the world of death offered a better alternative. Or perhaps my lonely walks were a desperate search for strong emotion of some kind, which would serve as a substitute for parental care. My brothers seemed to be able to endure our difficult family circumstances, but I could not. For better or worse, I had a strong sense of being different from all other children. This made me lonely and angry.

I would sometimes spend an entire night sleeping on a grave. I wished that the beings in the dark world of death would come and give me the strength to live and bring some sense into my life. Sometimes in the afternoons I would creep into the mortuary near the cemetery and touch the dead bodies. They had a kind of magical attraction for me. I was aware of a powerful force inside me, the power of despair and hate. I hated my mother, and all adults. I hated the surrounding world, the school, the teachers, and this hatred grew into despair.

My longing to explore the world of the night was especially strong whenever there was a full moon. Sometimes, my initial moves to escape the house, by going up to the attic, were made in an unconscious state. My mother would find me sleep-walking upstairs and march me down to my bedroom. During the time I was forced to spend in my own bed, I was tormented by insomnia and dark thoughts. I would twist myself up, or scream from mental pain. I did not belong to any world; I felt no love around me. The lack of love hung over me like a threatening shadow transforming light into blackness. Everything that I remember from that period today carries the stamp of coldness, emptiness,

Klaus – always unhappy

sadness, loneliness and fear. There was nowhere that I felt really at home. I did not understand why I existed in this senseless world. How could I imagine that God had a plan, a purpose, a mission for each person? If anybody had suggested such a thing to me, I would have thought it ridiculous.

Sensing that I was a highly unusual creature, the other children of the neighbourhood began to abuse and humiliate me. I had no interest in joining their football games, but they tried to force me. Sometimes they kicked me as though I were the football. This was a form of torment not just for my body, but also for my mind and spirit. I was left helpless by their savage games, unable to protect myself. If even a single one of them had accepted me … but no one seemed to want me.

I did not know what it meant to have a friend of my own age, or to belong and feel comfortable somewhere. I was suffocated by the so-called love of my mother. When I had been out for the day, I felt afraid to cross the threshold of our house and meet that woman, who called herself my mother but always talked about wishing she could die. My private name for her was the "woman of darkness".

Her mere presence frightened me; her gaze even more so. My sense that something terrible was going on inside her was, as I have since realized, perfectly correct. One day she took my brothers and me into the kitchen, and turned on the gas, determined to kill herself and all of us. I have no conscious memory of this incident; she told me about it on her deathbed. In any case, the attempt somehow failed. Not for the first or the last time God brought me out alive from a situation of mortal danger.

In my extreme need I began to build up a world of my own, a world full of dazzling heroes who fought to right wrongs and reverse injustice. The very idea that justice could exist in the world was something that I mainly derived from comics. My favourite character was a prince known as "Ironheart", whose life was one long battle. I began to fantasize about exacting my revenge on all adults and repaying them for what they were doing to me.

Thus I began to create laws of my own. Attempts to instil in me the accepted laws of human behaviour were a failure; I was written off as "unteachable". But that did not stop me inventing my own code of conduct. I listened to no one, neither my mother, nor the nuns who worked in my kindergarten – and humiliated me by putting plaster over my mouth if I spoke too much – nor my other teachers. Nor did I have any respect for the police, with whom I very soon came into conflict.

When I reached adolescence, my rebellious attitude began to attract the attention of other youngsters, who sensed that I possessed the charisma of a leader and very soon I was surrounded by other "street boys", and so I became the head of a gang. We used to mount shoplifting raids on the local stores. Sometimes there were vicious outbursts of fighting between gangs wielding sticks and stones, ending in bleeding heads and black eyes.

In order to survive without being punished, I became an artful liar, hiding my street adventures from my mother and teachers.

When things became intolerable at home, I would retreat into the nearby woods, where I had discovered a natural hideout, which I made quite comfortable with a bed of leaves and twigs. No one could find me there – it was a place where I could devote myself to my schemes and fantasies.

I was determined not to submit to authority. But sometimes authority caught up with me, and I faced terrible punishments. In a state of fury, my poor mother would beat me with a fire tong, ordering my brothers to help. They would stretch me out on the floor – one brother holding my hands, the other my feet – and she would beat me continuously until the body which lay in front of her was covered in blood and no longer able to move. My brothers cried from shock at what they were being forced to do. My mother knew no other way. Which of the two of us, I now wonder, was the more helpless?

When a group of people love and respect one another, their human energy and dynamism is like the water in a well-made hydro-electric system which cascades in a positive direction and unleashes huge creative power. But in my world, the water seemed to trickle endlessly downwards, to a moral level that was lower and lower.

My hatred for the world, and my determination to wreak revenge, became ever stronger. Under the continual rain of beatings and pain, I swore to myself that I would never ever cry or show any kind of emotion. Had I done so, it would have proved my "weakness" and others would have been the victors. I did not want to concede such a victory to adults. Indeed, from the age of just five, I swore never to shed tears, and I kept that promise for another 28 years, when something happened to unleash my accumulated pain and grief.

Instead of showing my feelings, I spent much of my childhood thinking of ways to get my own back. One day, I was sure, I would be more powerful than anyone. But I calculated that to achieve my goal, I needed first of all to learn how to influence people and make them like me. I became a chameleon, able to show any colour or wear any mask. I began to feel that by this technique I would be able to penetrate people's souls, and enter into their skins. Sometimes I would play the buffoon – or whatever other role was needed to win my way with people. I resolved to develop these skills until I became powerful enough to prevail over all my tormentors.

In my later adolescent years, however, some dark psychological tricks were employed against me: things so sinister that even I was not cunning enough to avoid them.

For all my problems, I had enough determination and intelligence to win a place at a good high school. But I misbehaved from the start, answering back, provoking my teachers and engaging in acts of hooliganism. I think I was one of the first of my generation to sport long hair and spray-paint slogans. After only one term I held the school record of 76 warnings in the class register and I was already on the brink of expulsion. I was desperate for attention and I did not care whether I gained it through positive or negative means. Although I was sometimes capable of academic success, it did not fill the painful void within me, left by a total absence of love.

Klaus was always the black sheep, blamed for every unfortunate event or petty crime. Sometimes I was accused unfairly, and this enraged me. Whatever sense of dignity I had was undermined by the readiness of others to think ill of me in all situations. I developed a feeling that whatever I did, I would be blamed. This gave me a sense of being trapped.

In the whole town, people started to assume that Klaus was guilty of all manner of crimes. My reputation became so dire that even during lessons the police would take me out of class, and down to the station for questioning. I can recall spending three days in prison, where I met some young Chinese who told me they were Maoists. Eager for a sense of belonging somewhere, I embraced their ideals and kept in touch with them for several years – contributing articles to their monthly paper, "China in Pictures". Being arrested and charged became a ritual. Even when the accusations were true, I felt a sense of injustice. I craved to be part of another world where a different idea of fairness existed. In that world, my desperation and loneliness would somehow be eased.

As my behaviour became more and more rebellious, my mother's psychological state grew worse. In a confused way, she was trying to combine an intense practice of Catholicism with dabbling in spiritualism and attempts to communicate with all manner of invisible forces. She would go to mass every day, and often cry in church. Only in retrospect do I realize how much pain she was suffering. Certainly she showed nothing but anger and irritation as I got into trouble with the police. Her words of advice were always the same, that I should admit to all the charges laid against me. We had both reached an emotional point of no return – we could not stand each other any more.

As a last resort she dragged me to church. I remember how she had knelt beside me, sighing and praying in a loud voice:

"My God I cannot endure this any longer. I do not want to live with this wretched child any more. Please take him away from me!"

Then she turned to me and said:

"Klaus, I want you to know that from this moment on you are no longer my child, neither am I your mother. I cannot bear you any more!"

After that she continued to pray, this time to Our Lady. I heard her say:

"Mary, Mother of Our Lord, please receive Klaus and be his new mother. I entrust him now to your care."

This was her way of abandoning all maternal responsibility. Perhaps she saw this as a liberation of sorts, and maybe it was for the best. This was not the only time that the Mother of God was called on to play a role in my life, but her guiding hand did not become fully clear until much later.

From my mother's point of view, a response to her prayer seemed to come quite quickly. A Roman Catholic priest whom she knew very well, offered me accommodation in his house. I would continue to attend high school but lodge with him instead of at my family house. He ran a youth organization in the city called, "New Germany" (*Neudeutschland*), of which I was a member. He assured my mother that he would undertake my education. She must have felt a great sense of relief that, at last, her insolent and unteachable son – so much more troublesome than her other two boys – was now to be in such "good hands". She would be rid of him forever.

Not long after this conversation I changed lodgings. As it later turned out, I was moving from a troubled and dysfunctional home to something much worse. But that was not obvious at first. I felt no particular liking for the chubby, middle-aged cleric who was taking me in, but at the time, anything seemed better than staying with my family.

Soon after my move, I received an instruction from the priest: "Klaus, come to my study at 8:00 p.m. with a passport photograph." Sensing something peculiar, I spent a nervous afternoon, waiting for the appointment.

It was indeed an odd meeting. As I sat in front of him, he put my photo on the table, took out of his pocket a small silver pendulum and held it above the image. The pendulum started to swing back and forth spontaneously, although he did not move his fingers. He then mumbled a few words, unintelligible to me. From watching him and hearing the tone of his voice, I presumed this to be some peculiar form of prayer. He seemed to invoke some kind of invisible source of help before beginning to ask me questions. I now realize that there was nothing good or holy about the help he was invoking.

"Have you done your homework today?"

"Yes."

The pendulum began to move to one side. I watched his fingers attentively.

"You are lying", he replied.

I had to admit to myself that he was correct, but I still felt that he was playing some kind of trick.

"Did you go to have lunch with your mother?"

"No."

Again the pendulum moved slowly. I lied deliberately to see if he could indeed discover whether I was telling untruths. It seemed that he could.

"Once again you are not telling me the truth."

Damn, how could he know that? What sort of strange game was this? Because I was unable to interpret his peculiar talent, I became very attentive. However, this did not help me resist the psychological pressure that he was exercising. The fact is he succeeded in breaking down my will after several more of these sessions.

It was during one of these evenings that I realized the deadly purpose of what he was doing. This is how events unfolded.

The priest issued a new, general instruction. "If you ever come back home after 10 o'clock at night, please come to my room, so that I know you are safe and nothing has happened to you. I shall then sleep more peacefully."

A few days later, I arrived home at about 11 o'clock. From a distance I could see that there was still a light on in the living room upstairs. When I unlocked the front door the light suddenly went off. He must have gone hurriedly to bed. What did this mean? I approached his bedroom quietly in order to "present myself" and say good night. It was obvious that he was pretending to have retired, as the light had been on only a moment earlier.

"Good evening", I said loudly, after stepping cautiously into his room. Why was he not answering me? I tried again: "I'm back, I'm going to bed."

A long silence followed, unending and awkward. Through the door which I had left half-open, a slither of light shone in from the corridor. I began to feel very uneasy. Again I heard that bizarre grunting, the same noises he had made when he was muttering those weird "prayers". A cold shiver ran through my spine as I stood there totally helpless. It felt as though an iron hand was clutching me round the neck, trying to strangle me. There was something corrupt and rotten here, something that in normal circumstances would have driven me out from the room – yes, driven me away – but suddenly I realized that I lacked the strength to do so. Where was my strength? Where was my will? All at once I felt rooted to the spot. Fear gripped me. Because of the panic I was experiencing my throat went dry, words were choked and a dark fear took hold of me. In a provocative, slimy and honey-voiced way, he issued an order: Come closer!"

Horrified, I realized what was in store for me and with all my inner strength I rebelled intensely against this horrible attempt to use occult powers to break my resistance. In my mind's eye, he was transformed into a repulsive, pig-like figure. I began to feel dizzy and faint because I was so frightened.

"Come here!"

The voice, even more repellent, took on a threatening tone. I rebelled. I began to feel as if I were in a trance. I fought in despair against the person and the powers that were trying to ensnare me. Everything within me was refusing to take the four steps towards that bed – the precipice which that bed represented – because it was clear that hell awaited me there. This odious individual also waited. He kept a threatening silence, grunting and growling from time to time. I was being lashed by a storm and my soul was tormented. I could not move.

How I hated my mother at that moment. She was responsible for what was happening to me there and then. I hated the police even more for allowing people like this monster to exist. I hated, hated and loathed the adults around me, who only knew how to exploit and inflict pain, as this pig of a man was doing now. I hated everything, the whole world and even myself, because here I was completely unable to defend myself. But I did not want to give up. Hate gave me strength, gave me the power to oppose this repulsive thing that was waiting to happen to my body. Hour after hour passed, as I stood there rooted to the ground, neither retreating nor advancing. An alarm clock was glowing in the semi-darkness. By midnight, I was utterly exhausted. Two o'clock in the morning … I could hardly stand up, my legs ached, the muscles had stiffened. Four a.m. – how can I get up and go to school? At five o'clock, I collapsed like a rubber tube without air, almost fainting onto his bed. It was then he violated me.

I was destroyed. In my dirty and defiled state, he let me go. I dragged myself upstairs to my room and stayed there until I had to get up and go to school. I spent that hour and a half tortured by frightening thoughts of murdering the person who had just murdered my soul. The serial abuse of my mind and body went on for the next seven years, daily, nightly. If my resistance broke, it was partly because I dreaded being sent back to my family house. Moreover, he knew I dreaded it. To this day, I suffer pain in my spine, legs and feet which I feel is somehow connected with the dreadful things I suffered as an adolescent. Hell, in the form of deceit, hypocrisy and blackmail, practised by so-called Christians, had found a new victim in me.

As a result of my appalling domestic circumstances, my school results took a dramatic downward turn. So the lecherous priest paid generously for me to have private lessons with a teacher he knew, and a fresh round of torment began. While I was doing my Latin exercises, I became aware of a cold hand moving under the table and creeping slowly up my thigh. My blood ran cold. As I studied Latin verbs, this beastly pedagogue had been carefully studying me.

About seven years later, when I was in my early twenties, I told my mother about all these horrors. Her answer was devastating: "You are telling a lie, Father R. is a Catholic priest and so he *cannot* be lying. *You're* lying!"

Such were my early experiences of organized Christianity. As though his own misdeeds were not enough, my clerical tormentor sent me off one day to a Catholic theological seminary in Rome. There he hoped that one day I would study for the priesthood. He told me it would be good to see the "institution" for myself. I was 21 at the time, but still in my last year at school. (My patchy academic performance had slowed up my secondary education.) I went, because I enjoyed travelling. One night, I climbed the stairs of a tower, unobserved, because I had heard some strange sounds coming from that direction. By slightly opening an iron door, which I did quite easily, I was able to look inside. The scene I glimpsed involved half a dozen priests I knew from the seminary. The acts they were engaged in made me shut the door rapidly and flee in disgust. A muffled cry of horror resounded in my soul.

That episode brings to an end the story of my early experience of Christianity, or what masquerades as Christianity. I resolved that for the rest of my life I would not merely avoid so-called

Christians; I would treat them with contempt and hatred, and try to destroy them.

In my rush to escape all the horrors I had experienced, I was at risk of falling into a very deep abyss, a point of no return. If Christianity was an illusion, or worse, were there any other values worth embracing? Were there no limits to human cynicism and deceitfulness? Everything, I felt, was a pretence and a disguise.

My late teenage years did not merely consist of erratic studies and humiliation at the hands of an unworthy priest. I had other lives too, both as a free spirit who liked to wander alone, and as an increasingly popular and superficially glamorous figure on the emerging rock scene.

LANDESÜBERBLICK   *Samstag, 14. Aug. 1965*   SCHWÄBISCHE ZEITUNG

Die Biberacher „Shouters" machen ihrem Namen Ehre

Baden-Württembergs beste Beat-Gruppe schlägt nur im Tanzsaal einen harten Ton an, sonst ist sie gemäßigt

In die Fußstapfen der Beatles, ihrer Vorbilder, wollen die „Shouters" gerne treten. Der Schuppen, in dem sie sich stolz präsentieren, wird ebenso wie das verstreut liegende Kleinholz (nicht von Fans) nur zu Dekorationszwecken benützt.   Bild: P. Mayer

Newspaper article about my rock group, The Shouters (August 1965) – I am standing on the right

At that time, I felt that I had no responsibility to anyone. I was as free as a bird. Who had the moral right to hold me to account, in a world that contained so many hypocrites? If a God had ever existed in my life, there certainly was none now. I was filled at times with a kind of desperate inner energy, laced with hatred, which drove me to seek power, because I was without peace and afraid of engaging openly with this miserable world. Another of my ruling passions was the desperate need to have a father. But the more I looked for a paternal figure, the more I realized that the ones on offer were quite unworthy. It was like trying to catch the wind.

In fact, one of the few things that I really liked was a storm. When the wind was blowing hard, I would sit on riverbanks or in fields and allow the gust to caress me roughly. I could feel it blowing through my hair and stroking my face.

The wind, in a way, was my father. I did, of course, have a mother in a more conventional sense, but I called her the "queen of the night", because from early childhood I sensed the blackness that enveloped her. I had a nightmare once, a vision of my mother sitting in a damp, dark grave, dug out of a rock. Her fascinating physical beauty held me as if I were in chains. I could not move. I was bewitched, and only when she made a sign with her hand for me to come nearer did I regain the ability to walk. But the closer I came to her, the more bestial her face began to look. From a distance, she had looked beautiful and glowing, but as I approached, a grotesque transformation took place. At the same time she extended her long claws, using them to pull me towards her, so as to suck out my blood with her fangs. I woke up screaming and terrified. In my conscious, daily life, too, I was frightened of my mother. But some mysterious inner drive prompted me to look for her in all the friends I knew, trying desperately to find love and possess it.

There was no worthy or good figure in my life from whom I could seek and gain respect. If I was to survive at all, I had to find a new sense of purpose and self-worth. I felt I might be discovering such a purpose when at the age of 17, I set up a beat group which became popular across southern Germany. I was already conscious of a musical talent, which I must have inherited from my parents. Our town hosted a famous annual jazz festival, and at the age of 15, well-known groups had invited me to play the banjo with them. So it came naturally to form my own group, somewhat influenced by the Beatles. We called it, *The Shouters.* There were, of course, plenty of things for me to "shout" about, and I was ready to do anything if it would shock people and in the process make me notorious or important. Suddenly, I started to gain a recognition that had previously eluded me.

My name began to be mentioned in school essays; newspapers wrote about my activities. In part, because of my shoulder-length hair – an affront to all established notions of decency – I became well known in the town. If all this filled me with pride, it did not solve the problem of loneliness. Neither did sex with female fans or groupies satisfy my longing for love. On many occasions, my rude manners provoked people to such an extent that they would throw stones at me.

This merely reinforced my resentful, negative feelings towards humanity in general. Nobody knew what was really going on inside me. On the one hand, I despised people and longed for revenge; on the other, my heart longed to be truly loved.

*I survived loneliness and desperation
with my guitar and girls*

CHAPTER TWO

RUNNING AWAY

THE GROUP'S SUCCESS helped a little to ease my inner turmoil. But I was still running away from my mother, from people in general, and from my own real self. I was convinced, sometimes with good reason, that everybody around me was sick, but I was far from well myself.

Given the conditions that I grew up in, it is a wonder how I found the stamina to endure so much during my adolescence and early adulthood. One of the things that drove me on was the powerful thought of revenge. One thing was very clear: I did not and could not launch into a conventional study and career path, as my brothers and school friends had done. I cannot even remember thinking out my future in any profession, because I knew that first of all I had to find out who I was and why I existed in this world. Despite all the vexations, it seemed that I still possessed a form of faith in something that had not so far been destroyed by the bad experiences I had lived through. This dim faith – in the possibility of something better – now became the target of the "prince of darkness". That is what I now realize.

Without much enthusiasm for my studies, I began a course at the University of Tübingen, which would have qualified me as a teacher of literature and sport. The move to a new town brought two big advantages: an escape from the lecherous priest and the chance to win fame and money as a disc jockey.

Life on campus also gave me a chance to dabble in the ultra-leftist politics which were sweeping through universities all over Europe and the world. Having heard lots of militant talk about the need for "all old traditions to be destroyed" and slogans urging people to "destroy what destroys you", I began to go each Wednesday to a series of meetings in a student hostel. The rhetoric at these meetings was all about bringing an end to the State. The main speaker was Andreas Baader, co-founder of the Baader-Meinhof group of urban guerrillas.

The group was actively recruiting, and it made clear that it would not hesitate to engage in violence, if that seemed an effective way of landing blows on hated capitalist targets. For me, their nihilist talk was like fresh water to a thirsty soul, because, in my mind, the State was made up of adults, in other words, the enemies who had destroyed my childhood. I joined the cause to the point of participating in sit-ins, occupations and minor acts of hooliganism, such as setting tyres alight. But I never came anywhere close to real terrorist action. For all the negative feelings I harboured, I did not have much appetite for inflicting serious violence. And in my *naïveté*, I failed to understand the true motives of Andreas Baader.

Even if there were limits to my desire to destroy others, I was still capable of self-destruction. Through the music scene, I began to experiment with drugs, albeit cautiously at first, and avoiding the heroin and cocaine which had become a habit for some people I knew.

At that time, I was working as a disc jockey in Tübingen from 6:00 p.m. to 2:00 a.m. There was never any shortage of female company, but one day I met a young woman who was somehow different from most of the people who used to hang out in that trendy night club. Her appearance and clothing were typical enough of our generation: a mini-skirt, long hair, a top with flowers. But she had a strong spiritual sense, which marked her out from all the women I had known before.

She spoke of the "inner light" of real values and of love. She brought me books on psychology, found reasons why I should begin a course of psychoanalysis. We had long discussions on philosophy.

She often told me, albeit kindly, that I was a "bad dog", but this was only on the surface, because underneath she could see a sensitive and precious soul. Soul? The meaning of this word was hidden from me. During the day I was a successful sports student at the university and at night a popular disc jockey, earning plenty of money. I was very proud of my notoriety. I would drive about in a turquoise-coloured American Chevrolet, wearing silvery shoes and a white fur coat, lined with pink, and surrounded by a bevy of young women. I was therefore unimpressed by her bizarre theories concerning my terrible spiritual life, as she described it. How could a braggadocio like me understand what this new girlfriend believed in? My old hatreds were still active, as well as my need to make use of others and to possess them. Because of this I was unhealthy to be around. It was nearly impossible for anyone to have a sincere relationship with me. However, Ursula – that was her name – paid an especially high price for her love. I was unable to understand her language. Locked as I was in a protective prison, I was not prepared to risk further suffering by opening up to the real love that she was proposing. It was enough to have experienced the "love" of my mother.

Ursula's wisdom was – if only I had understood – a sort of healing pill, which I should have been willing to swallow in its entirety: the sweet coating and the sharper-tasting, curative part that lay inside. But that was not my way. In any relationship, my habit was simply to enjoy the sweetness on the surface and spit out the rest.

Ursula endured months of suffering as I showed her my darker side and refused to try mending it. She was the only person I had met thus far in my life who could have given me lasting love. But her attempts to soften my heart came up against an obtuse barrier. Finally, having no strength left, she was driven to attempt suicide. For around six hours, I watched her fighting death from an overdose of sleeping pills, and left her in the end choking on her own vomit.

Part of me – a big part of me – wanted to be rid of her. She disturbed my world with her love for me. When she was around me I felt guilty, and so I hated her more. That was all I was aware of.

However, at that moment, God's loving care was strong. When she was only a few minutes from death, a feeling arose within me that I am unable to describe. Perhaps God intervened to save Ursula's life – and my soul. I went to the telephone and called an ambulance. But I had not turned into an angel. Such was my cynicism that before the ambulance arrived, I drove off to Nice to see another girlfriend.

At that time, I broke off my studies in Tübingen and stayed for a few weeks in Nice. I had had enough of philosophy, psychology and all the other subjects that Ursula and I used to read about. What was the good of my having devoured so many books? Maybe they had devoured me instead. My problems remained unresolved and like a blind king I was sitting on the throne of my pride, seeing everyone else as guilty and stupid except myself. This miserable, cursed situation I was in became unbearable. Once again, I was sullenly asking myself, where, if anywhere, happiness existed in the world. Like the traveller in Franz Kafka's novels, I was hoping to find a purpose at every turn, only to realize that nothing new had happened.

One day I decided I had to pull myself together and set out again on my journey. In a sudden moment of hope I left Nice and went straight to Hamburg, which was Ursula's home town. I heard that she had recovered. To my own surprise, I was deeply moved by the news. So I began to wonder, could the relationship which began in Tübingen continue on a new footing? Perhaps, after all, it was possible for Ursula and me to have a long-term future. Although her ideals had often irritated me, I also knew that she had something which intrigued me: a yearning for ultimate truth and a refusal to settle for anything less. I decided to give convention a try. We got married. I was still torn. On one hand, I was seeking stability, on the other, as a devotee of hippie culture, I detested the "bourgeois institution" of marriage. Perhaps both of us wanted to teach her father a lesson, who was high up in the legal profession. He couldn't stand me (especially after her suicide attempt) and tried to break up this "wild affair" that his daughter was having. So, one day Ursula and I went to the Registry office.

"Good morning. We want to get married today."

"Hey, not so fast – you can't do it just like that."

"What dates do you offer then?"

"Next week, Saturday morning."

"The morning is too early for us. We are late risers. Could you marry us as late as possible?" we requested.

"All right. It is an unusual request, because our office is closed in the afternoon. But we will make an exception in your case and for once we will come in to work later. Do you have any witnesses and do you have a photographer?"

"No, we haven't. And in any case, I don't want to remember this day", I answered.

"But you must have witnesses to conclude the marriage", replied the clerk.

"Then your secretary can do the job."

The week passed and the following Saturday we presented ourselves for our wedding, without anyone else accompanying us. The Registrar was very friendly and said that in his opinion we were well suited to each other. He tried to be nice. After a short ceremony he gave us his good wishes, but during the conversation which followed, I let slip a remark which told him what my real attitude towards marriage was. "In any case, you know, we'll be divorced very soon."

I wanted to show him that I did not take the act of marriage very seriously. His facial expression, having hitherto been friendly, suddenly changed. He was flabbergasted. That was just the effect I wanted: to disturb, to destroy people's assumptions, wherever there was an opportunity.

The next step was taken immediately after the civil wedding. We formally left our respective Christian churches, Protestant in her case, Catholic in mine. I had read some books about the history of the Catholic Church, about the Crusades, the Inquisition, Pope Pius XII and his ambivalent attitude to Nazism. My reading had convinced me that I wanted nothing more to do with such an institution.

Instead of receiving the Church's blessing, I sought healing and happiness in the hedonistic, cosmopolitan atmosphere of

Hamburg, which seemed at that time to be a more promising prospect. What I did not realize is that the devil is a sophisticated maestro, who can endow self-destruction with such a pleasant-seeming aura that we do not even think of the price he is asking.

What did the destroyer offer in the name of happiness? What were his tactics? An obsessive quest for happiness, brought on by the use of drugs, had begun to dominate my life, even whilst I was in Tübingen. But here in Hamburg, the evil one had become my real master. For the following six years my mind and my will would be under his influence. My relationship with Ursula lasted barely a year. My mind and reasoning were increasingly taken over by an obsession with sexual pleasure, along with alcohol, and intoxicants ranging from mushrooms to marijuana, as well as chemical substances. My desire to dominate people, because I was frightened of meeting them as equals, was undiminished. I was falling ever more deeply into the trap of false happiness offered by these illusory enticements. If I was right about anything at all, it was in my understanding that the cold and analytical logic of the West was not the whole answer to life. Ursula had helped me to understand that. But the alternatives I sought were a deadly deception. Perhaps the most terrible effect of a life based on chemical pleasures was that it once again catapulted me into deep loneliness. Under the influence of the drugs I had become hardened, and with a diminished sense of responsibility was continuing to justify myself, and deny what a terrible situation I was in.

After several years of self-destruction, I was having terrible and frightening visions, the kind of pictures that can be seen for instance on "Heavy Metal" album covers. Such was my mental state that even after one joint of marijuana, I would see my friends transformed into monsters. This had nothing to do with them, I was simply projecting my own inner demons onto the people around me. Things reached the point where all the human faces around me turned into skulls. During these experiences or "visitations", I became short of breath and sweated with fear. I was desperate for happiness, but the future looked increasingly hopeless.

Or to put it another way, I was shipwrecked and thirsty, but could find nothing to drink except salt water from the ocean. The more I indulged in chemical "pleasures", the more they constricted me. The vicious cycle was becoming impossible to break. My willpower had been annihilated. Instead of finding the promised happiness, I was not only destroying my body but also my soul, which was much worse.

Sadness was all I knew inside

Things would get even worse. Living as I did on the fringes of society, it was inevitable that before long crime would raise its ugly head. To support my drug habit, I began shoplifting and stealing pornographic material from shops in the Reeperbahn – Hamburg's notorious red-light district – in the hope of reselling it to tourists. I was arrested and taken to court repeatedly, although I never spent more than a few days in prison. Pornography became my new world. My naked body appeared in all the gossip magazines. I was always willing to model to make some extra money. Was that the kind of "love" I was searching for? At night I would sing in folk clubs and nightclubs in Hamburg and drink alcohol to excess, to forget the loneliness and lack of meaning and friendship in my life. One memory of that period tells me how deep and painful my solitude was. As I wandered round the backyards of the Reeperbahn, prostitutes would sometimes caress my hair or my cheek – not to seek business but to acknowledge a familiar figure. These tiny gestures would sometimes melt my heart: they were the only real tenderness I had experienced for a long while. Most of the time I was still running away – from myself, from the police, from my mother, from the world, and God. I had come no closer to the longed-for happiness.

I had never had a father at whose behest I could proudly go out into the world and fend for myself. There was not even a paternal figure whom I could defy, like a "prodigal son". For all his rebellious bravado, Klaus was little more than a crumpled leaf, carried along the streets by the wind until it disappeared from view.

As a student at the University of Hamburg (albeit one who didn't spend much time on campus), I enjoyed taking part in demonstrations against the State and Capitalism, even if I didn't take them very seriously. I needed little persuading that society was responsible for the situation I found myself in. The slogan was "anarchy" and that sounded like a solution to all my problems. Anarchist ideology allowed me to transfer all my grievances onto a social system that was rotten, corrupt and still dominated by the Church. I never realized that the "blow" could rebound: political hatred as well as personal hatred could easily be transformed into self-destruction as I became a cold, insensitive and lonely wolf. My suffering was imprinted on my face, though I did not want to admit it. When I looked in the mirror each morning what stared back at me was a frightening apparition, disfigured and grotesque.

My defiance of the law became increasingly more daring. It was harder than before for anyone to stop me. After all, what had I to lose? In my soul there was a great hollow, full of bitterness and unable to find satisfaction in alcohol, sex or other drugs. I could no longer face this inner misery and I needed to find a way out of the situation. Was there ever any path at all, I asked myself, that led to real happiness? In any case, I could not continue to live as I was.

One day, during the time I was living alone in Hamburg, I reached a point of utter loneliness where death seemed to be staring me in the face, offering the only available escape. I tried to commit suicide. But perhaps my body had built up resistance after having taken so many drugs. The sleeping tablets had no effect and my "wish" was not granted. My system was used to poison and did not react. I immediately tried again and swallowed a large amount of drugs with alcohol. Half undressed, drunk and staggering, I went outside into a temperature of -22 Centigrade. I lost my bearings in the inky blackness of a park, and I started to imagine that the snow and hoar frost were Caribbean sand. Not much later I found myself convulsing from side to side, through bushes full of thorns. In the darkness of the night, I stumbled and crawled through the brambles, scratched, dirty and covered in blood. I shivered and lay down to die in the cold, but in the middle of that black night someone I knew found me, brought me indoors and coaxed me back to life. Having survived once again, I felt that perhaps I was cursed not to die! Since I could not succeed on my own, let others try! I resolved to behave so outrageously that I would be killed as a result.

For example, on one occasion I stole some petrol. Within minutes I was surrounded by a group of garage owners looking as strong as bears. I saw them coming, but did not think to run. A few seconds later, I was literally beaten to a pulp with iron bars. It may be that God got me out of there, otherwise how else would I have survived? Another time, in a nightclub in Hamburg, approximately ten sailors who looked Chinese fell on me, after I strongly provoked them. In an instant I was covered in blood, left for dead and thrown under a table. But I was taken to the harbour hospital – only to flee, half an hour after arriving, because I was afraid of being followed. Despite suffering concussion and terrible headaches, I managed to drive 1,500 kilometres to Marseilles.

On another occasion, God protected me when a man whose wife I had seduced held a knife to my throat. His murderous motives were clear and I knew perfectly well who was at fault. How was it that I escaped that time, too? It was inexplicable. Later on, a revolver was stuck in my chest by a dangerous criminal, on whom I had played a nasty trick. He had been following me for days, threatening to kill me. Suddenly, he was standing in front of me, in the dimly-lit corridor of my house. What terror! Again I survived. During the same period of my life, I had another narrow escape, in New York, when I ventured into the black stronghold of Harlem. I had been warned that this was dangerous territory for white people, but I marched into the district dressed in white shorts and bare-chested. I was surrounded immediately, twice in fact, by groups of black men trying to rob me at gunpoint. Each time I emerged unscathed. I sometimes ask myself: Was Satan protecting his collaborator, or was the help coming from a God

I did not yet understand, whose loving mercy did not want to see the destruction of His creation? I hope the latter was the case.

One day, in Hamburg, there was a ring at the door. I peeped through the curtain and saw that it was my mother – she had travelled over a thousand kilometres to see me, her son. It was a long time since she had heard anything about me. But unfortunately I hated her, and her possessive nature, so much that I could not stand the thought of seeing her. I felt she should go back where she came from. I saw her through the curtain, but kept quiet. My door remained firmly closed. Soon after my mother's abortive visit, I made a really serious effort to take my own life. This time I must be sure that if they found me at all, they would find me dead.

It happened after I woke up one afternoon around three o'clock. I usually slept until about that time, after a night of alcohol and drugs in a club. I found myself sinking into a deep, dark hollow. I simply could not live like this any more. Finally, I decided to jump from the balcony of my fourth-floor apartment, onto the concrete courtyard at the back and thus put an end to my agony. Everything within me had died. I prepared to jump into the abyss, my whole body shivering. I was truly alone – there was no "risk" of anybody rescuing me.

Then something extraordinary happened. The moment I went towards the door leading to the balcony to accomplish this fatal act, I felt the presence of Somebody behind me. Yes, that is exactly how it happened. The memory is as clear as daylight. I felt that "Someone" was behind my right shoulder – Someone who radiated and threw out an indescribable warmth all around me, a warmth that penetrated deeply into my soul. To my astonishment I heard a loud voice saying, *"You are not alone."*

That "voice" was so full of comfort, hope and warmth, that my obdurate and solitary heart and soul melted like ice in the summer sun. I could no longer throw myself over the balcony.

Ursula came truly as a gift from God

CHAPTER THREE

DARK ARTS, NEW WORLD

DESPITE HAVING RECEIVED such a powerful message of comfort and reassurance, I was not ready to accept it fully. I simply did not quite understand what it meant. I did not know Who was speaking to me. The message was enough to save my physical life but not, at that point, to save my soul. Soon I found myself once more on the wrong road, embracing a false spirituality that was leading again towards death. As I now realize, the "angel of light", Lucifer the great deceiver, was preparing a series of traps for me, by creating the illusion that I could find happiness in clever human devices alone.

I began travelling more and more widely. I managed to save some money in Hamburg and started out. I felt I had to leave my country and the rationalism of the Western world. Paradoxically enough, my search – at least for a while – took me westwards, to the United States. But it was not mainstream American culture that interested me, but the culture of the Native Americans, as I imagined it. I was determined to explore "the New World" and I travelled approximately 40,000 kilometres, the length and breadth of the United States of America, Mexico, Canada, and even up to the frozen north. I found it was quite inexpensive to travel around the United States – either by hitch-hiking, riding Greyhound buses, or driving cars for people who needed their vehicles moved to a new place.

In my confused way, I was hoping that the Native Americans would provide me with a better understanding of life, of human nature – and of how to gain power over people. Nothing special happened, although I had a series of adventures and meetings with the Navajo Indians. Whatever the reason, I could not find any strength, love or wisdom in the things they told me. Sometimes I came across an attitude of racism towards white people, perhaps an inevitable result of a tragic history. I did find knowledge and expertise of a kind, but where was the Spirit that had saved me from death in Hamburg?

Even while I was still in Germany, I had gobbled up five volumes by Carlos Castaneda, the Mexican writer. I was intrigued by the "altered states of consciousness" that could be induced either by taking mescaline (the favoured drug of some indigenous Mexican peoples) or simply through physical and mental exercises. Indeed I had experimented with these exercises, and reached a state of mind comparable to that experienced by users of drugs like heroin. So the idea of travelling in Mexico was very enticing.

But initially I was refused entry into Mexico. Hippies with long hair were not allowed in because of "Acapulco-Gold", in other words, drugs. The moment had arrived for me to find out if the spirits described by Castaneda existed or not. If they did, then surely they could now help me to get across the border. I concentrated hard and called on those spirits to assist me. Lo and behold, a sort of "miracle" happened. The very same customs officer who had first refused me entry into Mexico was now arranging transport for me. My amazement was absolute. While I was still waiting on the American side of the border, I looked over the Mexican side and saw a large sinister black limousine, and I sensed that this car was coming for me. My intuition was correct. The Mexican customs officer, who had been so unfriendly when we first met, came up and told me that there was a place for me in this vehicle. I was both intrigued and frightened. I could feel strange forces coming from the car's dark interior, warning me not to approach. I felt an acute and disturbing pain in my chest as the powers emanating from the car seemed to assault me physically. From the moment I stepped into this monstrous vehicle, I entered the world of the occult.

We drove many hours under Mexico's scorching sun, eventually arriving at a camp of armed men hidden in the mountains, miles from anywhere. I was given a wooden hut to live in, and during the week that I stayed with this mysterious group, I had repeated conversations with the driver of the car, who turned out to be a "brujo" or wizard, just like the ones I read about in Castaneda's books. At very first glance, his appearance and clothing were that of a typical middle-aged Mexican, but I soon noticed he had a penetrating gaze. His walk and demeanour suggested a strange inner confidence. He and his comrades claimed to have assassinated a leading figure among the Mormons in Utah. They also told me in all seriousness that they wanted to overthrow the American government. The brujo had several "wives" living in different towns nearby and he drove me around with him as he visited one spouse after another. In between bursts of laughter, he told me, and indeed showed me, that he had magic powers. He reminded me of Don Juan, the teacher described by Castaneda. For example, he could make objects appear and disappear. I cannot tell what was physically happening, but I experienced – in my own field of vision – the effects of his tricks. All this intrigued me, because I felt that I might be able to master his techniques and hence bend other people to my will.

After many years and sadly much too late, I understood that by getting involved with the occult, I was closing the door to discovering true spirituality. Everything that followed in my life simply serves to prove this point. In subsequent phases of my search for ultimate meaning, I was to encounter real demons, worse things than I had met in Mexico.

When I set out on my travels from Hamburg, I was filled with a determination to free myself from Western intellectualism and materialism. In some ways, this was a sound impulse. I was hoping that with the help of some kind of spiritual power, I would be able to live a life without fear. I interpreted my spiritual experience at the Mexican border as a clear sign of support from invisible powers.

But help that comes from "fallen spirits" is not freely given: that was something I was unaware of at the time. My engagement with dark invisible forces was to bring me, over the years that followed, to a dreadful point where my personhood nearly disintegrated. Although I did not realize it, my involvement in the occult amounted to a headlong rush towards death, and the only real cure for my deadly dabblings lay in committing myself to Jesus Christ. But I felt no desire, at that time, to look towards Christ. The pain I had experienced at the hands of people who called themselves Christians still clung to me very powerfully, and had given me an exceptionally keen nose for Christian hypocrisy: I had been profoundly alienated by my early experiences with individuals who claimed to be followers of Christ, but were themselves in the grip of something very dark. The very word "Christian" triggered a negative reaction in me. Still, I knew I was searching for answers and I felt, at times, that I was prepared to try anything – except Christianity.

Klaus in Teheran, Iran

Like many people of my generation, I looked East for religious inspiration. My early travels took me to many Muslim countries, including Iran and Afghanistan, where I stayed for a time with some nice and friendly people, but I never considered converting to Islam. My friends were not allowed to think for themselves, but had to accept unquestioningly the teachings of their leaders, which translated into an intolerance of other faiths. It seemed that they were somehow "protected" by the law, as by a fence around a chicken run, which prevented them from running away. This was not necessarily wrong, but I felt that God had created man to be more like an eagle, to fly high in the air – the air of Love. And love doesn't break the law. Love and Mercy were what I was looking for. Instead of the Merciful Allah, I found a religion that placed heavy emphasis on laws and punishment, and my rebellious spirit reacted against this. I had received enough punishment in my lawless childhood. So, in spiritual terms at least, my journey eastwards took me straight to India and the religious traditions of that country.

In fact, my involvement with the religions and traditions of south Asia began while I was still in Germany. Even as I studied the works of Castaneda, I was also practising transcendental meditation and yoga. How did that begin? One day in Hamburg, I met a man at the university who looked like Jesus: he had long dark hair, a long beard, a warm smile and wore a long robe. He was Maharishi Mahesh, the founder of the Transcendental Meditation (TM) movement. I was very strongly drawn towards him. His words struck a chord when I heard him speaking about his hopes of achieving world domination through TM. He was eager to tell me about the bank accounts and palaces which his organization possessed. At first I was convinced that he was referring only to spiritual riches; only later did I realize that he was talking in a very concrete and material way. Given that I was still engaged in a search for meaning in my life, I was ready to believe in his promises of finding inner peace through TM.

This was despite the fact that "His Holiness", as his followers referred to him, had recently tried to demonstrate his powers to a

German audience, but failed miserably. With press cameras present, he had attempted to "walk on water" in a pool, but instead simply plunged downwards. This fiasco failed to dent my willingness to follow his path. I steadily overcame my reservations and decided to take instructions from this new leader in my life. At least provisionally, I put my trust in my "master" and was convinced about his mission to the world. After all, he believed in himself too, didn't he?

From the very start I had a sort of mystical experience which confirmed, to some extent, that there was a place for me in the spirituality of TM. It happened like this. At the close of the first of Maharishi's two conferences the university auditorium was evacuated, as his second conference would be by entry ticket only, costing the equivalent of 15 euros or 20 US dollars. I sat in the middle of the hall knowing that if TM was for me, then it should be given to me without payment. My inner self was saying that "freedom" must not be bought, so I was unwilling to leave the hall, and indeed I felt unable to do so.

What followed was somewhat similar to the weird sensations I underwent at the Mexican border. All of a sudden, I felt my body being surrounded by an impenetrable shield, which rendered me invisible to other people. The stewards and supervisors passed through the rows of seats requesting the last visitors to leave. The next meeting was due to start two hours later. However I, sitting on a chair, remained unnoticed. People simply could not see me. Once the hall doors were closed and the lights extinguished, I spent the interval between the two meetings as if in a trance. However I became visible to others again when the lighting came on again and the people flooded back into the hall. I had no explanation for what had happened, but this experience of "invisibility" was to be repeated time and again.

It was not just that I felt invisible. When I had this sensation, I literally seemed to disappear from other people's perception. The experience in the hall tempted me to believe that I had been freed, for a time, of Western logic and materialism – something I did want to be rid of – and I had achieved this with the help of some other "beings" who, as I thought, were serving me. What I failed to understand was that I was also serving them.

Entry into the world of meditation – the third eye

The time had arrived for my initiation into TM. How did this happen? In a semi-dark room, the teacher made spiritual contact with the "grand master", called Guru Dev, who had been Maharishi's master. His portrait, surrounded by flowers, was placed on an altar. One had to offer fresh flowers to this "grand master", bring fruits and place a white scarf nearby as a symbol of purity. The fragrant joss sticks and candles brought a sense of sacred mysticism. A sum of money equal to a month's salary (with a reduction for students) and a promise of absolute discretion were required. After bowing before some unknown Hindu god, my teacher whispered a "mantra" in my ear – a syllable in Sanskrit.

When I reflect on this moment, I remember the teacher's gesture of prostration with a shudder, thinking of the early Christian martyrs who preferred to die rather than bow down before Greek or Roman gods.

The teacher assured me that every mantra given was unique and absolutely personal. This, as I discovered later, was a plain lie. Maharishi used only a certain number of mantras, which were distributed according to age and gender. His mantras came from an old form of Sanskrit that had been adapted by Maharishi for the Western tradition. To clarify this point, I record here a few mantras I heard from some disappointed people who had left this practice: "ema", "aoum", "aïm", "ijenga" (for the age-group 22–23 years), "shamma", "shiring" (for the 30–34 year olds), "shirom", "keng", and of course the well-known mantra, "om". "Aaing", for example, is the name of a Hindu god, combined with "namah" – pronounced 26 times at the initiation rite. It means, "I bow down to you." Later on, the word 'Shri' is added, and you would then say, "Shri Aaing Namah", which means, "I bow down before you, noble Aaing". All this was taught to Maharishi by his godly Guru Dev, with the order to convert the world to Hinduism. In the world of TM, entry into paradise was not free. The fee that students had to pay to undergo a basic initiation was the equivalent of 200 euros. Books by Maharishi cost a bit extra.

However, for a few years I patiently meditated on the word – which was my mantra – waiting for enlightenment, freedom and wisdom. I was still meditating at the time I went to Mexico, and tried absorbing the tricks of my wizard teacher.

I remember from my Hamburg days being told that plenty of other TM attractions were on offer if the basic initiation proved insufficient. Maharishi advertised courses such as "Siddhi", where one could learn to levitate, at a price which could be as much as

5,000 euros. Also proposed was advice on how to obtain "health and immortality", as well as courses on a new "world order", "economic enlightenment", "foresight" and "passing through walls". The price of any of these courses could range as high as 20,000 euros.

One morning I did indeed have a surprise. During my TM session, the figure of a fascinating woman appeared in my mind's eye. Her alluring expression seemed to paralyse me. That same night I was invited to a party by some friends. Finding myself to be the first of the guests, I rang the hostess's bell. When the door opened there I was face to face with the woman I had seen in my vision. Delighted by this "apparition" I needed no further confirmation that TM really worked. During the years that followed, a number of bad things happened to me as a result of my association with this person. Without knowing that she was a "center of evil spirits", or let's say, a "witch", I fell into her trap, in a way that reminded me of what I had experienced with my mother, and several times in the months that followed I feared for my life – a fear that was accompanied by a real sense of suffocating. This lasted for several years, though interrupted by long periods of separation (of 7 to 9 months at a time). It was extremely difficult to "get rid of her", and just before I thought I would die, someone came to rescue me from her spiritual grip. (Though even today, I feel that this woman is still "looking for me".) All of this was enough to convince me that TM had an evil and diabolical influence on my life.

In the ensuing period of my TM practice I slowly began to see the movement's emphasis on the commercial, money-making strategies of the West, rather than the real needs of man. Nevertheless, I continued to meditate faithfully for twenty minutes each morning and evening. After some time doing these exercises and practices, I began to feel that my mind and thinking were taking strange turns. Or was it my soul? My transcendental experiences were penetrating deeper and deeper. Sometimes I would have the feeling of being in a long tunnel at the end of which there was light, or I felt as if I were paralysed, passive and unable to challenge anything, even had I wanted to.

Instead of the inner peace that I should have been experiencing, I found myself in a sort of mental fog. I was becoming more and more impatient. I was becoming indifferent to worldly concerns, but that made me nervous, not peaceful. The teachers of TM said this state reflected a dissolving of stress. They were never short of an explanation. But sadly as time went on I found myself sinking, not only mentally, but also physically. I was entering more deeply into my inner being, but this brought unrest rather than serenity. I did not know what was happening. I was still convinced that this was a way out of the analytical logic of the West, as well as an effective escape from my problems. Perhaps it would be possible to get through to a more genuine self, I continued to hope. The idea was that with the help of the mantra, I could gently push aside all incoming thoughts – even those about the hidden tactics of my master! – in order to open up the locked realms of my soul. As a result of this I, Klaus, was expected to merge with the "All and One", with the entire cosmos.

Maharishi and TM – A fake saviour

My master talked all the time about the dawn of the "Epoch of Enlightenment". Little by little, something completely different was dawning on me. When I learned more about Maharishi's organization – with the help of people who had some inside knowledge – I discovered things that made me suspicious of the total dependence of the pupils on their master. There were devotees who formed a strict hierarchy around their master and took vows of faith to venerate him. As in other religious and authoritarian systems, there were many moral strictures and other formalities. For example, one had to walk barefoot in the presence of "His Holiness". Men were obliged to shave their beards, and women to wear saris. These rules were strictly enforced by the higher echelons. Members of the inner circle behaved with coldness towards one another, and maintained a wall of silence towards the outside world. Huge assets – in the form of land, hotels and castles – were purchased throughout the world. All these things made me think of the organization as a financial emporium rather than a centre of meditation.

As there was no positive change within me after several years, I suspected that once again I was caught up in a hopeless net. Later on, I met people who had had prolonged experience of TM and who had come to the conclusion that this practice can turn into self-destruction. Professor G.E. Schwartz, from Harvard University, in his research with TM participants, had concluded that "using a reduced quantity of oxygen, slowing down the breathing, being in a balanced bodily state with a reduced pulse and a higher electrification of the skin were phenomena symptomatic of people who had just returned from the beach." My experience showed me that TM's release from some forms of stress had become quite "suffocating". I began to feel a growing, irrational fear of the ordinary things of life. I also felt a deeper spiritual anxiety, a sense that some force was waiting in hiding to attack me. Something was very rotten in all this. The more I practised, the more my nerves were strained.

Another change I noticed was a growing pride, a sense that I could now become my own god. I hoped that in this way I would have access to spirits and demons and would then be their apprentice and collaborator. I now realize that in Maharishi I had found a false "Christ". The idea of leaving this world – which TM promised – seemed half-attractive to my young self, but another part of me did not want to abandon this world. I wanted to remain on the earth, but I had to find a way of going upwards, not downwards.

What could I do to improve my situation? Had I truly been able to manipulate forces that could help me to reach my "never forgotten" goal, to have power? Was it not *me* who was really being manipulated? As I now understand, there was no source of restraint or guidance, which could have helped me to avoid traps. The Holy Spirit was not active in my life, and therefore I was badly equipped to discern the influence of dark spirits.

I might have thought that I was on the path towards holiness and purity, but what I had seen was just a series of false halos and false enticements. After several years of TM, my nerves were strained to the utmost. I was full of inner tension and paralysing fears. My conscience – my sense of right and wrong – had become obscured and foggy. Despite all that, I held to the belief that my TM practice was more important than university studies, which I abandoned. My best hope of escape from a miserable existence seemed to lie in the states of ecstasy and trance I sometimes experienced. But because there was nothing divine in TM, I always woke up feeling possessed by my vices: sex, lying, cheating. I was left unbearably frustrated.

CHAPTER FOUR

SEEKING THE LIGHT IN INDIA

IN THE END, in order to find the true roots of TM, which are in
Hinduism, I went to India, the source of these teachings. There I
came to know the multitudinous forms of Hinduism. But the first
thing I found out was that Maharishi, adapting to Western needs,
was teaching a personal version of Hinduism, whose real devotees
were often wary of. The technique of levitation (or Siddhi),
which the TM movement teaches, is something that mainstream
Hinduism warns against.

Seeking spiritual depth through music – in Calcutta

In 1975 I decided to try living in India. I had already paid several long visits to that country. But at the age of 30, having quit my studies at two universities and failed to find any permanent spiritual or physical home, I felt that somewhere in India's vast religious tradition, I might find lasting peace and the ability to live without fear. Unfortunately, I still imagined life without fear as a life of domination over others.

When I settled in India, I had great hopes for a future in the world of Hinduism. I wanted nothing more to do with sects, only a religion, such as the one that is practised by believers in India. Perhaps there I would resolve my problems. Would I also find in this religion the answer to the mystery of life? I meditated and prayed to the eternal being, Brahma, in many ways, by practising yoga, calculating festive days astrologically, going through the temple rituals before statues of Hindu gods, demons and demigods. Someone had calculated that there are some 33 million Hindu gods. In the next seven years I travelled more than 30,000 kilometres, the length and breadth of India, from high up in the Himalayas to the southernmost point of the country. I visited the temples of Brahma, Shiva, and Vishnu, the three most important Hindu deities. I also met renowned teachers, such as Sai Baba, whom I found to be a huge disappointment.

During my time in India, through intensive meditation, I acquired a certain ability as a medium, and I developed the ability simply to look at people and tell things about their psychic state. I was able to use my newly acquired skills to speak to teachers from the other world, such as Swami Vivekananda, Sri Aurobindo, Ma, Paramahansa Yogananda, or Ramakrishna. They gave me messages from beyond. I was virtually taken captive by some of these experiences: they filled me with pride, convincing me that I really was a somebody, perhaps an important guru. But although I laboured intensely, nothing positive happened to my spiritual state.

In the Hindu teachings, I learnt a series of philosophical axioms such as the doctrine of karma, the idea that "as man sows, so shall he reap". I also picked up the idea of reincarnation which seemed logical, to begin with.

But I found a religion foreign to a European mind. Anything you like could become a god and be prayed to: cows, monkeys, elephants, money, people, rats, yes even myself. But how could I establish a personal relationship with such gods? It was also clear that demons who exercised divine power really frightened the Hindus I met. But I could not find any form, order, system or clarity in this situation. From one point of view, the lack of order seemed positive. It represented a release from the rationalism and materialism, and the analytical thinking of the West, which seeks explanations and wants everything classified. I was already convinced that it was impossible to access, through logic alone, the mysteries of inner being, and I wondered whether Hinduism, in all its complexity, might provide an answer.

I began to see that the system of castes, which divides faithful Hindus into five groups, was particularly discouraging. So was the teaching of karma, which at first helped to explain things. In fact, I concluded, karma locks man in a predestined fate by linking him with his past and that of other lives before him. The dire effects of karma can be observed among people "re-embodied" in the Dalit caste: they have no right to education, to certain kinds of work, they are despised by the four castes above them, and they experience that contempt right from birth.

To these poor people even entry into a temple is forbidden, with the excuse that they will defile it. For the same reason a Brahmin from the caste of priests would never shake hands with a Dalit. Was it possible that Hinduism was a form of apartheid? Logic convinced me that if Hindus have striven for thousands of years to attain a "positive karma", then surely after all this time, some positive results should have come about and be visible somehow. I thought that India ought to be a flourishing country, full of happy people. My one-year stay in Calcutta revealed another world: the fatalism of Hinduism, as a result of which the wheel of history goes backwards instead of forwards. In the life I saw around me, I could see little sign of people freed from the constraints of "selfhood". When even rats were adored and worshipped as reincarnated holy souls (as I had observed in Calcutta), where was progress? It seemed more like a downward slope, not a path of regeneration, and for me this feeling was confirmed by the external misery of the city around me.

None of these things stopped me from going further towards Hinduism and from thinking that here and now I had a chance of being freed from my long-suffering destiny. Here I was, living in the house of an Indian family, which had virtually adopted me, because I was a good friend of one of their sons who now lived in Germany. My hosts were members of the Indian middle class: the mother of the family was a headmistress. She gave a lot of practical advice about what was going on in the world of Hinduism in Calcutta – when a famous teacher would be coming to town, for example. So to a degree that was unusual for a European, I had become integrated into the life of an Indian family and their wider social circle. That seemed to present a perfect opportunity to learn about Hinduism in all its forms.

I still felt the Indian spiritual path had something to offer. I did not belong to the Dalit caste, nor was I an aristocratic Brahmin or a member of the merchant class. Logically, I felt I ranked among the warriors or Kshatriya. In order to avoid being reincarnated, one had to egress from the samsaric state, the circle of reincarnation. My task was to purify myself in order to escape endless reincarnation and reach a state of non-being. I had to redeem myself, to achieve separation from the materialistic world, which I recognized as an illusion (*maya*). The exercises that I practised and saw other Hindus performing, seemed rich enough in content, although they were different from temple to temple and from guru to guru. Thus one could go from such painful rituals as self-castration to going on pilgrimages on one's knees around the Kailash mountain. I practised everything from sacrifices in the temple to burning joss sticks, from washing in the holy waters of the Ganges to reading the sacred book of Bhagavad Gita. Like countless other Hindus, I hoped to be freed from the humiliation of a rebirth.

On my Hindu journey I discovered something new. Perhaps it was just a different form of meditation, but yoga seemed to offer me a useful form of help in my struggle to attain freedom from suffering, fear and guilt. Through my involvement with and practice of various rituals, I expected that one day I would become "guiltless". As to the real nature of guilt, no guru was ever able to give me an answer.

To begin with, my devotional practice and exercises seemed to help on a daily basis with the stress and burden of my duties towards the world around me. I chanted, visited temples, went to holy places. Yoga and other forms of meditation are relaxing at first, bringing peace to the nervous system, allowing the individual to control his mental and physical energy. This offers hope for transformation into a more positive state of being, a higher level of consciousness.

It can be easy for a Westerner to accept yoga as an answer to psychological problems, because it promises inner peace. This is a more attractive proposition than what is offered by some Christian priests, who seem to think more of their stomachs than of their parishioners. But who can tell whether or not the promised "deep peace" obtained through the practice of yoga or Hindu meditation is only an "anaesthetic"? This pain-killing effect can, as I later concluded, lead to spiritual paralysis, because it takes away the incentive for purification and growth.

In my case, I found that the anaesthesia offered by Indian techniques and practices had alienated me from my true self instead of enlightening me. I improved my ability, first developed when I was learning TM, to turn all incoming thoughts away. But this proved to be an emptying and depersonalising process. I now believe that every form of Hindu meditation is in the end connected by a sort of umbilical cord to the world of multiple gods, idols and demons, who offer to end the worshipper's suffering, but only through bringing him into a state of non-being, which is not in fact a state of non-being at all, but rather a state that signifies the disintegration of one's personal or hypostatic integrity.

In any case, all the spiritual "attainments" I had achieved, which included levitation, states of weightlessness, out-of-body experiences, brought me short-lived satisfaction at best. My own passions kept resurfacing. There was no sense of needing or obtaining forgiveness. My thirst for money, sex and power still had me in its grip. In no way had I obtained more freedom, in fact everything had become worse: the deeper I immersed myself in Hindu practices, the stronger were my feelings of fear. In particular, I was frightened of dying in a bad spiritual state. Instead of conquering death, I could not put it out of my mind.

This was not what I was truly seeking. In other words, instead of being a means to end my problems, all this yoga, meditation and astral journeys had only suppressed them for a short while. When I awoke from the "anaesthesia" these practices offered, all was just as it had been before. For me, such spiritual self-control was nothing other than a technique to keep away unpleasant thoughts for a certain time. In no wise did they offer me a way of mastering, much less dissolving, my stubborn passions and contemptuous hatred. The unknown mystical forces I experienced through yoga totally absorbed me for a while, but this had the bad effect of making me more self-obsessed than ever. There was no way of communicating or sharing these experiences with anyone around me.

The one thing that kept growing was my ability to act as a sort of guru, to whom many Indians as well as Western seekers would turn for advice. Only a very discerning person could have told that I was a fraud, that underneath the mask of my psychic tricks there was still a very troubled soul. In fact, I remember one occasion when a Christian woman from Germany saw through me and resisted my powers. I was disturbed by this, because it happened so rarely. I myself was convinced, most of the time, by my abilities as a guru. But my compatriot's wise reaction triggered some healthy doubt in me. Perhaps I wasn't as clever or as perfect as I thought?

I had seen and perceived some extraordinary things through esoteric experience, philosophy, psychology, the religions of Asia, mysticism, magic and occultism, as well as some astrological dabbling, palmistry, experiments with exotic symbols, and contact with voices from the underworld, which I transmitted in my role as a medium.

By being involved in these quasi-spiritual practices, Klaus the guru was attracting others who were seeking the truth. When

I convinced myself that I was a real guru, I felt I was reaching my goal. Having been cruelly dominated by others during my childhood, I now wanted to dominate the people around me and force them to adore me. As a guru, I would at last be powerful and influential – or so I often felt.

I often found myself talking to Westerners about the idea of reincarnation, which many of them found attractive. People who are attached to whatever they enjoy in their current life – sex, power and money – have difficulty accepting the idea that they need to sacrifice something for the sake of eternal life. But the doctrine of reincarnation allows such people to say, "I will become virtuous, but only in some future life." If a man believes that he will be given another chance, allowed to live again, he may conclude that he does not have to try too hard now. He can even afford to be lazy. Reincarnation permits us to hide our heads in the sand. Only in the next life will we "truly" start again. If now you cannot decide, well, never mind, there is always tomorrow.

Whenever I returned from India to Europe, I propagated esoteric ideas about reincarnation and found that people were very receptive. With all the experience I had gained it was not difficult to find the weak points in my interlocutors, to discover what they were controlled by, what they depended on, even to read their thoughts, to get under their skin unobserved. Such people respected me as their teacher – much more than I deserved – but in reality I was their spiritual oppressor. I was playing the same diabolical power game which had been played against me when I was a child, and the effect was deadly.

To some degree at least, I must have fallen, during my stay in Calcutta, under the influence of Kali, the goddess who gives the city its name. Kali – the dark one – draws in, through her erotic attraction, both human beings and other Hindu gods. They feel unable to resist. Then using a large sword, she decapitates them, so that she can ultimately suck their blood. She adorns her neck with the heads of those she has slain. This is how she is represented in clay statues during Kali-pujas or celebrations of the goddess.

The fearful godess Kali and fearful Klaus

None of the Hindu gods is able to stop Kali, nor can she stop herself. When I prayed to her, I saw her as a destroyer. Of course, for the ordinary Hindu believer she may represent something quite different. I can only speak of how Kali appeared to me. She became my new "queen of the night", my new mother. I might have thought that at last I had escaped from the claws of my natural mother, but it was Kali sitting on her throne who was holding me in her power.

One day, something truly remarkable happened. I had been meditating longer than usual in the Kali-temple, the only temple in India where blood sacrifices still take place. Shortly before my arrival, some animals had been decapitated, as part of a sacrifice, and there was blood everywhere. The faithful in their fear had sacrificed these animals to the goddess Kali, in order to keep her away from them. The entire floor was red with blood and I was sitting in the middle on a stone platform. After a period of meditation, I fell into a trance, and immediately I sensed death approaching.

It seemed to me that I could now challenge death by making use of my own powers. Once and for all I had to conquer my fear of her – I saw death as feminine - and gain victory over her. But how could I do this for certain? I have never been a theorist. It was not a question of conquering death in some symbolic way. I felt an urgent desire to meet death face to face and then to gain victory through my own strength. But where could I find death? Where was this terrible energy to be met? I remembered how, when in my teens, I used to play in the cemetery and made fun of the corpses in the mortuary. But at the age of 33, I had still never experienced the presence of death personally, nor had I seen anyone die.

Whilst I was meditating in the Kali temple, in front of her black statue, I suddenly fell into a trance. I had lost all my usual sense of control and instead an indescribable power or energy entered me. All of a sudden I found myself outside my body. I felt as if I had been wrenched and pulled upwards, thus separating my soul from my body. From the temple ceiling I could see myself sitting below. It was an "uplifting" feeling. Was I dead? While completely conscious, I wondered whether I had at last been freed from my suffering in this world. It certainly seemed that way. In the state I was in, space and time were nonexistent. I was neither afraid nor happy. Everything seemed "natural". There was a sense of, "Well, that's how it is" – no more, no less. I began to feel amazed only when I returned to my body.

After this experience the thought of death came flooding back. What was the meaning of it all? Was it something to do with death? And again, where could I meet death? What did death look like? Then, an idea came to me.

During my stay in Calcutta, I heard people talk of Mother Theresa, but beyond that I had no interest. At most, her name was known to me, because she had something to do with the Nobel Prize for Peace. Of course, I knew she was a Christian, but things connected with Christianity were nowhere in my line of sight. Then I remembered that she had the care of several establishments in the city, which were called "houses of the dead". It was then that I made the connection. As if it had been specially arranged for me, one of these places was in the basement of Kali temple, where I happened to find myself at this moment. Clearly what I should do was find this "house of the dead". With a strongly pulsating heart, I stopped my meditation in the hope that I would at last encounter the reality of death in this tomb-like cellar. I encouraged myself with the idea that this was the only way out of my situation. In my fantasy, I could already hear the shouts and lamentations of the dying and I was imagining their sufferings before death. Bit by bit a great fear arose in me at the thought of this meeting. What else was left for me? I had to find death, so that I could find life. I had to conquer death, and so had to go to that place.

On entering a vaulted cellar bathed in semi-darkness, expecting to find something hellish, I was surprised to be confronted by a deep peace both outwardly and inwardly. How can I express this? In this place the horror of death was not "at home" – I knew that immediately. But in a peculiar kind of way I myself felt very much "at home". Was this the "unknown" peace I had been looking for? Where did it come from? All these things were beyond my understanding. It was most strange and I remained rooted to the spot for a short time, surrounded by the semi-darkness of the cellar. At that moment, I was simply engaged in being, in living and breathing the fact that I "existed". How very strange! I think I was so taken aback by this unexpected sensation that I had quite forgotten the purpose of my being there. At that moment one of the missionary sisters came to me and I asked her:

"Where is Mother Theresa? I have some questions to ask her."

A new idea came to me as soon as I said this. Could I find in her a new "guru"? It might be that she could help me in my continuing search.

"She is outside working on the streets."

"But when can I see her?"

"We don't even know if she will return here today. However, each morning, at 5:00 a.m., she goes to Lower Circular Road, No. 35, and that is where you can meet her."

As that place was only a few minutes away from where I was living, in Park Circus, it wasn't too difficult to decide to go there the following day.

I set out early next morning, curious as to what I would see. As Mother Theresa was quite renowned, I half-imagined that she would be the same as most of the gurus I had met. I fancied her seated on a raised throne, surrounded by her favourite nuns, who would be permitted to sit at her feet. I imagined her adorned with garlands of flowers and smiling sweetly from time to time at some person or other, thus blessing their innermost being. At least that is what I was used to when visiting the "great" Hindu gurus.

Full of curiosity and hope, I stepped over the threshold of that place. Bang! Can anyone imagine what it was like when I awoke to the reality around me in that hall? When what I saw instead of a throne was a frustratingly simple wooden table. In that great hall there was no grand lady sitting on a throne. Instead, there were about a hundred nuns, all dressed in the same blue and white saris. Even more strangely, they were all praying.

I had not seen any picture or photograph of Mother Theresa and therefore had no idea which one of them she might be. All I really wanted was to wait until all those present had finished their prayers, so I could ask about her. There was a special atmosphere. With my lingering prejudice against Christianity, I didn't feel at ease in the midst of those Christians and their prayers, so I slipped away, creeping slowly towards the exit.

A moment later, a small, unassuming, robed figure came up alongside me and handed me her prayer book, so that we could pray together. "This is where you are wrong", I thought, "I have nothing to do with any of you Christians or your worship." At that moment my eyes fell on the words of the prayer on the open page. It was the famous prayer of St Francis of Assisi, which suddenly really made sense to me. At just the same time, something even stranger happened.

When I was a small boy, I had sworn that I would always be tough and never ever cry. Despite all the beatings and brutality, wounds and humiliations, I never showed my feelings, I never cried, so that adults could take on a superior attitude. But now, after twenty-five years, here I was with a trembling lower jaw and my chest beginning to throb as if an inner explosion was about to occur. What was this? Something was nullifying all my resistance. I was like a leaf carried away by the wind in a storm. At last I was crying! I was being overwhelmed by a force, which left me totally unprotected and helpless. I was so deeply moved that my whole body shook, and I felt as if I were giving up inwardly and collapsing. But the most astonishing thing was that I could not feel any form of embarrassment. I was in this state, sobbing and choking continuously, for three quarters of an hour. During that time a priest arrived who served a Mass for the nuns. When this was over, I couldn't utter a single sound. Trance-like, I left the place hurriedly and went back home. I had not found what I was looking for – namely, an encounter with death – but I had come across something entirely different.

Back at home, I began a round of Hindu meditation in the hope of settling things down. In reality, I had no idea what had happened to me just before. What did all this mean? Had I become a kid, a cry-baby? Unimaginable! That could not be. Was there some other "force", different from death, that was stronger than I was? As there was no obvious explanation, I decided to explore further and go back to the nuns the following morning. This time I would be stronger. I could not allow such a thing to happen again. After leaving the service, I felt utterly ashamed of the weakness that had been laid bare. So I prepared myself for the "meeting" with that someone or something through a deep meditation. I was determined not to submit myself once more to that unknown force, which, although not death, was stronger than I was. I attributed my sudden weakness to the fact that I had been completely taken by surprise.

The next morning, I went there half an hour earlier, in the hope of seeing Mother Theresa before the nuns started their prayers and Mass. To my surprise, the nuns were already at their morning prayers. I felt I should withdraw to the back of the hall, close to the door, but suddenly the elderly sister – whose heavily lined face I had first seen the previous day – came up to me and once again put her book in my hand. "Pay attention", I said to myself. This time *nothing* was going to happen! I was on high alert. But what use was this? As soon as the book was in my hand, my lower jaw trembled and the shaking started. Inconsolable tears poured from the deepest recesses of my soul. For the second time my whole world fell apart like a tower of dominoes. How could this be happening to me! However strong I had once thought myself to be, I was now touched as if by an arrow in a vulnerable place, without my knowing that there even was such a place. How painful! I was hurt! What force was even stronger than all my accumulated experience? Why had I not yet learned to control it? Crying bitterly and unable to speak, I had to disappear again, feeling vanquished. I had no words to explain what was happening.

Once again, driven by determination to solve this puzzle, I went a third day, and this time at *four* in the morning! I was sure that I would be there *before* their prayers and Mass. But I once again found them at worship. When do they get up! I asked myself in amazement. The elderly nun once again offered the book. Do I have to repeat myself? I wept for the third time, without stopping, until the end of the Mass – two hours later! I was somehow no longer part of this world, but was caught up in this place "that had a spell on it". I was helpless and unable to stop my mind, my thoughts, my soul: everything within me kept whirling about the room. I simply wanted to scream and escape. But I wasn't given the chance. When I handed the book back to my elderly helper, she grabbed my wrists and began speaking to me gently. From the moment she looked at me, I realized that this was Mother Theresa herself. She had witnessed me crying now for three days! As she began speaking, my heart was beating so powerfully that I felt my chest would split open. Suddenly, I realized why people in India called her a saint. Mother Theresa's soul gave off so much love and warmth that she had been able to melt my ice-cold heart. This heart, for so long one of stone, was transformed then and there into a heart of flesh and blood. She was a true mother to the poor, and at that moment I was the poorest of them all. She was my mother. I had never had a real mother, and yet I felt that she was the one and only mother for me.

Mother Teresa – encounter with love – my first mother

Still looking at me with great love in her eyes, she asked me first what was my name, so she could speak to me personally. Having witnessed my distress over the last three days, she now questioned me, with an intense look, as to why I was there:

"What are you doing in Calcutta, Klaus?"

At that very moment the "wise guy", Klaus, resurfaced. Proudly I tried to impress her. Don't forget, I had had extraordinary experiences in my search for the truth and I was even considered a guru. Like a man of great intellect, I answered:

"I am searching for truth!" That sounds good, I said to myself. Now she will receive me, of course, as one of her dearest disciples. She would be proud to meet a person as clever as me. Now I was worthy of her.

Instead, as she had not heard such nonsense before, she laughed loudly, and so heartily that tears came into her eyes. Without answering, she took me into her arms and said still laughing:

"For this you do not need to come especially to Calcutta." Holding me in her arms and with the tips of her finger tapping my chest where the heart is, she continued: "Deep down here is where you have to search. Inside here is the Truth. What you see there on the altar as the tabernacle is nothing more than a sign or symbol of what is here within, in your heart. The tabernacle is in your heart."

There was something so powerful in her words, and her simplicity was so surprising that it revolutionised my way of thinking. Klaus, the self-appointed guru, who thought himself so clever, was for the first time speechless. Two forces had come together, and mine was the weaker. What I had just experienced was sufficient for me to accept Mother Theresa as a person. But she was a Christian! I thought that maybe she was a Hindu without knowing it, because in my mind Christians who showed love were nonexistent. So for the next three weeks at our morning meetings I tried to convert her to Hinduism, which for me represented hope, despite the fact that my belief in it had begun to waver. She, on the contrary, was trying to bring warmth to my analytical mind, so lacking in love. She did not waste time enumerating arguments for or against Hinduism, but simply told me about Jesus and Mary and their divine-human relationship with man. After a few weeks it seemed that she felt I had not "succumbed". My search was destined to lead me once more into the "world".

"Come here", she said one morning, and taking my hand she opened it. "Look here. In the middle of each person's hand there is a capital M formed by the lines in the palm. So think of Mary, the great Protectress, as if she had engraved this letter so that you would never forget that she is the Mother of Jesus and praying for us to her Son. When you are in difficulty, or things are going badly for you, open your hand and ask for Mary's help. She will be close to you and protect you."

She added, "If you want, you can say a prayer that I also use, and it will protect you. 'Mary, mother of God, be mother to me and lead me to your Son.'" At the time, overwhelmed as I was, I was still not ready to say these words myself. But I never forgot them.

After some weeks, we said our farewells. And God only knows she was right about my need for the Mother of God's protection and intercession. But I still had to endure five more years of suffering before I could fully understand her words. I had been too deeply wounded by blind, mentally-sick or hypocritical people who called themselves Christians. It was not yet time for the complete repair of that which had been broken. My wounds were still open.

CHAPTER FIVE

RIDING ON THROUGH ASIA

I left Calcutta to take up the search for truth and adventure once again. I rode on an elephant for two days through the age-old forest in the Assam region, passing over freshly-made tiger spoor and through swirling rivers, until it seemed that this powerful animal had reached the end of its strength. When it rained, I would reach out and grab a giant umbrella-sized leaf from the nearby foliage and cover my head. At times, the elephant's head and trunk were straining to stay above the water, and my legs were all but submerged. I imagined myself drowning in the powerful eddies. Nevertheless the giant succeeded, albeit with great difficulty, in reaching dry land. Parts of the journey were so exhausting that I fell asleep on the pachyderm's back. These were certainly not spiritual experiences. More than anything they implanted in me both pride and confidence in my own strength and resilience. But there were limits to my interest in purely physical tests of endurance. I decided to travel to Kashmir, with the intention of heading for Ladakh in the Tibetan plateau. By now my spiritual interests were turning away from Hinduism towards Buddhism.

I took an indirect route, visiting several other places in India, before heading northwards. During the journey I had a mishap, which somehow symbolised the confusion and incoherence of my spiritual search. I was on my way from Poona to Mumbai. If you ask ten people for the way in India you will get eleven different answers, and this is just what happened to me on arriving at Mumbai station. I asked which was the platform for my train and straight away received the wrong information. It was almost midnight and the loudspeaker was announcing that the last train would leave in a minute. It was already too late for me to get to the opposite platform through the labyrinth of subterranean corridors. Each platform is separated by a three-metre metal fence, which is fixed into a ditch fifty centimetres deep. The Indians spat into these ditches the spew from the red betel leaf they chewed, used them as a public lavatory, and also threw in there the dregs of their tea and their broken clay teacups. In addition, people supposedly from the public health and hygiene office swept all the filth from the platforms into those same ditches, and then filled them with water, so as to stop the pestilential smell of human detritus wafting upwards from those horrible crevices.

Afraid that I would miss the last train, I threw my luggage over the fence on to the next platform, but it caught on the railings. I decided to do a high jump on to and then over the fence. Foolishly, I grabbed the edge of the railings and entwined my arms around them so as to get a grip. But the fence was rickety and I lost my balance. I then unhitched my rucksack, only to see it fall into the ghastly brown water with a great splash. Then the whole structure gave way, and soon I was up to my neck in murky sludge. Nearly immersed in that stinking filth, feeling bitter, miserable and soaked to the skin, I managed to drag myself out, along with my dripping bag. Was this my "crowning glory" for all the time I had spent with the gurus?

Chastened a little by this experience, I finally reached Kashmir and the Indian Himalayas. Through dust and never-ending snow, I crossed mountain passes as high as 5,000 metres, reaching the Indian side of Tibet by following the course of the Indus river to its source. Access to this zone had only recently been opened to foreigners, and there were still plenty of soldiers, who quite often came to check on travellers. But the area was fascinating and beautiful, and it whetted my appetite for adventure. Again I wanted to prove to myself that I could find what I was searching for without help from anyone else. Having arrived on the roof of the world, I hired a Land Rover with a driver. He took me to the Buddhist monks who lived in the wonderful monasteries on the ribs of the Himalayas, like vultures in their nests. There was an exotic fascination in the landscape, with its scenery and its shades of blue, white and brown.

At the foot of the mountain called Nanga Parbat (8,126 metres) I hired a horse and a guide, rode up the mountain until the guide became so frightened he refused to continue. He was afraid of bears and white tigers, but did not want to leave me the horse. Without guide or horse I could ride no further, so I continued my ascent on foot through the snow. My feet were almost frozen. All alone, I pressed on, until I reached an altitude of 6,000 metres. I had two purposes. I was seeking out a peaceful place to meditate, but I was also looking for adventure, because I wanted to demonstrate to myself and the world that I needed no one. My pride had not been shattered, even though Klaus, the guru, was on the point of losing his balance.

Going up into the Himalayas – my new home?

I did try meditating at that extreme altitude, for two hours or so, but I found it hard to breathe, and the cold was penetrating my body. I knew that if I stayed till nightfall, there was a real possibility of freezing to death. The cold was so powerful that no mental tricks of mine could prevail over it. I did, however, realize certain things on that journey, which took me so close to the highest point on earth. I was taking my leave from Hinduism, and perhaps also from the life of directionless oscillation, which I had been leading for most of my three decades. Time after time, I had looked for certainty and security, only to lose my foothold. Hinduism had its innumerable truths, its sacred cows and monkeys, its thousands of gods, and also countless sages, some of whom, without doubt, had led a far more ascetic and pure life than many a Christian. This incomprehensible religion and fascinating philosophy did not in the end provide me with what I was looking for. It did not bring lasting inner peace, joy, or freedom to my soul. Nor had I found anything I could recognize as love. On the contrary, each new form of meditation that I tried only confirmed the limitations of the old one. Everything remained in a state of "anaesthesia" that allowed me to forget the pain provoked by loneliness. I had to admit that I was still a prisoner of my own ego and unquenched desires for money, sex and power. Everything was the same as it always had been: selfishness, suffering and fleeting happiness, followed by emptiness. How could I teach others or be a guru to them if I myself had not experienced the fulfilment that I was trying to preach? That was exactly my own complaint about the other gurus I met on my long journey through Hinduism! Was I a hypocrite? In the end, all those experiences had only helped me to forget my problems momentarily. If that was all that yoga was good for, namely, to distance one's self from unpleasant thoughts, then it was certainly of no use in bringing about a real transformation. I was beginning to understand the need to avoid becoming enclosed in a world of self-absorption, and the last thing I needed was to accept a substitute for life, instead of true life, whatever that was. I had not achieved what I would now call union with God, despite my seven years of intensive experimentation. Something did take place during those seven years, but it was only a sharpening of my appetite for spiritual thrills, the sort of thrills whose purpose, unfortunately, was to turn my egotistic self into a kind of god.

The air was wonderfully clear, albeit somewhat thin, at those high altitudes. But there were still plenty of spiritual fog in my mind, the sort of fog which prevented me from understanding what was really going on inside me. And the meditation I regularly practised was not, in the end, much help. It promised enlightenment, but in fact it obscured the true path towards the light, and kept me from finding it. Instead, I was still chasing after false imagery, obsessed with my own capacity as a medium, with astrological "confirmations", and with the so-called cleansing of the karma chain.

In this state of mind, I visited several Buddhist monasteries on the ribs of the Himalayas, staying no more than a few days in each one. I found much to intrigue and delight me, but these were not places I could have stayed a long time. There were amazing paintings on the monastic walls, scenes from the life of Buddha, and images of the human path towards perfection. As I gazed at them, I was intensely aware of the contrast between these beautiful scenes and my own confusion. The monks were quite welcoming. They had few visitors in those days, and I must have seemed as exotic to them as they did to me. Some of them spoke basic English, and I had conversations with them, albeit not very deep ones. There were moments when I felt that here among the Buddhists in the quiescence of the mountains, I would find it easier to attain inner peace. It must be helpful, I reasoned, to be so far away from the sex shops and the supermarkets.

However, the unbalanced diet – long on greasy tea and short on vitamins – and the thought of eight months of winter, isolated from the world with temperatures of 45 degrees below zero, put me off the idea of a longer sojourn. I could not return to India, to Hinduism. I decided to try another stronghold of Buddhism, at the recommendation of a person who had mysteriously come back into my life.

Shortly after returning to Calcutta, I met up with my former partner and wife, Ursula. I had been in touch with her only occasionally over the previous seven years, but she knew where to find me. Her life had not been quite as checkered as mine, but she had experimented with several religious sects, including the Children of God. Despite or perhaps because of the terrible things we had lived through together, I was overjoyed to see her. On the surface, she looked no different from the average Western traveller around India, in jeans and a tee-shirt. But she was at least as keen a spiritual seeker as I was, and she seemed to have made more progress than me. She told me she had just come back from a visit to the monastery of Ajahn Chah, one of the great Buddhist masters of Thailand, and intended to go back to enter that monastery for good. It was located at the eastern edge of the country, near the border with Cambodia and Laos. Ursula suggested that this community of men and women might be a good place for me to settle, too.

During Ursula's stay in Calcutta, I introduced her one morning to Mother Theresa. Like me, Ursula had grave reservations about Christianity. But I will never forget the exchange of glances between Mother Theresa and Ursula: it was like two soul sisters, who had known each other for years. Long afterwards, Ursula told me that the memory of her meeting with the famous nun sustained her, indeed kept her alive, at very difficult moments in her life. I decided that I would eventually follow her to the monastery, but not immediately. I was afraid of new disappointments. So for a year I kept on travelling through Southeast Asia, seeking adventure and self-confidence, until I could at last come to terms with the failure I had suffered in Hinduism, and turn to something new. Early the following year, in February 1978, I was at last ready to enter the silent, timeless world of Buddhism. I now exchanged the adventures with monkeys, scorpions and snakes in the Malaysian jungle for the inner jungle, which was also full of spirits, demons and poisonous vipers. I could no longer attempt to believe in any theistic religion – whether monotheist or polytheist – after all the letdowns I had suffered. So what else was left, I reasoned, but trying the non-theistic philosophy of Buddhism? I now felt I should stay with Ajahn Chah and his monastic community until the end of my life, hoping that ultimately I would find that long-desired goal of inner freedom and peace.

Ursula had told me that Ajahn Chah was one of the greatest living masters of Buddhism, and that under his guidance she was making more progress in finding some ultimate meaning and truth than she had in any other phase of her life. There was real enthusiasm in her voice when she spoke about him. But I still did not have a clear idea what to expect when I arrived at Ajahn Chah's temple, known as Wat Pah Pong. It was located at an isolated spot deep in the forest, but the buildings were impressive. The main place of worship was a concrete structure which had cost a lot of money to build. Clearly the institution had generous benefactors.

On the day I turned up, a certain Buddhist festival was being celebrated, and the monastery was full of monks and visitors. The great leader, Ajahn Chah, was sitting in the middle, naturally, surrounded by important personalities and elders. Out of respect for his illustrious spiritual powers and fame, one had to stay at least two metres away from him. When I stepped in front of him to be presented, I did a "testing of the guru" act, as had been my custom in India. Was he just a "man of high rank" who relished his lofty status or was he someone who was really experienced, genuine and honest in what he taught others? Was he dignified enough to respect me or was I face to face with yet another hypocrite, covering up his inner emptiness? I wanted to test his reaction, in order to decide whether I would stay or lose interest and leave. I looked at him. He was short, with a broad, flat nose and face, and a high, shaved forehead – not particularly good looking. To provoke him, I said in a loud voice, "Who is this ugly dwarf, looking like a road-worker that is sitting here in front of me?" Amazingly enough, at that very moment, Ajahn Chah took a liking to me. To be liked by this man was a far-off dream for countless monks and lay Buddhists. I seemed to gain that prize from the first instant of our acquaintance. I spent a week living at the monastery in ordinary clothes, and I was then allowed to don a brown robe like everybody else in the community. Life was made easier by the fact that the master looked on me with favour. Permission was given to me to sit at his feet, and in a short time he was giving me special lessons.

The famous Buddhist master, Ajahn Chah (died 1994)

I still remember some of the things he taught me. One day I was sitting in front of him, on the steps of the temple, and he picked up the full cup of tea which had just been served to him. To my surprise, he poured more tea into the already brimming cup, making it overflow. Then he tipped out the entire remaining contents of the cup, letting the liquid trickle downwards from one marble step to another. There was silence for a while, and then he said something like this: "Before a vessel can receive something new, it has to be emptied first." I began to understand the Buddhist notion of "self-emptying" – a concept that also exists in Christianity, albeit with a somewhat different meaning.

Despite the privilege I enjoyed as a favourite pupil, the way of life for all the monastics was a demanding one. Our daily round began with three hours of meditation in the small hours. Then we would walk six to eight kilometres barefoot through the local villages, begging for food. We would usually receive a handful of rice each, sometimes hard-boiled eggs which had been dyed blueish-green, and sometimes leaves from trees which could make a salad of sorts. At the weekend there would be gifts of meat and fish from the visitors who came from all over Thailand.

From 9:30 onwards, after the morning meal, nobody was allowed to eat again until the following day. There was no talking, no reading, no listening to music. No possessions of any kind were allowed. Normally, I had to wash the spittoons of the monks, which was a healthy exercise in humility. Then we had to draw water from a well which was 24 metres deep – there was no electricity or running water. Each action had to be performed in a spirit of meditation. The rest of the time one had to sit in one's own hut and meditate in different ways. There were several main forms of meditation that we had to master. One involved breathing, and careful observation of the flow of air as it passed from the nostrils to the lungs. Another was walking meditation, which required focusing on all the muscles that have to be used every time we take a step. This was supposed to give the mind something to concentrate on, and keep stray thoughts at bay. In another technique, the word Buddha was endlessly repeated.

I used to see Ursula, who lived in the women's section of the community, about once a week. The rules laid down that another sister always had to be present during our conversations, and we had to maintain a distance of three metres between us – that was the monastic rule for any interaction between men and women. These meetings brought both of us great comfort. She was having a hard time, because many of her fellow sisters were fleeing from violent husbands and had no real spiritual vocation. They chattered continuously and disturbed her. But I did not discuss my own monastic or spiritual journey, nor did she talk much about her inner life.

For one night every week, we monks had to engage in walking meditation from 10 o'clock in the evening until six in the morning. This was mostly performed indoors, because in a place so infested with snakes, scorpions and stinging ants, walking outside was very hazardous. For those who had difficulty staying awake, Ajahn Chah had a radical solution: a large glass would be placed on the monk's shaven head, and it was a matter of honour not to let it fall. Avoiding such a disaster, in the dim candle light of the temple, took lots of mental energy. If this failed to cure sleepiness, there was an even more drastic remedy. The somnolent monk would sit on the edge of the well, with his feet hanging about 20 metres above the water level. Anyone who fell asleep in that state would certainly fall to his death. I underwent this frightening exercise several times. Such measures were not imposed in a spirit of harshness or discipline – that was not Ajahn Chah's way. They were simply "recommended", and monastics readily obeyed because they were determined to succeed on the spiritual path, and were generally willing to do whatever was necessary.

One of the weirdest things Ajahn Chah advised me to do was to contemplate death in the most literal way, by gazing on human corpses. Other monks received this advice, but as far as I know, I was the only one who actually followed his counsel. To renew my visa, I had to go to Bangkok regularly. As a monk from a well-known monastery, I obtained a permit to visit a morgue, which would have been impossible for an ordinary citizen. I also paid visits to a hospital where I would observe autopsies. I saw human bodies chopped to pieces with a saw, young and beautiful ones as well as old and wrinkled. My teacher thought that such experiences would bring home to me the transitory nature of beauty. I was perhaps less horrified by what I saw than most other people would have been – even as a child, I had felt a strange curiosity about dead bodies, and I was familiar with the sight of them. On many occasions in my life I had felt closer to death than to life. I was already intensely aware of the reality of physical disintegration after death, and these morbid visits simply reinforced this sense.

I remember my time at the monastery as a period when I lived at an extreme. In my wild, drug-taking days in Hamburg, I had lived at the other extreme: a life of hedonism, decadence, utter lack of control, and finally utter despair. Now I was testing my ability to endure an intensely disciplined regime, of a rigour that is hard for most Westerners to imagine. I probably felt the need, at least unconsciously, for some very strong medicine in order to counter-balance the influence of my troubled past. In any case, I had never been a person for half-measures. But the aim in Buddhism is not to live at an extreme of self-torture. Indeed, it is to eliminate all extremes, contrasts and dualities: good and bad, black and white, happiness and misery. The idea is to reach a state where both poles lose their importance.

Long drawn-out meditations for the next three years

Ajahn Chah no longer went on the daily begging round, but he still carried a begging bowl, and he gave it to me to carry. In our walks, he would take my arm, and once, at a weekly discussion he held for the community, he said he considered me to be a true monk, much more genuine than the 400 others. My fellow monks were left stunned. He then explained to them: "Unlike yourselves, Klaus goes straight from the heart in everything he does – he does not make conscious calculations."

I was flattered by these words – and perhaps not sufficiently conscious of the danger of excessive pride. My fellow monks were intensely jealous. Without claiming that I deserved these words of praise, I think I can understand why Ajahn Chah spoke as he did. By that time, I had become disappointed by theories and theologies, and my experience taught me not to believe in either. I simply judged things by my own experience. If something one had lived through had a palpable result, well and good. If the results were negative, then it was time to renounce that particular path or theory. That was my way of thinking. Now, Buddhism had appeared on my mental horizon. I felt that to achieve anything as a Buddhist I would have to put aside all learning acquired from books, to see if there was any truth or spiritual value in a world where the intellect and formal education played no part. I presumed that Ajahn Chah had sensed what my attitude was when I greeted him with the name of "ugly dwarf". I was impatient with formalism and hierarchies. I wanted to get down to the essentials. In the following months, I threw myself, body and soul, into the Buddhist way of life, full of new hope. A fresh wind and a renewed feeling of courage gave me wings.

The purpose of life in the monastery was to attain nirvana, an indescribable state of release from all attachment, and indeed from existence itself. Ajahn Chah used to say, "Whoever succeeds in meditation, even for six minutes, without any interfering thoughts, has realized nirvana." This meant, at a minimum, that such a person would be freed from all his problems. What kind of state nirvana was, he didn't say. Was it being and non-being at the same time? Sometimes it seemed that no one had yet attained this state. But what of the master himself? Some monks said he had reached enlightenment, which might mean the same as nirvana. In general, Buddhist masters are very hesitant to describe their own attainments. (For example, Buddhist teachers I met later in China and Korea avoided answering when I asked them what spiritual state they had reached – some Western practitioners are not so modest.) Ajahn Chah followed the Asian tradition of reticence.

But he answered as follows when somebody asked how he had become a master:

"When I eat, I eat, when I walk, I walk, and so on. Everything is and becomes meditation: to speak, eat, walk, sleep, work." I still think that there was some real wisdom in these words. We in the West talk at table, think while we sleep, walk while we read – our thoughts are here, there and everywhere, always preoccupied with something else. Forty-seven per cent of our thoughts belong to the past, forty-seven per cent to the future, and rarely do we give enough attention to the present. As Ajahn Chah helped me to understand, scattered thoughts are in opposition to concentration and meditation. Too seldom do we find ourselves in the "present", in the literal meaning of the word.

Even now, I still ask myself: What is Buddhism, a religion, a philosophy? How is it that this religion is praised so much by some Christian theologians? Why has it been so popular in the West, beginning with the hippie period? Why have New Age thinkers taken so much from this religion?

Siddharta Gautama was a wealthy prince, noble and honest, who lived in the years 563–483 BC. One day he came out of his father's palace and, for the first time, encountered illness, poverty, injustice and death, and as a result suffered a shock. He felt that the Hinduism which surrounded him was only a ritual, until he met a monk whose asceticism impressed him greatly. He devoted himself to asceticism and gained enlightenment on his 35th birthday. Through this, he discovered how one can distance one's self from the bad aspects of human life. Some people have seen a parallel between him and Adam, who was expelled from Paradise, but wanted to return there. In the mire and suffering of our daily lives each one of us seeks, in some way or other, to re-enter Paradise.

Gautama, now called Buddha, the "Enlightened One", summarized his knowledge in *Four Noble Truths*. These truths place man, not God, at the centre of everything. The Noble Truths of Buddha are as follows:

1. The truth about suffering: Everything that passes is characterised by suffering.

2. The origin of suffering: Suffering is the product of sin (greed, passions, desires).

3. The truth about breaking this suffering: Renouncing desires will end suffering.

4. The way of renouncing pleasures, greed and passions, or of the extinguishing of desires, is the "Noble 8-fold Way".

If we look at that "Noble 8-fold Way", we can understand much better how it is that so many people start on this road with great hopes. The steps are as follows:

1. True faith, upright opinions, that is, the understanding of those four noble truths.

2. Right decisions, honest intentions, that is, keeping our motivation pure.

3. Correct speech, that is, telling the truth.

4. Honest actions and demeanour, that is, a mode of behaviour directed and impregnated with sincerity and a peaceful attitude.

5. To earn our living honestly, for example, not to sell weapons or drugs.

6. True effort, that is, *ascesis* and self-discipline.

7. Real concentration.

8. True meditation.

If this path is followed, then, in accordance with the statements made by the "Enlightened One", it is possible to escape from life's worries and attain the state of nirvana which frees one totally from all desire. Following that, all suffering ends. I feel it is possible that the first seven points come from divine inspiration. The eighth point, I now think, presents the same problems I experienced in Hinduism. As shown above, the mind control maintained during meditation – whether Hindu or Buddhist – is achieved through methods such as Zen, yoga, and various forms of an ecstatic state. Other techniques include listening to the wind, bells, mantras, training the eyes either to focus or to avoid focusing. All of these have the ultimate purpose of achieving a merger with the whole universe, so as to become one with the forces of the cosmos and in this way overcome all the dualities of life. However, the same old problem arises: How can I find "myself" if in this impersonal universe no "one" exists, or if my individuality disappears, and is dissolved?

There is a certain egocentricity, I would now say, in the Buddhist belief that man has to free himself on his own, by his own strength. "You yourself are your own light", was Buddha's advice, expressed not long before his death. The problem I faced as a young seeker was that I had not found my "own light", and no teacher or technique had been able to help me discover it. The Buddhist Klaus had hopes of discovering an inner light by retreating from the world forever. To live the whole of my life in a monastery was not what I had imagined, but for a time I thought it was necessary. Even as I did my exercises under Ajahn Chah, the thought came to my mind that four-fifths of the world's population was forced to engage in daily manual labour. It seemed unfair that these people were disadvantaged from the beginning and had not much prospect of reaching nirvana. Apparently, they had not been created for the monastic life, but to work in order to keep life functioning on the planet.

In fact, the teaching of Buddha is something between philosophy and religion. Siddharta Gautama himself was strongly opposed to the idea of people turning him into a god. But the need of simple people for deities was stronger than anything else. After all, in modern times people managed to make god-like figures out of criminal devils like Stalin or Mao Tse Tung. This impulse is always present as long as "human nature" is considered the measure – and centre point – of all things.

As I settled in to the rhythm of life at Ajahn Chah's monastery, I began to experience palpable results from the intensive practice of meditation and other disciplines. But what had I attained by successfully creating "inner emptiness"? Was it the case that my doubt, anger, lust, hate, envy had finally weakened to some degree, or disappeared altogether? Had I become free or at least a little freer? I really wanted to see this working. It seemed as if peace and freedom were winking at me. But the road had already proved a hard one. I had seen poisonous snakes, rats, scorpions, giant spiders and termites, not only in my little hut or kuti allocated to me on my entry into the monastery, but also in my soul. The fight against these unwanted "lodgers" was going on within as well as externally. It was a battle on two fronts. The physical challenges were also formidable. One day when I was meditating in my kuti, I saw a snake slip down from the roof on to the steps leading to my room. Under the monastic rules, I was not supposed to move, or to touch an animal. But I watched in horror as the snake advanced in a lightning movement and burrowed under my pillow. When I came back the following evening, I had no idea whether the snake was still around – that was an exceptionally sleepless night, although I never saw the serpent again. Friendly creatures inhabited my hut, too. There was a chameleon clinging to the shutters that I would greet every morning, as I returned from the temple, wondering what colour it would have turned. I preferred this inoffensive creature to the rats that regularly ate my soap. One encounter with the region's lethal fauna very nearly put an end to my earthly life as well as my monastic career. I was engaged in our early morning meditation in the temple, which was lit only by feeble oil lamps. Some impulse prompted me to turn my pocket torch on, and there on the floor, about a metre away from me and heading in my direction, was a bandit krait – one of the deadliest snakes in that part of the world. In fact, there was a mother krait with two smaller ones in her care, an even more terrifying prospect. If I had not turned on the torch, it would have burrowed under my legs and bitten me as soon as I moved – within five or ten minutes I would have been dead. This time there was no respect for monastic rules. As soon as I spotted the danger, I jumped up and let out a scream. All the other monks turned on their torches. They managed to sweep the snakes into a metal container and throw them back into the forests. I was later told, by a holy man I respect, that this was one of the occasions in my life when Mary, the Mother of God, protected me.

Despite these hazards, I took my disciplines seriously, and became skilful at plunging myself in a deep void, refusing to pay any attention to my passing thoughts, let alone dissect or analyse them. But part of me was questioning the purpose of this deliberate pursuit of emptiness. In its denial of all contrasts and dualities, Buddhism seemed to be denying many of the things that I yearned for. How could there be joy, if there is no real distinction between joy and sorrow? How can there be love, if there no distinction between love and hatred? Even the stated purpose of the whole exercise – which was to eliminate suffering – had not been attained in my case.

I was troubled by the idea that fulfilment consisted of discovering that everything and everyone amount to nothing more than an illusion, or at best a sort of constant flux which leads towards non-being. The idea of eliminating the distinction between good and evil seemed to portend a complete absence of moral responsibility. There was no sense that man must freely choose between right and wrong and live with the consequences of his choices.

The more I penetrated Buddhist practice, the more strongly I felt that there was an unhealthy nihilism in this philosophy. This could not be life, I told myself, and I resolved to escape and seek life in other places. I visited other monasteries and paid more frequent visits to Bangkok, trying to find out whether I could retain whatever I had learned in the monastery while living in the world.

This made me increasingly unpopular among my fellow monks. They became angry, sarcastic and aggressive in their behaviour towards me. That in turn made me all the more disillusioned with them. Where was their wisdom now, where their self-control? I came to feel that this was a place where nobody felt or talked about love, everything was only theory or theology. I came to see the monastery as a kind of concentration camp. One day, I climbed the walls (walking out of the gate without permission would have been against the rules) and after a few minutes encountered a disturbing sight. A father suddenly losing his temper with his two sons, aged about ten and twelve, and beating them furiously. So much for Buddhist self-control, I said to myself. It was time to sample some real life again.

CHAPTER SIX

REGAINING "REAL" LIFE

With shaved head and fluttering robe, I went to Bangkok, some six hundred kilometres away, uncertain of when, if ever, I would return to the monastery. There I stayed in one of the innumerable urban monasteries. One day, I happened to be in the old and much valued monastery library looking for some important ancient writings. Reading was not thought of as a good thing for monks to do, but this piece of research was tolerated because it pertained to high culture. Whilst I was skimming through some pages, a monk whom I had befriended came and nestled close to me on the floor. An astrological discussion began and Santachitto – that was his name – asked:

"Klaus, by the way, what is your zodiac sign?"

"Taurus", I answered.

"Ah look, now is the period of Taurus!" He lifted his eyebrows and asked me which day was my birthday. I had not thought recently about such worldly things, but I answered:

"May 15th." To our astonishment, we realized that this would be the next day. This fact was of great interest to him and he made me a crazy proposition. What he said impressed me more than any other suggestion I had received in my monastic life. It encouraged my belief in some inexplicable force, which directed everyone's life.

"You can say no if you wish. Don't feel pressurized. What I am going to offer you on your birthday is not just something simple."

"There must be some risks in life", had always been my motto, and for that reason I asked him to tell me what he had thought up for me.

"I am on my way south, and I have about one thousand kilometres still to go. Would you like to accompany me?"

A long journey? There was no need to ask me a second time. Of course I would like to go!

"But", he continued, "there are specific conditions. We shall not be travelling in the normal way." I became rather curious.

"The thing is", he said, "I am proposing that we walk the one thousand kilometres!" This left me open-mouthed.

"No, it won't be that bad", he said, trying to calm me down. "I am anticipating that during our journey we will not have to ask anyone for anything, except for water, which is vital. Everything else will be quiet and problem-free."

I was still tempted by the journey, but on second thoughts it seemed an unreasonable, even impossible idea. A little while later, I started to feel that I had no real choice, if I wanted to make progress in my personal journey and broaden my experience. I accepted. After that I began to sweat, but I had agreed and there was no going back. Human logic said that it could be suicidal to undertake such a journey, walking in temperatures around 38°C with nearly 100% humidity in the atmosphere. I had very little time to linger, as Santachitto announced:

"We will leave in two hours' time, just before dark, when it will not be so hot."

We got ready in a hurry. There was hardly anything to pack except our robes and begging bowls. The journey before us was destined to become an important landmark in my life. It was significant, I felt, that I had conquered fear and put faith first. Faith in what? In the first instance, just in a human being, and in my powers of endurance. As I set out, I had no idea of the extraordinary turns of fate that would occur on our long march.

As darkness approached, we began to walk through the chaotic traffic of Bangkok, with its perpetual cacophony of car horns and narrow streets full of filth, chatter and much commercial activity. A few hours later, at the edge of the city we were stopped at a police control post. There were no questions, no explanations – only intense, heavy heat, and a tedious wait of more than two hours. What was the meaning of it all? Finally, one of the uniformed men approached us and asked us to follow him. What had happened? Santachitto was asked where we wanted to go. Then this tight-lipped official began asking other drivers, while checking their papers, where they were going. Eventually a driver was found who was willing to take us on to the next large town, where there was a monastery and where we could spend the night. We climbed into the car, meditated and smiled throughout the next two hundred and fifty kilometres of our journey. When we bade our farewells, thanking the driver, he told us that it had been a great honour for him to have begging-monks in his car.

The next day things became more difficult. After doing our begging rounds and breakfasting we began our journey once again. It was a *very* hot day indeed, far away from the protecting shade of the forests, no shelter to be found anywhere. The scorching sun burned the tops of our shaven heads as we marched in single file, hour upon hour along the never-ending road. The air quivered, sweat poured from our faces, thirst tortured us and as far as the eye could see there was nowhere to sit, nothing: no water, no shade, only cars passing us at great speed. I was afraid now as our physical condition was becoming critical. My throat was dry, my tongue was stuck to my jaw and I was beginning to feel dizzy. All this, I knew, was leading to acute sunstroke. Why had I been so stupid as to accept the monk's offer? I was reproaching myself bitterly. Did I really have to do this? I was overcome by a powerful feeling of doubt and asked myself how much longer my feet could last out before they stuck to the scorching asphalt. I was almost in a trance because of the boiling heat when I heard a car horn next to me. The driver not only invited us into the car, but also took us to his house. It turned out that he, unbelievably, was an

Pinda Bath – begging with my fellow monks in Thailand

ice cream salesman. He proceeded to offer us some of the best and most expensive of his wares. Had I been a Christian then, I would have uttered a "hallelujah". As it was, I was struggling to be an "excellent" Buddhist, who was supposed to receive all things with stoic indifference. Of course, I could not hide my feelings of joyful relief. The man's kindness went further. To make sure we would remember him – and without any request on our part – he gave us enough money for the bus to take us on to the next stage of our journey. It was unbelievable. Finally, that night, we arrived in a place where everything was closed, and there was no room in any monastery to spend the night. We decided to sleep under the stars in an old ruin at the top of a hill outside the city, hoping that we would not meet any snakes or scorpions, of which there were plenty everywhere. From above we were surrounded by scores of monkeys leaping around the trees, making strange noises and gaping at us inquisitively.

After three days, we had reached our destination and I was happy to have taken up Santachitto's suggestion. We spent some time in a monastery carved out of a rock in the south of Thailand. While my friend was suffering from a bout of malaria, I heard that the abbot of the monastery had a few things to attend to in

Bangkok the next day, and I was asked if I would like to accompany him. This was just too good to be true, I said to myself. However, not long after I found myself sitting in a luxurious American limousine with air conditioning, and there I was, speeding back to the monastery in Bangkok. Faith, not fear, had been vindicated.

Over time, some features of my old, worldly self began to reassert themselves. I developed a platonic friendship with a glamorous Thai woman from a privileged background, and she often invited me to stay in her house. I had met her when she visited Ajahn Chah's monastery, and I was able to advise her on some very personal problems. Even back then, she had often asked me to visit her in Bangkok. Now that I lived in the capital, there was no obstacle to pursuing the acquaintance. When we felt like it, we would go out at night to enjoy ourselves in a disco, incognito of course. I would exchange my monastic clothes for more worldly garb, and she also took care that nobody would recognize her. We would dance rock 'n' roll to exhaustion. Both of us were relieved to have an escape from the formal environments where we spent the rest of our time.

Life had taken hold of me again. What a delight! Was there duality there? Were there any prohibitions against this in Buddhism? None that I knew of. After all the time spent in the forest and behind walls, I felt a longing for some sun and beaches. While I was staying with my rich woman friend, she recommended the seaside resort at Pattaya, the nearest one to Bangkok. So I went there to "recover" and searched for a room. As I enjoy dancing, it was not long till I found myself at a discotheque.

What happened next is of a rather intimate nature and I would ask the reader not to misunderstand it. It represents an important way-station on my journey. When I left the discotheque, three young Thai women took hold of me and invited me to their house. Their intentions were evident. They clearly came from very poor families and were working as prostitutes, because they had no other way of surviving. For such women, every Westerner they meet represents the hope of earning some money and eventually leading a better life.

Initially, they assumed I would simply be a client like any other. But they soon realized there was something different about me. I wasn't wearing monastic apparel, but my plain white clothes were different from those of the usual disco-goer. I was confused when I realized what they were expecting. Despite my rebellious tendencies, I was a monk and truly had no thought of "such worldly things". In any case, the idea of paying money for sex has never appealed to me, at any stage of my life.

I simply did not know how to behave in the situation I found myself in. I sat on the pavement in front of the discotheque, and meditated, asking for help from the spirits. What do you think? I had a reply! I heard the following message from the mouth of a person I understood to be Ajahn Chah: "Do what you are doing and do it completely and well, as you have always done. Take no half measures." I felt as if I had been struck by lightning and looked around to see if Ajahn Chah was behind me. As far as I could see, there was no one there. Was it he who had spoken to me, or the demons imitating his voice? Only now, as a Christian, I can say with confidence that it was probably *not* Ajahn Chah; he was too sincere in his monastic calling to have given me such advice. It may be more accurate to say that what I heard was a clever imitation of Ajahn Chah's tone and voice. Nevertheless, I could not, in those days, tell the difference between his true voice and that of the imitator.

In any case, my situation changed immediately. The first young woman *offered* me a lot of money (some $70) to be *her* "guest", which meant that I had to go home with her. I hardly need to say that this seemed very strange to me. The second woman offered me even more, showing me $100. I must not follow the other one but *her*, she insisted. It was incredible. This went on for a while. I imagined the kind of place where they lived and worked: a dockland bar, in some dark narrow alley, full of smoke and an atmosphere of crime, where you could get stabbed in the back. Everything seemed very strange. Once again, I heard that voice clearly repeating: "Do just what you are doing!" After suppressing the powerful fears raging inside me, I decided to follow the first woman, whose name was

Dang. The other two followed us anyway. We entered a rough area. Sensing danger at one point, I decided it was time to stop for a while before somebody put a knife in my back. I went into a seedy drinking house with bare floorboards, and ordered a beer. I wanted to see the womens' faces close up, and so regain my self-confidence. I started to feel better. Obviously, the "voice" had not been a trick, and my doubts gradually disappeared. Not long afterwards, I changed my monastery cell for a shabby room in the house where my three new friends lived, along with dozens of other prostitutes. I started living among them. Seeing me as a protector and counsellor, the three of them gave me money, food, clothing and fulfilled my every desire. In exchange, all they asked of me was the "blessing" of Buddha and the benign effect of my medita-tion. They also wanted me to lend them a sympathetic ear when they told me about their personal problems and travails. It was not hard to understand why they needed this friendship. They would come back at dawn, exhausted and with a look of repulsion on their faces. I would then hear from their own mouths stories, revealing the lurid acts they were forced to perform and the awful trap they were caught up in. How much I despised the male tourists who frequented Pattaya when I heard those stories.

I became a chameleon, just like the little creature that used to inhabit my monastic hut. I abandoned monastic dress altogether, and my women friends ordered some gorgeous, embroidered silk clothes for me from a local tailor. I was one of them, part of their group. They called me Baagh Wan, Sweet Mouth. If at first I tried to restrain myself from accepting their blandishments, this phase soon passed with the help of those "inner voices" apparently from my teacher who repeatedly gave the order: "Do what you are doing. There is neither good nor bad, everything is one." Such, it then appeared, was my true Zen practice. This was real life! I continued to yield to the advice I thought I was receiving, and carried on.

But what exactly was happening to me? Sweet as it superficially was, this new way of life began to suffocate me. I had to leave this place of so-called "love". For one thing, there was a real risk of being attacked by jealous women. Everything was getting more and more troublesome, and I feared that in this house I would truly sink and drown. Finally, I returned to the monastery in the forest, in the east of the country. I was unshaven, sweaty and smelly. The road there had been tortuous, and half-way along the bus I was travelling in caught fire. I was sitting in the back, and I was the first to see the flames licking upwards from the blazing engine. At first the driver paid no attention when I told him to stop. When I screamed at him to let the people out, he finally put the brakes on and we escaped in the nick of time. I remember watching people run in terror from the fire-ball of the exploding bus. This was one more occasion when I believe the Mother of God saved my life.

I had to complete my journey barefoot, having lost all my possessions on the bus, and the soles of my feet burned as they touched the hot, rough asphalt. My fellow monks were not pleased to see me. I don't think they had any way of knowing exactly what I had been doing immediately before my return, but the mere fact that I had quit the community for a more worldly life was enough to enrage them. They seemed full of hatred and poisonous jealousy. I could see daggers in their eyes. This reaction deepened my general disappointment with the supposedly enlightened monks, whose life I had tried to share. I was enraged that not a single member of the community, neither my erstwhile master nor any of his humble underlings, took a moment to ask me how I had been, what difficulties I might have faced during my absence. The effect was to revive my old hatred for religious authorities and theologians. I began to see all the monks as a bunch of poor soulless hypocrites who made everyone's life unbearable by their dead theories. Yes, I was used to suffering – had it ever been otherwise? But was there no justice or love in the world? Did it always have to be so painful? I hated those monks, just as they seemed to loathe me. But where should I go? How could I continue my search? The only way that remained was the stillness of meditation. But who could say at what age I would arrive at that point?

In the end it seemed to me that everyone, including monks, thought only of themselves. Perhaps, I felt, that was inherent in Buddhism. In this world, the "other person" was of no interest to the aspiring devotee, except in a negative sense: they would react sharply against any Klaus Kenneth who provoked them in order to bring certain unspoken truths into the light. My bitter private laughter, the unshed tears, which flowed within me, those were my karma! To suffer, to be in need and to die – that was my predestined karma. "Mai pen rai" – that was an expression in the language of Laos, which one heard endlessly in this monastery and the villages nearby: *That's how it is*, *It doesn't matter*, *There is nothing to be done*, *Let it be*. To express any emotion was considered a weakness, a loss of face, and despite the customs of giving food to monks, there seemed to be a complete absence in this part of the world of real human mercy. That is how I felt. Even if I had my faults, I longed for somebody to treat me with a minimum of love and understanding, to show that they cared about me.

At this time of intolerable suffering, a moment of grace suddenly came. My Unknown God wanted to show Himself to me, His tortured child. Perhaps He knowingly led me into situations through which He could reveal Himself in a particular way. After my unpleasant reception by the monastery, I felt so morally annihilated that I decided to escape once more from that place, which felt more and more like a concentration camp. I climbed over the thick brick wall at the back of the monastery, where nobody could see me, and traversed the forest, running through the rice fields, feeling abandoned by all "good" spirits. In my utter loneliness I sat down on a patch of dry ground, deeply troubled within. By chance, I put my hand in the pocket of my robe and felt an object with hard sides. I took it out and discovered that it was a small New Testament, which Mother Theresa had given me. How on earth did it come to be in my pocket? Only God knows. In the state I was in, meditation techniques were no help in overcoming my feelings of hatred. So instead, I opened the book at random, and began reading.

As I read the passage about the woman caught in adultery, I understood immediately why these bad, hypocritical "guys" could not stand Jesus and wanted to get Him into trouble. For me, at that moment, the Pharisees represented the monks of the monastery. My heart stopped beating as I imagined the situation the woman found herself in. She had committed adultery. Perhaps her husband was one of the merciless Pharisees who beat their own wives but were themselves adulterous in secret, and this was "love". I had met many such people in many world religions. Faced with such a law, the poor woman had no chance. What was going on inside her at that moment?

I could easily identify with her, because in the past few days I had done even worse things than she had, and according to their "law" I myself would have been condemned to death by stoning. This thought brought me great pain and a vehement revolt against her tormentors. Deep down I felt that those of us who were outcasts, who had reneged, were "driven to it" by the harshness and lack of love of those hypocrites who publicly display their virtues and purity. Were we truly so "sinful"? Did we deserve to die for this? Those merciless Pharisees and monks, by their very presence and "law", formed an impenetrable wall of prejudice. They were caught up in their own hatred, and in my mind I could just see them joyously wishing to see the woman's bloodshed, gasping with delight as they waited for the event. The spectacle would satisfy their twisted sense of morality. Such unforgiving observers of life would never pay attention to "our" arguments nor indeed would the monks behind those walls who study their "holy" theories in front of the dead statues of Buddha. I was desperate to find a way out. On the verge of tears, I continued to read and my amazement grew. This Jesus silently wrote something in the sand. Was it the names and sins of those already holding stones in their hands? Had He Himself convicted them? Then I heard Jesus' answer:

"Let him who is without sin throw the first stone."

At that moment I was overcome with gratitude and relief. Now there were real tears of joy in my eyes at this reconciling wisdom, confirmed by Jesus. In my mind's eye I could almost see how each one would have dropped his stone, withdrawing abashed and subdued. Clouds of hatred must have boiled up inside them. Jesus had spoilt their entertainment and they were going to take revenge when an opportunity arose. The One who had spoilt their game, He would have to be eliminated, sacrificed. That's what they thought. I could see them.

For a moment, I felt again that indescribable nearness and warmth, the same sensation that I had experienced in Hamburg, when I was about to jump off the balcony. With renewed hope I leaped back over the wall of the monastery and went to my cell in the forest. I have never forgotten that "meeting", not to this day. The voice within me was calling out too powerfully. Even if Buddha had never answered me, because he was dead, "Someone" did respond – a Person who was alive, Someone who seemed to know me and knew that I was on this earth.

CHAPTER SEVEN

MOVING WEST

WHEN I RETURNED TO THE MONASTERY from the rice fields, I felt strong enough to endure the taunts of my fellow monks. In the absence of any other clear goal, I was still determined to reach the spiritual heights which the monastery in the forest seemed to offer. In the period that followed, I was indeed destined to scale spiritual heights, of different kinds, but they were not exactly the ones that I was expecting. In any case, the immediate effect of my moment of comfort and reassurance, reading that Gospel passage, was that I felt better able to make a distinction between the hostile monks around me and the gifts which I thought Buddhist meditation could offer.

During this time, I was convinced that I would have to stay in Thailand to the end of my days with Ajahn Chah, in the hope that maybe in old age I would find peace, love and the knowledge of who I was.

But I could not stay all the time in the monastery. I felt it was important to sample life in other places and countries, without abandoning my monastic calling. I was beginning to feel strong enough to travel outside the monastery without lapsing into a worldly life, as I had done during my first long stay in Bangkok. My most memorable trip outside Thailand, during this period, took me to a region of the world where holiness and religious conflict have always existed in a highly concentrated form.

I accepted the invitation of an old German friend, a woman called Edith, who had been a singer in my band in Hamburg, to visit her in Tel Aviv, where she was living with her Israeli husband. We had remained in touch, on and off, and she had often urged me to visit her. Suddenly some impulse told me that the moment was right.

It was during this trip that my Unknown God sent me another sign. But as I set out, I would have found it hard to explain why I was making the trip. I did not have a very high opinion of Judaism as a religion, because it seemed excessively legalistic and too close to Christianity, of which I was still suspicious. Maybe the reason I would have given, if somebody had asked, was that I wanted to make my general spiritual knowledge more complete, so that in the end I could forget about this experience, too. I now believe that a much higher power – "Someone" – was guiding me to Israel.

On arriving in Tel Aviv, I yielded to a strange impulse which had always been present in my psyche: to challenge and provoke death. My friend, Edith, left me her car, a little Deux Chevaux, while she was absent from Israel for a couple of weeks. With no hesitation I took the car and drove straight to the border between Lebanon, Syria and Israel. After passing through Acre, I headed towards Lebanon and then drove about one hundred kilometres along the length of the border, straight along the barbed wire, past the camouflaged tanks. In due course, I reached the Golan Heights. I kept being told to go back by Israeli soldiers wielding machine guns. They warned me that the "other side", the Syrian army, was likely to fire without hesitation on anything it saw moving. My car had a yellow Israeli number plate. My heart began to race, but I felt I must press on. I had to know if I was vulnerable to death, mortal. An irresistible power pushed me on. After a certain point, there were no roads, only tracks made by tanks. I found my way through the dust, mire and shrubs, without a map, always staying close to the barbed wire fence. Either I was a stubborn provocateur, or just plain naïve – that's how I must have seemed to anybody who observed me. If I was to die, then so be it. I have never been able to do things by halves. I had to test the limits of my ability to survive, or simply die – there was no other choice. I arrived at Qunitra, on the Golan Heights, a town which had been completely erased from the face of the earth, leaving only ruins and ghosts. I was reminded of the sights I had seen as a child after the bombardment of Germany at the end of the war. The scene was strangely familiar to little Klaus, who had played in the ruins of the bombed cities, who was hungry and drank water from the puddles after a rain shower. For a moment I almost seized up with fear and horror. I was engulfed both by a natural fear of death – the normal human instinct which I sometimes seemed to lack – and by the horror of war. At great speed I drove down from the Golan Heights into the interior of Israel, where I would feel protected. Fleeing those ghastly landscapes, with cold sweat on my neck, I went straight to Jerusalem. And there I was struck, as if by lightning.

In Jerusalem

The curious intimations began as I walked along the Via Dolorosa, the path trodden by Jesus on the way to His Crucifixion. I had the profound sensation of being "at home". Everything was somehow familiar, as if I had been brought up here, and it reminded me of my early years. There was an overwhelming sense of *déjà vu*. Had I been a Jew in a former life? My Eastern beliefs about reincarnation led me to think so. Everything was wreathed in a kind of mist. I could see nothing clearly. As I passed by the noisy souvenir shops, something guided me to the front of the Church of the Holy Sepulchre. I would not have called myself a pilgrim, just a curious tourist visiting another historical monument. But it soon became evident that there was something else in store for me.

My invisible guide directed me into one of the many chapels, the one called the "Flagellation Chapel", after the flogging endured by Christ before he was crucified. There I sat for a few moments to rest and absorb everything I had seen. Then I spotted an influx of pilgrims accompanied by a priest. A religious service took place. I looked at the tired and weary faces of the pilgrims who, perhaps like me, were glad to escape from burning heat into the coolness of the chapel and unburden themselves of life's various cares. I simply observed the prayers, not expecting anything in particular. After a few minutes, when the priest was ready to serve the Eucharist – a rite whose meaning I had virtually forgotten – I was somehow lifted up from the bench where I was sitting. I found myself standing up without having made any conscious decision to rise from my seat. The "Force" which lifted me up then moved my legs and guided me, Klaus, to the front where people were waiting to receive Communion. This was a totally new experience, unlike anything I had lived through in life. Whatever relationships I had formed during my life, I had always felt alone, incapable of giving or receiving love. But this was a moment of union, although I hardly understood with whom or what. Some of the pilgrims looked at me with curiosity.

But that was not all. When the group of pilgrims had left the chapel, that same "Force" sent me back to the bench where I had been sitting. It was *impossible* to leave. I had the impression I was no longer master over my own body. It almost felt as though I no longer existed in bodily form. I simply let things unfold. Not long after, another group of pilgrims, with a different priest, came in. Without having made any conscious decision to do so, I participated in a second service. Once again I felt that I was floating. Something was going very deep within me, and it felt as though time and space had been annihilated. My heart was beating furiously. Then another surprise came. Once again, I was led by that "Force" to take Communion. Perhaps something out of the ordinary was visible on my face, because afterwards several pilgrims, instead of leaving the room, came up to me and asked me to pray for them or their children. I felt dizzy and hardly heard what they were saying. The state I was in could not be compared with the ecstasies I had felt in India or Thailand. This was power, warmth and peace. Had I been in some other place, I might have thought that these people were making fun of me. At that moment, I had no such feeling. What was happening to me? "He" was not giving a clear answer. Neither could I give an answer to those people who came up to me – I just nodded my head in affirmation. It was a kind of miracle. I was very powerfully moved by what was going on inside and around me. In any case, "He", whose name I did not know, was not allowing me to leave His presence.

The "Force" carried me back to my place once more. Again I was allowing myself to be led. I had never felt so joyfully lifted up, so full of enthusiasm. A third group of believers came in and ... there was one more religious service! This time I felt an indescribable warmth within, much stronger than in the two previous services. This Presence, whatever it was, had absolutely mastered me. While I was looking at the pilgrims it seemed that I could feel their suffering, their worries and needs within my very soul. I shared the moments they were going through. Their suffering had become mine – it was a kind of cosmic experience. With power, that Force guided me to Communion for the third time. This time, more than before, I had a sense of being one with the "poor" and the "weak", the sort of people whom I had previously scorned in my proud spiritual state. The unbelievable happened. Now all the pilgrims came up to me, shaking me by the hand, touching me and asking me to pray for their parents, children, families, worries and needs. Only the priest looked at me in distrust. I was suddenly overcome by such an intense dizziness that I staggered outside into the blazing sunshine, so that I would not lose sight of reality. It was becoming too much of a good thing.

I went down towards the Dome of the Rock. Blinded by the strong light of the day, I stepped into what is known as the third holy Muslim place (after the "Kaaba" in Mecca, and Medina), went down into the basement (where normally no non-Muslim would be allowed), and for two hours meditated on the rock, from which legend says, Mohammed was lifted up into the heavens, together with his winged horse. To my amazement, during all the time I was meditating I was invisible to the guards. I wanted to feel here once more the Force which these kinds of special places impart. But I found neither peace nor stillness.

Despite all the extraordinary experiences in the Holy Land, my home was still in Thailand, and I was still determined to pursue Buddhist meditation. I had received some powerful intimations of the Christian mystery, but my deep grudge against Christianity in its established form was still intact.

I immersed myself ever more deeply in meditative practice, achieving a kind of "perfection" which led to three significant spiritual experiences. One night, I again had the experience of leaving my body, as had happened in Calcutta. I looked down on my physical self as though I was looking at a stranger. I felt I was turning into pure thought, and it seemed that everything I thought of I would become: if I thought of a tree, I would become a tree; if I thought of a stone, I would become a stone.

Then I had a series of sensations of the kind which are often reported by people after near-death experiences, albeit with some differences. I felt I was floating down a corridor. The walls of the corridor were not ordinary walls. They consisted of people, scenes and thoughts from my entire life up to that point. Nothing from my life was missing. If I had ever nursed a bad thought about somebody, it was somehow present on that wall. The wall was the totality of my earthly life, of the "I" which was Klaus. But this presentation of my life was not, I felt, something that my memory had generated. It was an expression of total reality, which did not in any way depend on my mental powers. Nothing could be hidden, nothing added. My Buddhist teachers had spoken to me of attaining a state of "non-being", but this felt like "total being".

I could see the mistakes I had made in life with absolute clarity. In contrast to some near-death experiences, I did not see any golden city or beautiful landscape ahead of me. Perhaps it was because I was still under judgment for the mistakes I had made. I discerned a blinding light ahead of me, but it was cold. And after seeing all these extraordinary things, I found myself again surrounded by black nothingness. Was this nirvana?

Another time, while I was meditating, a white lotus flower appeared in my field of vision. At first, in accordance with the practice I had been taught of "letting go" of things, I tried to dispel the image and refocus on my breathing. But the image would not go away. In the religion of south Asia, the lotus plant is a powerful symbol, because it rises out of the mud and produces flowers of great delicacy and purity. The image kept returning to my mind's eye, with such intensity that I started to "look" straight at it, until it seemed to engulf my whole sensory field. Then I felt something more physical, a kind of scratching in the palm of my hand. Always wary of snakes and other unwanted visitors, I opened my eyes and looked at my upturned palm. There was a small lotus flower. I thought I might still be in a dream world. I pinched myself, and then touched the flower. Everything was real and tangible. I heard my teacher's voice saying, "Let go". So I closed my eyes again, and when I reopened them after several more hours of meditation, there was no more flower. I was grateful for the revelation I had received. But it pertained only to nature, the created world (including man, and his ability to achieve great spiritual feats) – it did not pertain to the Creator. That is what I now realize. Later in my life, I was to meet a holy man who convinced me that revelations of the beauty of the natural world do not necessarily lead us beyond creation, to the realm of the Uncreated. Nature can sometimes lead us to God, but it does not always do so, especially if man places himself at the centre of things. And at that time, I was still following a philosophical path which was man-centred.

In my Thai monastic life, I tasted not only the heights which that spiritual system can offer, but also some of the darkest abysses. Once while sitting in my hut, I was visited by demons. Green smoke started coming through the wall. The smoke condensed into figures and faces with the most horrible features and expressions: glowing red eyes, blood coming out of their mouths, long fangs. They crowded me in ever greater numbers. I closed my eyes in terror, but when I opened them again, the demons were still there. My lasting impression was these demons were stronger than me, and I could not escape them. Soon after undergoing this experience, I became physically ill, tormented by pains in my head, back and knees.

To put it mildly, I had not found inner peace or freedom through Buddhism, but I held out the hope that I might eventually receive these prizes if I hung on at the monastery. Perhaps I would have to wait till I was 80? So I flew to Europe for the last time, to bid my farewells to the people I knew there. In particular, I wanted to say goodbye to some friends in Fribourg, Switzerland, who had been "pupils" of mine during the days when I was practising TM. When I left Thailand, Ajahn Chah gave me two beautifully cut diamond stones as a token of his confidence that I would return. It was highly unusual for someone to leave the monastery, but he clearly felt that it was appropriate for me to travel to Europe at that time. I entrusted the two precious stones to some very good friends in Hamburg, Petra and Norbert. Later they told me that they had taken the stones to be valued by a jeweller and their high value was confirmed. They packed them up and put them in a small metal box for safekeeping, until I was ready to take them back to Thailand.

Things took a different turn. Just as I was about to return to Thailand, a beautiful young woman disclosed that she was madly in love with me. I can't say that I was equally in love with her. Indeed, I don't think I knew what love was at that time. But I enjoyed her attention. I was 35, she was more than ten years younger. I was not going to resist her flattery or her sexual attraction. I suppose I was hoping to learn about love, to make progress in that realm, through a passionate relationship, even if the passion was rather one-sided. I agreed that we should live together, thinking that if this did not work out I could always return to the monastery. For the first time in twelve years, I settled down for a while.

We rented a large, rustic country house near Fribourg with another woman friend, in a gorgeously picturesque area on the Greyerz lake. In the beginning our little community seemed very promising and full of hope. It became even better when I found a job as a teacher in a well-known private school in Greyerz, which paid very well. Heaven seemed close at hand, but I could not quite grasp it. I had not reckoned on the unseen powers and demons. At earlier phases in my life, as a so-called guru, I had used their powers to make others dependent on me. But now they had made me their victim: they were attacking me, giving me no peace. I continued meditating, and despite the beautiful landscape around me, the visitations of demons became more and more frequent. Sometimes I was brought back to the death's-head images that I had seen as a student in Hamburg while smoking marijuana. It sometimes seemed as though the face of everybody around me was turning into a skull. In our little community, there was discord, because of my strange behaviour. Communion became separation, harmony gave way to conflict, and mutuality to loneliness. In other words, the killers had arrived.

My women friends were not fooled by my theoretical Buddhist wisdom; we were living so close together that they began to understand the tactics I used as a so-called guru. For me, my two house-mates had become like mirrors in which my cunning machinations were reflected. They rendered visible some of my selfish qualities, which I tried to hide, even from myself, using Buddhist theory as a smokescreen. Deep down in my soul I knew that they were right in their severe criticisms of me.

One part of me longed to escape from the dangerous game I was playing, or even from my own skin. But I could not do so, because the ugliness inside me had been exposed and seemed impossible to remove. I had invited in the demons, just as my mother had once done, and I was to be the next generation cursed by God. My mother had also tried to love, but she only managed to spread fear and sorrow around her. I too was a prisoner in a cell I had made for myself. This is the most horrific kind of prison, because there is no way out.

There were days when my two house-mates grimaced with pain if I so much as looked at them. There was something so hostile and menacing in my gaze that it affected them physically. Sometimes they literally fell to the ground under the impact of my dagger-like stare. The tragic thing is that something equally hostile and menacing had been present in my mother's gaze, especially after she started dabbling with spirits. My hostility towards them deepened as I realized that they were successfully and accurately deconstructing my claims to be an enlightened Buddhist. Indeed, the whole fabric of my Buddhist philosophy was being torn apart. "Klaus, just listen to what you say and compare it with what you do", they would say, and I knew in my heart they had a good point. I needed nothing else to convince me that I was a hypocrite who knew neither love nor inner peace, the very things I always liked to preach about.

With great pain, I came to the conclusion that I must quit Buddhism and everything that belonged to it. Once again, I had tried to discover something solid and lasting, a house built on rock, and the thing I found proved to have been built only on sand. What a terrible disappointment! All that moral teaching, the 2,200 laws, the theology, and in three and a half years of trying, it seemed that I had not found one Buddhist who was in any way free. I felt that not even Ajahn Chah was free, for all his great accomplishments. They were all great masters at discourse, but never followed up with deeds. If you listened to the Dalai Lama, how perfect his words sounded, about tolerance, love, respect and happiness. But I still felt that Buddhism could not provide the answer, the real way to get rid of sin and passion. In Zen Buddhism, there was a lot of talk about doing: when I eat, I eat, and so on. But why did those Zen Buddhists never find their objective? Was the path itself their objective? Was there something missing? In the end, I didn't want any more explanations, I wanted life. Just to live and love!

My two women friends moved out. They could not stand being with me any longer, and I can understand the reasons why. They had become convinced that my Buddhist persona was a fraud, so I had no religious calling to fall back on when I was left alone. My life appeared senseless and without meaning, I had reached the end of my tether. My hands were empty, because what I had tried to grasp just slipped away. My heart had wasted away. I felt I had made the horrifying discovery that neither love nor freedom really exist, and all the religions of the world fail in the end. This was the most shattering moment in my long religious search. I decided that all theories were useless, and therefore I had no purpose in life whatsoever.

But it turned out that those demons had not yet finished their work on me. They now whispered who my next "saviour" would be: I became addicted to alcohol.

I drank at least a litre of wine a day, often more, as well as spirits which I bought cheaply in Italy. I was in a state of permanent intoxication. As soon as the high from one drinking session began to wear off, and depression started returning, I would reach for the bottle and guzzle down some more.

My mind grew fuzzy, and I was unbearably lonely and embittered. Was my idiocy and that of others what "cosmic unity" really meant? I could no longer bear the injustice in the world, the ubiquitous desire for power, the eagerness for sex. I raged over the misdeeds of banks, which were taking over the role of churches, over environmental pollution, even over the petty gossip which poisoned human relations in the village where I lived. Most of all I raged against myself. The enormous quantities of alcohol that I was taking would kill me sooner or later. Having been treated so badly, my body began to take its revenge. I felt permanently weak and sick, with a pain in my side which suggested that my kidneys had reached their limit.

I did not entirely lack human company during this period, but the relationships were abusive and exploitative. Winning people's confidence and then playing games with them, disturbing them, became another addiction. I started frequenting discotheques all over Europe, from Hamburg to Ibiza. My sole purpose was to show off my powers as a seducer and wrecker of people's lives. Like a vampire, I began to dig my teeth into others' souls. This was my "shot of heroin", the thing that made life worth living and stopped me putting a bullet through my head. I lived through others, leeching off their strength, after which I disposed of them. As a self-appointed guru, I sought to deprive people of their free will and to make decisions in their place. I now realize that this was something similar to the sort of abuse which that lecherous priest had inflicted on me twenty years earlier. Restless, haunted and tortured within, I ran, full of suffering, from victim to victim, in nightclubs, on beaches, everywhere in Europe where young people liked to gather. Behind a mask of "wisdom", I brought suffering, destruction and discord among people, and meanwhile I was the unhappiest of all.

By now it was obvious that I would never return to the Buddhist monastery in the forest. So on my next visit to my Hamburg friends, Petra and Norbert, I asked them to hand me back the two diamonds given to me by Ajahn Chah. There was no question any more of my bringing them back to Thailand. I simply wanted to reclaim the gems, so as to sell them and make some money to support my hedonistic lifestyle. They went to the cupboard and took out the metal container, in which the diamonds had been wrapped in simple paper towels. My friends were not the kind of people who believed in safes with giant locks. We took the lid off, unwrapped the paper, and, to our utter astonishment, all we found were two little heaps of ash. We looked at each other in disbelief. My immediate reaction was to see this as a sign of the worthlessness of my Buddhist journey: it was a waste of time, and so was just about everything else.

My cynicism about religions and religious organizations was fed not only by disappointment with Buddhism, but also by things I was learning about various other cults and creeds that were popular among young people in the West. The Hare-Krishna movement I knew from within, having visited its European headquarters near Frankfurt. In fact, the Indian leader of the movement's European branch had been a fellow student and fairly close friend in Hamburg. Both in Frankfurt and at the global headquarters in Calcutta, I saw enough to convince me that the whole thing was a childish fad, not something for serious adults. The so-called Church of Scientology, with its prying manner and full coffers, seemed little better. I drew a similar conclusion about the Unification Church, run by the super-rich Reverend Moon in South Korea. For a time I was interested in

Baghwan Rajneesh, who at his peak had a vast following in the West. Then there was Guru Maharaj Ji, a chubby teenager, who claimed to be a reincarnation of God. On investigation, one of the attractions of his organization was the opportunity for plenty of promiscuous sex. All religious movements, I thought in my sceptical moments, were motivated by some combination of sex, money and power.

Moreover, the demons had begun to visit me more often and torment me in the night. There were many occasions when I dared not open my eyes for fear of seeing some hideous or repulsive face. I was beginning to feel the result of my involvement in witchcraft at many different stages of my life. The noose around my neck was being steadily tightened, and it was on the point of strangling me forever. I had moments of such incredible loneliness and depression that I even wanted to call my mother and ask her to come and help me, but I could not bring myself to pick up the receiver. I would simply sit by the telephone for long periods of time, helpless and in despair. My spirit was paralysed, my hand was paralysed – everything in me was dead. I had nothing and nobody.

The moment had come for the enemy to make his final attack. He wanted to possess not only my soul, but my body as well. So he planted in my mind new thoughts about a deceitful stratagem for obtaining freedom and peace. If he had succeeded, I would have become a useful collaborator in his work of destruction. What I now resolved to do was return to Latin America. I had never forgotten the extraordinary experience of visiting Mexico, and being taken into the confidence of a wizard who showed me some of his tricks. Now I decided to make further investigations of the secret occult teachings and magic powers which were practised in South America. I had only a vague knowledge of these things. I wasn't sure whether I should look to the indigenous people, or the voodoo-like cults practised by the descendants of slaves. I simply felt that somewhere in South America I would find new survival tricks. I had long known the power of "spirituality", of real magic, witchcraft practices (imported by black slaves from cults out of Africa), ecstasy states, and the paranormal. I had also long known the power of ecstasy through dance, as a way of seducing people, and of defiling women. Full of cunning and hope, I decided to fly to Peru.

But before I left I had a very unexpected sort of encounter with a person who had been one of the guiding lights of my life since we first met 15 years previously. Ursula came to see me in my village home in Switzerland, where I lived alone surrounded by liquor bottles and dark thoughts. Instead of a brown Buddhist robe, she was wearing a white sari. She was no longer emaciated by a monastic diet; her weight had gone back to normal. It was a delight to see her, and I knew at a glance that her life had been transformed. Her smile had always been warm, now it was radiant. To this day, I shudder to imagine what she must have thought of my wasted appearance.

In fact, I already knew from her correspondence that a big change had taken place in her religious affiliation. She started to tell me what had happened to her in the monastery and what she related sounded quite breathtaking:

"Remember the library in the monastery?" Of course, I did. "They had all kinds of spiritual books there", she went on, "and one day I found on one of the shelves something which attracted my curiosity. The title was something like, *The Way of a Pilgrim: A Russian Orthodox Hermit's Path*. So I went through the pages and thought that I had found just another 'mantra' in order to change our endless 'buddhaa, buddhaa, buddhaa', or our breathing or walking meditation. 'Let me try it, just for a change', I said to myself. I took only this sentence, *Lord Jesus Christ, have mercy on me*. But as you remember, I did not believe in Christ at all. I just wanted to practice with another 'mantra'. This I did several hours a day, for a period of two to three months. And then the shock happened! Suddenly, in a horrible agony, I clearly saw and realized that eternal death was waiting for me! I began to panic and fell into deep despair. This 'mantra' seemed not to have been a simple mantra, but had some hidden power in it, and this power revealed my inner hell. I realized that the 'fall of Adam' had been repeated in me, and the terrible fear of death could in no way be eliminated. This was the worst of all! My former meditation was absolutely useless in getting rid of this dread. I ran to see the master, Ajahn Chah, but he and the other older monks said in a banal tone that these were 'just thoughts', and that they would pass away after some time. Unfortunately, this was not the case. Luckily at that time a group of Christian missionaries visited the monastery and started to pray for me. I still did not believe, but through their prayer things became more bearable. It wasn't much longer before I left the monastery for good."

In fact, since the time she left the monastery she had begun sending me letters from where she was staying in India with a Christian family. She would write about the saving grace of Jesus, in what I would now recognize as an evangelical Protestant mind-set. In my cynical state of mind, I was irritated by these missives. I wanted to tear them up, but at the same time I had to admit that these letters tore at something within me. They had opened an old and painful wound.

Why had she turned up in Fribourg at that particular moment? Perhaps Ursula had sensed that I was depressed and in all manner of danger. Perhaps, I would now say, God sent her to ward off some bad event. In any case, she told me everything about her "wonderful experiences with Jesus". I couldn't quite believe it. I was impressed, however, by the way that the expression on her face had changed. She looked more peaceful and healthy than I had seen her for a long time. I knew her well enough to realize that she was not the sort of person to talk for the sake of it, or to say something thoughtless. As her words began to strike a chord in me, she said something grave:

"Klaus, if you still refuse to understand where life can be found and insist on going away, despite all my warnings, you will undoubtedly fall into the clutches of the spirits that you have searched for all your life."

"Yes I know. This is exactly what ..."

"Stop, stop! There is something you *must* know. These are destructive spirits, they only bring death. This will be your death! Your soul is already dead, and if you go to South America you risk being attacked bodily and then dying physically."

"Oh, leave me alone!"

But she did not do that.

"I keep on warning you, Klaus. You will not return from there alive. Please don't go to South America. Come to us! I, as well as you, have searched for so long. It is only in Jesus you'll find everything!"

I was too stubborn to follow her advice. Another force was at work in me, and it made sure I remained as I was. Ursula's words had thrown me off balance, but they were not powerful enough to make me change my plans. After she had left I became very confused, but nevertheless I bought my plane ticket. It would be some time before I realized how right Ursula was.

Before saying goodbye, she gave me a small gold crucifix on a chain, adding that its power would protect me from any "evil". I took it, but more in a spirit of superstition – after all, it was gold! She also gave me a book, *The Cross and the Switchblade*. It was the life story of Nicky Cruz, a onetime gang leader in New York, who had returned to Jesus Christ. Some of it I read during my journey. Thereafter destiny took its course.

CHAPTER EIGHT

THE LANDS OF THE PUMA

VERY SOON I LANDED IN LIMA, not as a normal tourist, but intent on sounding out the spiritual atmosphere and using my inner antennae. Where will the "message" come from? Was it the mysticism of the magic stone and Machu Picchu that had attracted me here like a magnet? No. Beyond all doubt something else was pulling me, it was pulling me to the north. Was it to be the wilderness of northern Peru? No, even there nothing seemed to hold me.

In Peru, as in so many other places, I played games with death. One day in Lima I returned to my hotel to find that a curfew had been imposed, because trouble was brewing. The atmosphere on the street was growing more tense by the minute. Sure enough, a full-scale gun battle was soon raging nearby. But I insisted on going out, walking straight to the city's main square, where some heavily armed soldiers warned me to leave as soon as possible. I complied only reluctantly. Some strange voice inside me kept giving the foolish advice that I was invulnerable, that nothing could touch me.

By the time I started travelling in South America, I was taking no drugs and very little alcohol. I was in pursuit of other mind-altering experiences. And from the moment I arrived on the continent, I felt strangely intoxicated. The feeling grew with every passing day. I had a decent amount of cash, having saved money from various temporary jobs in Switzerland, from archeological digs to teaching. I soon became used to travelling on overcrowded

buses, full of kitsch religious images and often carrying livestock
as well as people. I journeyed north to Ecuador over a mountain
route, gasping every time we took a hairpin bend and learning
not to notice the music that blasted endlessly in my ears. In a
village outside Quito, while strolling through the market-place, I
suddenly saw a man fixing me with a piercing gaze, the sort of gaze
that I used on people if I wanted to control them. I went up to him
and spoke to him in Spanish, and we became acquainted. Soon he
agreed to drive me up to the highlands in his goods van. He put me
in the back, in the open, while he took the steering wheel and his
friend sat beside him.

In a village outside Quito, the capital city of Ecuador

I followed my new friend to his home – a large tent – and was
conscious that he was bestowing a great honour on me by taking
me there. Inside the tent a group of men, perhaps eight or ten of
them, were sitting in a circle. They started to pass round a pipe,
offering me a drag, which I declined. There was a long, heated
and friendly discussion between the men. Suddenly, something

changed inside me, as though a sword had suddenly dropped from the sky and cut me off from all friendly contact with my Indian acquaintances. I would now say that I was possessed by some dark power. This was not, I believe, because the Indians tried to cast some spell over me. On the contrary, their intentions were nothing but friendly, as far as I could tell. Whatever happened must have concerned my disordered internal state. In any case, the result was that I could no longer participate in what was going on around me. With my heart thumping hard, I realized that I could no longer look anyone in the eye. It was similar to the worst of the worst of the "horror trips" which I had experienced ten years ago under the influence of drugs, back in Germany. The strange thing was that I had not taken any sort of intoxicant.

The conversation was stifled. Clearly my companions realized that something odd had happened. Overcome by panic, and without saying a word of farewell, I bolted out of the tent, rushed away from the Indian village, and down the mountain, going nowhere in particular. I ran on and on as if a giant magnet was pulling me and there was no escape. As I later realized, I was fleeing right into death's open arms.

I felt impelled to head northwards to Colombia, and I hitchhiked as far as the border. As soon as I passed the customs post, I was overcome by a sense of gloom and desolation. Was this because of the strange things going on inside me, or was the spirit of the country having an odd effect on me? Everything inside me seemed empty, rigid, cold and dead. I longed for some gleam of hope or relief. But I know that my soul was not completely covered in darkness, even at that moment, because I wrote a song on the way to Bogota, as we rattled through the night on the bus. I held in my breath as I penned the words. Knowing no God, I addressed the song to an anonymous recipient: YOU. The last verse at least sounded a note of optimism.

It won't be easy for me to come back.
'Cos I believed in what I'd done,
But I've been hurled away from my track,
Now I know that soon we shall be ONE.

Little realizing what a crime-ridden city it was, I arrived at night in Bogota, the capital of Colombia, and was immediately swallowed up by the fever of its eight million inhabitants. A certain heaviness pervaded the air and I felt as if everything was immersed in crime and violence – one did not have to be especially intuitive to realize this. Large and small shops were guarded by armed men. The cinemas showed violent films. Walls and kiosks were adorned with giant pictures of violent scenes. Guerrillas, drug-lords, and organized crime bosses created a climate of fear and corruption. I am not easily scared by violence, but the place unnerved me. Within hours of my arrival, there was a bad sign. I was crossing on the wide boulevard, jay-walking in between cars, with a rucksack on my back, when a shadow loomed behind me. It was a young man who fell on me like lightning and pulled my gold chain and cross from around my neck. In a flash he disappeared in the hurly-burly of the traffic. I felt as if I had been hit by a bomb. It was not that I cared about the material value of the cross. I simply remembered Ursula's promise that this keepsake would protect me. Clutching my way through a mental fog and barely able to move, I suddenly sensed a frightening thought entering my head. I was now so "naked" that any spirit whatever that wanted to take hold of me would be able to attack, and during this trip I had already sensed dark forces swirling around me.

I sat down on the strip dividing the two lanes of traffic, shaking and shuddering to the very core of my being. I remembered in a flash every single word that Ursula had spoken to me. I had long known that nothing happens by chance. From now on, I was in a very serious predicament. Some fateful moment, some high noon of my life, was approaching. I would have to be exceedingly attentive. To snap out of my half-paralysed state, I went to the police station, so I would at least get a document for my insurance company. What I saw and heard in that station made my hair stand on end. "Young man, I advise you to take off your wrist-watch. We have several cases each week where these bandits cut off their victims' arms to steal their watches. They tear off earrings from women's ears, as well as half the ear. I tell you, violence in this country is sadly a very great problem."

To top everything, in the room next door, a gangster was being held at gunpoint by a policeman with a machine-gun. Was I watching a movie? Was I in the Wild West? No. It was bitter, everyday reality. Before becoming totally panic-stricken I decided at once to leave the city and bought a ticket for Caracas in Venezuela. At 5 o'clock on a Friday evening, I climbed into a half empty bus, feeling relieved to have escaped from a nightmare. But even more sinister things lay ahead.

It was July 24, 1981. As we left the Colombian capital, twilight was rapidly turning into night and the offices were closing. Businessmen and police officers who lived on the outskirts were heading home, the weekend awaiting them. After about 90 minutes, we were deep in the countryside and I was just falling asleep, exhausted from the heat and humidity of the day and the troubles I had just lived through. And then it happened: Shots, screaming, shouting, thrashing about. To begin with, I had no idea what was going on, but then, after being brutally awakened by a blow on the head, I was punched and kicked. One of the gangsters stayed close to me and pressed a gun to my temple. He shouted loudly:

"Hands up! Don't move!" My heart was thumping.

"If anyone even thinks of moving or doing anything at all, I'll shoot!"

I counted five frightening figures. They were going to rob the passengers – there were eleven of us – using their guns, and they clearly did not mind at all if they injured or killed some of us in the process. This was something more than a routine act of theft; they seemingly wanted to take us captive. The gunmen forced the bus driver off the main road and told him to turn up a small side road towards a lonely mountainous area. In the meantime, the darkness outside was profound. Oh, hell! This time it's happening to me, I thought. I began sweating with anxiety as I remembered Ursula's warnings, and wished I had heeded her advice not to go to Latin America at all. I kept saying, "Why me?" Thus far, I had always been lucky, or mysteriously protected, in dangerous situations. But I now felt that I might be running out of luck.

I felt I had no alternative but to seek the help of occult powers. On several previous occasions, they had protected me from guns and knives. Surely they would not abandon me now; they would get me out of this mess. It only needed one thing: I had to look my enemy – the gangster who was threatening me – in the eye, and then I could frustrate him. This would only take a couple of seconds. I reckoned that before the other four gangsters noticed anything, I could push back the window, which was already half-open, and then save myself by jumping out into the bushes. The bus was travelling at a speed of 50–60 kilometres, slow enough. And that was my only chance. As if reading my mind, one of the other gangsters came to my window, closed it and pulled the curtain. Oh no! But I would not give up. To make things worse, they forced me to bend my head down and keep my hands on the back of the seat in front. All I could see were the gangster's legs and shoes; I could feel the barrel of the gun pressing on my temple.

It was now or never. I had to lift my head to look into his eyes, so as to "hold" him in my gaze, using a familiar technique. As soon as I made the slightest movement, the gangster hit me on the head with his gun. I saw stars dancing before my eyes and wished I could kill him. Suddenly, everything went black and I felt the warm blood flowing down my face. Only then did I fully realize that this was very serious – deadly serious.

Having glimpsed the bloodlust in the gangsters' eyes, I felt panic settle in. I was no longer in control of anything, but doubled up in my seat, in a ghastly state with blood dripping onto the floor. My heart was thudding furiously and I began to think I was heading towards eternity. Time stood still. I thought of my unhappy life going back to the beginning, to my birth. All I could see was pain, sadness, misery, loneliness, and more loneliness.

Again I pressed my arm on my head-wound to stop the blood from flowing, as the more blood he saw, the harsher he became. I had seen that "thirst" to kill in all the gunmen. I sensed their unrelenting hatred towards us "gringos" (people from the capitalist

West and the USA). Among the hardened killers in this part of the world – whether they were guerrillas, drug-traders or simply bandits – there was a callous feeling that "the only good gringo is a dead gringo" – that was what I had often heard. Feeling pain and humiliation, I began settling my accounts with life.

Suddenly, in that atmosphere of death, something new happened inside me. A vision appeared in my mind's eye, and it was very clear and precise. I saw a huge building, a skyscraper, collapsing. (When years later, I saw the World Trade Center falling down, on television, it reminded me intensely of this experience.) An enormous quantity of debris was crashing down to earth, and it was steadily extinguishing a flame glowing underneath. But while a tiny flame was still flickering, a fraction of a second before its imminent extinction, a voice was heard asking:

"Klaus, are you ready to die?"

I had heard that question before. When I was in the monastery in Thailand, wanting to become a monk, the abbot had asked me this same question in front of all the other monks.

"Klaus, are you prepared for death?"

A "yes" was expected from any sincere monk. But I only shouted out loudly, laughing in their faces:

"No, I want to live!"

On hearing this bold, rude and unexpected answer, they all burst out laughing, although monks are always meant to be very sober. Of course, for them I was a stranger, and a stupid one. They knew that people like me had to learn many things in the monastery and that this would take a lifetime. That is what I thought too, but in a different way: I wanted to learn how to live and was not heading for the kind of Buddhist disaster *they* represented to me. For me the monks were scaredy-cats who needed to learn more about real life. I was confident enough in those days to think that I was a better Buddhist, or at least on the way to becoming a better Buddhist, than they.

But here and now the same question was put to me. Am I ready to die? How much bitterness and disappointment I must have felt as I answered to myself: "Yes, I am ready to die, because I have tried everything on this planet." This life was an unending chain of drudgery and torment mixed with fear and hatred. "Peace, love, freedom, God" – these did not exist! They were only the theories and fantasies of certain philosophers or fake gurus with the gift of the gab, but nothing real. That is how I felt then, at last having reached the end of my long journey at thirty-six years of age, even if I might have wished or imagined it to be otherwise. I was prepared to continue my suffering "into the next world", just in case reincarnation was possible. Perhaps it would be better there.

In any case, what did I have to live for? I had never understood the answer to that question. What else could be hoped for? My life had been a journey through darkness from beginning to end, and was at that moment falling into the deepest precipice, from which there would be no escape. I would have to give in to my fate. Money, wealth, power, sex, success, *ascesis*, loneliness, periods of acceptance by the world, periods of being forgotten by the world, life in palaces and slums, life with women and witches, being chased away with stones, war . . . I had known them all, success and downfall, and had never found freedom, peace or who I really was. Acclaimed and beaten, tasting honour, humiliated by ugly words and shame, starving or with an excessively full stomach – it was always harsh within. I sought the adventure called "life". But here I was, beaten and bleeding, with only one thought in mind. "Pull that trigger, you wretch. Go on, do it! Perhaps you will be my liberator."

Then another extraordinary thing occurred, albeit only in mind. I had the feeling that someone from above the precipice into which I was falling had thrown a rope to save me. My hope came "from up there", without my deserving it, without my doing anything or using any strength. I learned later that this is called "grace". At the moment I was ready to die, it was as if I heard a voice speaking to me: "To die, you will first have had to live!"

It was so unexpected and yet so logical. That proposition reminded me of a maxim I had heard as a child: "God is life!" What does this cliché mean to anyone anyway? So-called pious Christians had always been careful to make sure that religious maxims and Bible verses adorned the walls of their sitting-rooms and even bathrooms.

I had never met anyone who took this sort of maxim seriously, so these were probably just empty words, a sort of rhetoric that conveyed nothing. But in my situation on the verge of death, such a statement sounded totally different. If God *truly* exists and is Life, I thought, *now* was the time for Him to show Himself. If He was not going to give me proof of His existence, and of the fact that "God is life", then it would be better that I died. I did not want or desire to continue my life, not knowing the answer to those questions. Out of the depths of a lost heart I shouted mightily, "God, if you exist save me now!" Even so, my unbelief was strong. I did not want to survive and then tell myself afterwards: "Old man, you have been lucky again, don't give me those theories about God. It was just a matter of luck or hazard." I wanted to know and I *had* to know! So much so, that I added a P.S. to my S.O.S. "God, if you really exist, give me palpable, visible proof, so that I shall know you are the One who has saved me. Otherwise I am better off dead!"

It was in this way that I first met my Unknown God. I could only accept concrete proof if I was to survive. To describe what happened, I should first explain that the most precious and meaningful thing that I carried with me on my travels, the thing I always clung to, was my diary. It contained all the songs I had written. This journal had been with me for the last twelve years, on all my journeys throughout the world, and it was like a palpable symbol of my own self. All my experiences, suffering, songs, drawings and important moments of my travels were poetically expressed in those pages. This diary was my "talking partner" in lonely times, the last and most faithful companion. It was unique and could not be reproduced, and I had taken good care of it for a dozen years. But now, this and all my other things were in the leather bag that the bandits had taken away, at the beginning of their assault. It would be useless to plead with them; they needed my bag, because they were just about to take everyone's money and passports and wanted somewhere to store the loot. Money and passport were less important to me than my precious journal.

Cash and documents can always be replaced. Besides, I knew ways and means of finding money, illegally if necessary, but the diary was a different story. The thought of losing it was unbearable. Even when my life was in mortal danger, I still fretted about that precious journal.

The bus trundled on, passing various settlements, along narrow roads, climbing towards the mountains. It was pitch dark. Far away from any kind of civilization, the driver was forced to stop and another unpleasant surprise awaited us. We were met by yet more bandits armed with machine guns. I counted seven of them. They came onto the bus holding up their guns for us all to see. One by one we were dragged out, with threats and beatings, and pushed into a freshly-dug muddy pit. I was sitting at the back of the bus and was the penultimate passenger to be hauled out, kicked and punched. We were all frozen, shaking and deathly quiet, there in that hole, until each one of us was pushed deeper into the pit. The bandits were now at the edge of the pit and above us. Their guns were pointing at us. ...

It is almost impossible to describe what followed next. Nobody spoke anymore. I was not even thinking. My last impression was of some black silhouettes, lit by the lamps of the two vehicles, like shadows moving frantically to and fro. There was an atmosphere of sheer terror. It felt as though the release of those guns, due to go off any second, would almost have been a relief. Now they were going to shoot ... and everything would end.

But what actually took place was so unexpected, that even the gangsters were dumbfounded. God is truly All-Powerful and what He does is not within man's reckoning – that is what I have come to believe. Suddenly there was a noise in the darkness. From the pit I was in, I could see figures approaching rapidly. They came from a dark clump of trees, but gradually their silhouettes were lit up by the headlights of the gangsters' vehicles. The new arrivals were Indians dressed in white, of all things, and they were riding bicycles! Instead of unleashing their guns on to us, their prisoners, the gangsters started to shoot in all directions. Clearly the Indians belonged to a rival group. A few of the gangsters rushed towards the

Indians. From the hole where I was cowering, I could see how one of the first Indians was beaten with the butt of a gun and fell to the ground. I couldn't say if he was dead or alive. His body was dragged to the edge of the pit and thrown in beside me. The rest of the Indians acted with lightning speed. As they were on bicycles, they managed to disappear into the night. This prompted the gangsters to follow them in a car. The gunmen were now separated into two parties: while one lot was still holding us in check, the second followed the runaways. But the cyclists apparently had enough of a head start to hide somewhere in that desolate area. After a while some shots were heard, and then a deathly stillness.

Were those the bullets which had been destined for us? Had my "Unknown God" directed them towards another goal? Whatever the truth, I felt life coming back into me, and I was ready to burst from emotion. What had happened? It might not be long till the murderers would return, but at that exact moment I felt that the tide was turning in our favour. Were the gangsters afraid now? Had they fallen into a trap? Had they been betrayed and recognized? All at once *they* became anxious and nervous, and appeared to have completely forgotten us. In great haste, they loaded up their car with the things taken from us and disappeared into the night. But ... what about my bag? My diary and my songs? I had seen them put *my* bag into their car.

Some time passed before we dared to breathe. Everyone was still afraid that the bandits would return, or that they had hidden themselves nearby to shoot us from behind. Bit by bit we became more confident and climbed out of the pit. My fellow passengers, who were ordinary "campesinos", uttered the first words: "We are saved! Thank you, Lord. What a miracle!" The air was full of joyful shouts: "Milagro, maravilla!" I was happy too, but still a bit confused. What was my own life worth, after all? Would I ever get a response to my request for a sign of God's existence? Survival alone did not seem enough. Full of questions, I climbed back into our bus and went back to where I had been sitting. I could not believe it. Everything was gone, *except* one single object, and as I came close I saw that it had been placed in my seat. I recognized it – it was my diary with my songs in it! It had been deliberately placed there, on my seat. It was obvious that it could not have simply fallen out of the bag by chance. The bag was solid and nothing could just fall out of it. If they had only wanted to take the valuables, then they would have poured out everything, the dirty handkerchiefs and smelly socks, as well as other old tat. I was utterly perplexed. How had this been possible?

For the first time in my life the great question really posed itself. I had received signs and messages of comfort at other critical moments in my life. I did not know how to interpret them, and they did not linger in my mind very long. But now the ultimate question arose in a way that I could not dodge or escape. Does "Someone" *really* exist above Who knows us? Was this whole story like a chess game, and this "Someone above" knew all of my moves in advance, respected my free will and decisions, but in the end always brought forth something "good" for my benefit? Was there "Someone" who had lived alongside me, through all those battles, and was now "answering" my question? The object in front of me seemed like palpable proof. The thought shook me to the core.

CHAPTER NINE

RETURN TO THE OLD CONTINENT

MY LATIN AMERICAN TRAVELS were not quite over. There were more troubles in store. I travelled day after day through the northern Brazilian jungle, hitching rides on timber trucks, which negotiated the dirt roads near the Amazon. Once I took a rickety coach through part of the Amazon region. We were warned that our journey took us through an area where it was not unusual for Indians to kill white people. Sure enough, one night, just as our vehicle was about to cross a river by boarding a sort of raft, I heard a terrible commotion and realized that our driver was being threatened. My fellow passengers, all locals, looked very frightened. But somehow divine grace intervened, the argument died down, and we were allowed to proceed. In the so-called asphalt jungle of Rio de Janeiro, I once again came across mediums who practised occultism, but because of the great fear I had experienced during that recent criminal attack in Colombia, I began to withdraw from the dark world. An inner voice was clearly warning me. After the Colombian incident I became very keenly aware that I would never find any resting place in magic and witchcraft. However, I could not yet free myself from the powerful forces that were holding on to me. In a hotel in Bolivia I experienced another devastating battle with the demons, which penetrated my room in the form of green smoke, making hideous shapes that paralysed me with fear and gave me a feeling of suffocation and panic. Only in Thailand had I felt psychic terror of such intensity. I now had an overwhelming sense that I never wanted to undergo that sort of experience again. The mixture of physical danger and mental turmoil had left me drained. To crown it all, not long afterwards, in La Paz, I was robbed in the middle of a market-place. There must be more to life than this, I told myself.

Feeling thoroughly jaded, I took a plane back to Switzerland in the autumn. I did not know it then, but that flight was to be the last stage in the relentless series of long, exhausting journeys that had consumed my life for the past 14 years.

The next phase in my life did not require air travel: it was an inner journey between head and heart on the road towards God. It began with a visit from my spiritual sister, Ursula, who was studying at the "All Nations Bible School" in London. Having heard that I was back in Fribourg, she came to see me and listened carefully as I related to her the gangster attack I had experienced in Colombia. Her response surprised me and left me rather sceptical.

"It was Jesus! He was the One who saved you!"

"I beg your pardon?"

"Yes. On that same day, in our school, all my fellow students and I had a very strong feeling that you were in great peril, and so we prayed for you."

My immediate reaction was to think that this could not be true. It was too cheap. Could she prove it?

"When did this happen?"

In answer to this question, she told me the exact day the attack had taken place, something she could not possibly have known. Had she read it in the papers? She answered in the negative. But I was not yet convinced; my aversion towards Christians was stronger than the proof she had given me. At that time, I felt that even if Ursula's Jesus existed, he would not be my type. I would have been afraid of him, of his moral rules, and certainly of his representatives. And anyway, I used to think, "the people up there" had no need of someone like me. I would only create a great disorder in the heavens if they were to let me in at all.

Yet somewhere in my soul I held on to a few of the things she said. I was uncertain how to respond and, as had so often been the case, there was something in Ursula's very presence which made me feel uneasy. She noticed this and withdrew for a short time. But after a week or so she came back to see me. Her Swiss home was in Lausanne, at the headquarters of a Protestant association for the study of the Bible. But she seemed ready to travel the 75 kilometres to my home in Fribourg as often as she needed to make her point.

"Klaus", she said once, "after all that we have been through, together and separately, I can understand that you do not want to try anything else which might disappoint you yet again."

"Yes, that's true, I have been disappointed on every previous occasion and so this time I will not allow myself to fall into the net of another religion."

"You will not be cheated, this I can guarantee. I am telling the truth. Look at me! But if you do not give me credit, perhaps you can believe my friends. Please do come and pay us a visit."

"I have no need of your God! I can help myself."

"It is obvious you can't, as you have found out for yourself."

She was very insistent and because I really liked her – after all she had been my wife – I agreed to visit her in Lausanne.

That was the first step on my new journey, one that did not involve leaving Switzerland but did have many unexpected turns. I went to her "Bible House" in Lausanne, but I found the other people there too insipid for my taste. So she invited me to a village called Huemoz, where there was a centre for drug addicts and alcoholics, and where they were freed of these addictions in the name of the Lord Jesus. With the residents of that place I had something in common – they knew life's rough edges. Ursula introduced me to many other communities and groups. With her I went to an ecumenical meeting where I talked with some learned priests and theologians, who told me many things about this unknown Jesus. For my taste, they used too many Scriptural passages. At times I felt like slapping them across the face with a copy of their own beloved book, whose point they seemed to have missed. After all of my experiences, I felt I had learnt that life is not a series of theories or mere theological ideas. If the Word of God made any real difference to anybody, these people seemed determined to keep the secret to themselves by blinding their listeners with excessive amounts of learning and theory. That is how I felt. As I argued with them, I felt full of self-confidence. Satan kept giving me powerful arguments against what they were saying. I was too proud and "experienced" to take these so-called Christians seriously. What experiences had they had? It seemed as if they were all trying to convince me of something that did not exist, at least in my world. Most of the pastors and leaders I met in Ursula's circle held long discussions, and this was where I could score by my craftiness, as I felt I was invincible in an argument. I sarcastically named them "baby-faces", because they kept inviting me all the time, with a broad smile, to have some tea and biscuits. Even now, although I would try to be more charitable in my judgment, I feel that there was a distinct falseness in the larger-than-life smiles that I came across in that Bible-minded world. At the time, being a young cynic, I used to look at their toothy grins and ask myself when they would turn into a vampire's bite. Gurus in India had inspired a similar feeling in me. Their tactics had no effect on me. Instead, I felt I had "finished" with them by trumping their arguments, and I went away after such talks feeling very proud of myself.

However, a gap now appeared in my "protecting wall", made up of pride, scorn and disbelief. One day, when we were both in Fribourg, Ursula asked if I could take her in my car to a meeting of the YWAM (Youth With a Mission) association in Lausanne and stay with them for that evening. I hesitated but eventually agreed. On the motorway between Fribourg and Lausanne, the engine of my Renault began to cough and splutter, refusing to go any further. I called up the Touring Club patrol for help. Even though the mechanic could not find the fault, we managed to arrive at the meeting place by keeping up a slow, juddering pace. It was a Sunday afternoon and I feared that at the close of the meeting, late at night, I would not be able to get home with a faulty car, so I resolved to leave Ursula there and return immediately. She said that all would be well and began to pray for the car. The thought went through my mind at that moment that she was mad, but out of respect for her I said nothing. After a long exhortation from my old friend, I agreed to stay and accompany her to the meeting. The atmosphere became unbearable when everyone in that hall lifted up their hands towards the ceiling, chanting and intoning "Alleluia". "What a band of fools!" I said, with disdain.

This was too much for me and I dashed outside. In retrospect, I would say that there was real spiritual power in that gathering and this was intolerable for my old self, which was still in the grip of dark forces. Only the tea and cakes being served at the end of the meeting were enough to lure me back into the hall. After ten o'clock, I said goodbye to Ursula and left for home. Somehow the car *did* take me all the way without stopping, even though it coughed and spluttered.

My amazement was great indeed the next day, when the garage mechanic lifted his head from under the bonnet and said:

"Hey, Klaus, can you explain how you got here?"

"As you can see, on my own: coughing and spluttering."

"Come on, be serious. You must have turned the engine off and free-wheeled downhill."

"What do you mean?"

"Well, the coil from the spark plug is broken on both sides. In all my life, I have never seen a car move even one metre without a spark distributor. This is a miracle!"

I was taken aback, and a bit irritated, by his choice of words, and yet now *I too* was truly amazed. There had indeed been a prayer for the car – and I don't know what else – but I kept quiet about that now, because I was embarrassed. It was something completely beyond my understanding – too crazy, unbelievable!

A few weeks later, Ursula invited me to meet a Swiss lady of sixty-seven years, called Edmée Cottier, whose chalet was in Rougemont. Edmée, who had lived for thirty-three years in Angola, had been attacked and kidnapped by a rebel group of the so-called liberation army UNITA. This lady, despite her advanced years, was dragged by soldiers through scrubland, for some 1,600 kilometres in torrid heat. At this point in her story she spoke of how she was saved by Jesus. He had accompanied her. He had given her strength to endure exhaustion. It was a very impressive story, and what fascinated me was the fact that this lady did not have a "baby-face". Her skin was tanned, full of wrinkles, looking more like the skin of an Indian. I liked her. Instead of preaching morality at me, her eyes transmitted a fantastic power. Her face was a constant smile and an incredible strength emanated from her soul. Slowly my defences seemed to collapse. Gaps appeared in the wall I had put around myself. Could it be that there was something real and true in what she was saying? No. I did not want to accept this. Maybe she was

Edmée Cottier (left),
with my friend, Diane, in Lausanne

mistaken, I told her. I returned home, thinking I had convinced her that she had been the victim of some illusion.

So it went, on and on. . . . How long was this going to last? I could well imagine that everyone who knew me in that Swiss Christian circle had concluded that I was a hopeless case. Indeed this seemed to my cynical self to be proof of my superiority over them. I thought I had given enough conclusive proof to affirm that I needed no one – and particularly not their Jesus. *Nobody* was stronger than myself! No one at all in this world! But at that point in the conversation, they would all interject, "Except for *one* man". As Edmée had mentioned in our last meeting, this was a man I could meet soon if I wanted to.

About this man, who was for some reason considered to be stronger than myself, I had already heard from other Christians. I was becoming familiar with the tactics of these people and it was obvious to me how such a meeting would end, which is why I refused to take things further. But on one particular occasion, despite my reluctance, they were unusually firm and, using great diplomacy, insisted that I meet this person. Appealing to my pride, they said that the speaker was someone renowned, who had written many books, and despite the fact that he was very busy and famous, was ready to receive me, as he had already heard much about me. All of this was very flattering of course.

"So this man is really stronger? And he believes he can do something for me?" I asked in a rather provocative way, anticipating my meeting with him. Gripped by a strong desire to "show" him - this "famous one" – what I thought of his wares, I agreed to see the great man.

The meeting took place some weeks later in Lausanne. It was Saturday 10th September, 1981. We were to meet at 10 o'clock in front of the cathedral doors, as had been arranged through a third party. In order to show this "famous man" that I had no need of him, I arrived late on purpose, at around midday. I sat in front of the doors and waited. Some time later he came out, accompanied by Edmée, Ursula and several of their friends, and he came straight up to me. As soon as I saw him, a feeling of alarm unleashed itself in me. I could see that the person approaching me had a powerful aura about him. Vain as I was, I had the feeling that two titans were about to meet. It had always been my custom to look new acquaintances deep in the eyes in order to find out if there was anything unsure or unsteady about them. In this case, I could detect no chinks in the armour. A man of nearly sixty-five years of age, with long white hair, walked towards me, looking intensely at me, but with a gaze that was also full of love. He looked at me without batting an eyelid. That said everything. There was no longer any doubt – it was him or me! There could only be one winner from this confrontation. And deep inside myself I thought: Ursula and her friends were right in

My first fatherly friend, Pastor Maurice Ray
and Ursula in the background

their assumption. This would be my last battle! That he would be the loser, I was quite certain. I knew my strategy.

Spoiling for a fight, I went up to him and provoked him by saying:

"Good day, *Maurice*! Can I be informal with you?" I wanted to test his sincerity. I had met puffed-up, "virtuous persons" before, who smiled sweet sheep-like smiles a bit too often. If Pastor Maurice Ray had shown me such a face I would have left without another word. The problem would have been settled. But he answered me in the same tone as I had used. "Of course, my dear chap." With a broad and friendly smile he invited me to follow him to a building next to the cathedral, where we would be alone and in a quiet place. I agreed, but I had no intention of letting my defences drop. I felt that I was guarded by an impenetrable inner armament. But Ursula and her friends were also determined. They said they would be praying somewhere nearby while Maurice and I spoke.

I began by telling him about my lifelong journey, full of suffering, and he listened attentively. After I had finished my story, he said dryly:

"This is very *bad* news. The time has come for *good* news. Don't you agree?"

I did agree with him and I was happy, because he had not tried to fob me off with biblical verses. He had the experience to deliver the "*Good* News", in this case, of the Gospel, in such a way that it did not put me off.

I told him how one of those "baby-face" pastors had asked me once to pronounce consciously and loudly the name of Jesus. I had to admit to Maurice that I had felt sick and ill at that moment, as if someone were strangling me, and that my mouth would not open. Even if interrogators had threatened to cut out my tongue if I did not immediately pronounce the word and name "Jesus", I would have found it impossible to do so. Maurice understood this perfectly; he could see that I was under the influence of demons. His insights were something I could not have foreseen. He realized that behind my aggressive exterior, there was weakness,

a weakness which had made me receptive to the demons and
therefore incapable of pronouncing the name of Jesus.

Maurice laughed joyfully, knowing he had made progress:

"Now do you see why our new friends sent you to me?"

"No, not at all. Why?"

"Because you are a 'puppet on a string!' All your life you have
been nothing more than that." I became upset:

"Maurice, please don't talk like that. Don't taunt me! You might
seriously regret it ... I warn you."

"No Klaus, this is the truth. You know, in life there is always
someone who pulls the strings. While God respects man's freedom,
Satan does not give you that chance, because with him you are *forced*
to give in. You have to follow him."

Something went "bang" inside my head. I was perplexed, but
as I looked back on my life I realized that Maurice could well have
been right. All this time I had thought I was my own master, but in
truth my real master had always hidden and never revealed himself
to me. He worked in darkness. Shivers went through me as I sensed
the truth of this statement.

"Don't even imagine that the smallest spark of strength you
have ever had came from inside you. For one thing, you are always a
servant of somebody – you cannot ever be neutral. I pity you if you
are serving the one whom you should not be serving. Do you realize
this – is this not so?"

"Well, life has not been a bed of roses up until now. In that you
are right."

"Klaus, all you need to do is to move over to the other camp, to
serve the Other One. But don't forget that God never forces! You
can only follow Him by your own will and if you really wish it. Then
you will never ever be disappointed again. His purpose is as follows:
love and life, freedom and peace."

I suddenly understood that I possessed none of these values.
Hitherto my "faith" had been in power, force, and freedom – in
the sense of rejecting all constraints. Now, that faith was becoming
more fragile. But the fear of being disappointed, yet again, at the
end of this road was also powerful. Maurice went on:

"You know, dear friend, you are not free, you ..." – here he hesitated – "are bound by occult forces. If Satan is once allowed to enter a soul, finding there a place to rest, then he does not willingly depart. He considers that soul his own rightful property and wants to dominate it. You, Klaus, have been a good collaborator with the underworld, and that is why you have received power from Lucifer. But you have paid for it with your life, and in your soul. Your qualities have been lies, hatred, destruction, loneliness and death. You do not know God – He is on the opposite side. And above all, He is stronger than Satan."

To my surprise, I found myself admitting that everything he said sounded reasonable. Then Maurice continued:

"Now I will tell you why you have been sent to me. God has given me the grace and commissioned me to free – in His Name – those who are caught in Satan's net. But this can happen only if they freely wish it. In other words, I am prepared to release you from your links with the occult. I do not do this in my name, but in the name of Jesus, Who is the One Who frees you. It is now up to you to decide whether you want this to be so or not."

At this point I baulked. I was absolutely certain of one thing:

"No, Maurice, no way! I don't want to become a Christian, not one of those "baby-faces", with plump full-moon expressions and a wobbly pudding-chin!"

"That is not what you will be", he added quickly. He was evidently certain of that.

I was still somewhat dubious. I asked:

"What precondition does this exorcism of yours require?"

Maurice answered quietly:

"None. And it does not automatically mean that you are a Christian."

"Then what's the use?"

"We are talking about being *free*. That's all. Free of Satan. You will first be 'released' so that you can decide what you will do later on." This was an honest offer. After hesitating slightly, I finally agreed to it. Later we would see what might follow. In fact, I felt I had nothing to lose. Yet another experience would be of little importance to me after all that I had gone through. I had heard about "exorcism" in a certain Hollywood film. Why shouldn't I go through that sort of thing as well? It would cost me nothing and afterwards I could just tick it off as one more life experience and simply forget about it. So I didn't object any longer.

"Klaus, we understand each other?"

"Yes, go ahead." Maurice knelt on the ground next to me and began to pray. First in French, the language we had been speaking, then suddenly he was praying "in tongues" – a language I could not comprehend. Doubts rose up within me. I felt that here, too, strange spirits were being called upon, the sort of spirits that had worked at one time for the paedophile pig who marred my youth. What was he playing at? A terrible fear gripped me.

As if reading my thoughts, he went on in French, so that I could follow him. Then I heard something like this:

"In the name of Jesus Christ, I bind up all the forces that are in Klaus. Through the power of Jesus, I order them to leave his spirit and his body, so that Klaus can be freed and come to know and accomplish God's plan for his life."

During this prayer, I felt strangely stirred somewhere deep in my inner self, although I remained perfectly awake so that I should not be taken in by anything spooky. Every fibre of my being was alert.

When it was over I asked him:

"What now?"

He answered:

"Now you are free. Go wherever you like and do whatever pleases you."

I thought it had all been a bit too quick. "What? Really? Have you finished?" I had imagined something more gruesome and thrilling.

"Yes, the forces of Satan in you are now bound up by the authority of Jesus."

Now I had really become curious and wanted to know more about this.

"Hey Maurice, now I am really interested in finding out if all those stories about this Jesus of yours are true – for example, that He knows everybody."

There were something like six billion people in the world! I wondered how much work this would mean for Him. He must really be worked off his feet. How was this possible?

"He knows more than that, Klaus", Maurice said, adding that, "Jesus also knows our thoughts, in fact, even before we have thought them."

Now what he expected me to believe sounded worse than science fiction! This was just beyond me.

"How can I know that you Christians are not lying? Who is to prove to me the truth of what you have just said? What must I do to find this out?"

"For this you must pray", he said laconically.

"What!?" I burst out. "You're not going to ask me now to begin reading empty formulas or beautiful words from a piece of paper, or to repeat something after you parrot fashion. I have never prayed and don't even know how to."

All I knew was how my mother and the other Pharisaical characters I had known in my youth had prayed. I continued:

"When I was young, I was always obliged to repeat words. You can surely understand that this is not what I want, can't you?"

He understood.

"No, no", he said laughing and calming me down. "To pray is much more simple. You can think or – even better – say out loud all that you feel within. Say only what you feel deep in your heart, tell the *truth*."

"Is it really that simple? Then I suppose I can do it too."

But I was already asking myself another question. The heart, where is it? Did I have a heart? As I remembered, Mother Theresa had placed her hand on my heart, that time in Calcutta, advising me to look for the *truth* there, deep down in my heart. Was it possible that through this exorcism the road to my heart would now open? At that moment I found, to my surprise, that I could pronounce the name of Jesus without having those attacks, as if someone was strangling me. So I closed my eyes and tried to look into my heart, before saying in a loud voice:

"All right, Jesus, if all these stories I have heard about you lately are true, and if you really know all the people in the world, including me, and my thoughts – even before I have thought them – then, Jesus, if all this is true, you *must* know that I do *not* believe in you. You also know that I would like to believe in you. But you must understand me, I have suffered too much in my life to believe anything or anyone blindly. Too often have I been blinded and cheated. OK? But look, I will now make you an offer. If You will speak to me, then I'm willing to believe in You."

But how would I know if I received the answer I was looking for? Immediately after I had pronounced these words, I began to experience seeds of doubt about the authenticity of voices which appeared to come from another world. On the other hand, I had been a medium before and had clearly heard voices from the other plane of existence, so I added:

"But watch out, Jesus. I don't want to be fooled. I can recognize the voices of the other world. I want to be certain that it is *You* Who is speaking to me."

Maurice had advised me to speak the truth, and that is just what I did. This was my first prayer, and it came from the depths of my soul.

"Jesus will speak to you", Maurice assured me laughingly. He seemed utterly convinced that it would happen.

Honestly, at that moment I thought Maurice rather naïve and a bit of a dreamer. Frankly, how or by whom could something like this be considered *seriously*? Certainly not by me. I mean, vain and self-centred as I might be, I still wondered who was I that this eternal and world-famous Jesus should deign even to think of me, one out of billions! So, provokingly, I threw out these words:

"Well, if that happens … I'll let you know." Poor Maurice. I felt almost sorry for him.

Who would have thought then that my last battle had begun, and that it would be a fight between life and death. It was as tense and nerve-jangling a standoff as any Hollywood drama. Without the Grace of God, and the support and prayers of my friends, the next twenty-four hours would have seen me ground down like a grain of sand by the power of Satan. I had decided not to return to Fribourg before I had received palpable proof that God existed. I would rather have died in Lausanne than to have returned and to have continued living in my ignorance. The battle began for real on Saturday afternoon.

In the Cathedral of Lausanne, that day, an annual festival began called, "Days of Repentance and Prayer". It was to last three days and there would be a series of celebrations and talks. Speakers came from far away, both pastors and priests, and numerous lay-persons came by coach to listen to them. "An important event", explained Edmée Cottier, who was taking care of me during those days and praying for me continuously. She told me very clearly that besides herself a whole group of people were praying for me, so that I would "overcome it all without damage to myself", because, as she warned me, "it will not be easy".

After six decades of life, Edmée was a true powerhouse and I had enormous respect for her. Because of this, I agreed to go with her to the cathedral on Saturday evening. We were seated rather too near the front. As I did not understand very much of what the speaker was saying, I became bored and slowly fell asleep, my head lolling from left to right and back again. I heard the speaker's voice from "far away", as if through a dense fog. Then my head dropped downwards, and I was about to start dreaming when something happened.

As if from some very distant place I heard the words, *"Be joyful in the Lord always"*. My sleepiness made the words sound indistinct. Anyway, I half-felt this was just an empty phrase – one of those Christian clichés, often heard but never lived. They went in one ear and out the other. Suddenly, the speaker looked in my direction and I was sure he was eyeing me. I woke up immediately; he may well have seen me dozing off. I felt trapped like a thief in a shop, caught in the act by the store detective. This startled me out of my apathy, I blushed and in the twinkling of an eye I became highly attentive to what the speaker was saying. His words seemed addressed to me *personally* and they struck deep inside me. The speaker must have noticed that I wasn't paying attention, because he seemed to repeat the exhortation especially for me.

"Once again, I repeat: Be joyful!"

Now I was really wide awake! At these words, my mind became dizzy. At great speed a film started playing in my brain. Why was that guy repeating those words? And why was he looking at *me* while he spoke them? It was obvious. Because he had caught me dozing. I blushed like a little schoolboy caught cheating. I recalled that even my teachers had to repeat everything twice before I would obey! So it was with this preacher here.

But now, what struck me much more than the first time I heard it was the command, *"Be joyful"*. The words were like an exhortation, an encouragement. Up until now my only experience of "happiness" had been when taking drugs or alcohol, or when I could exercise my power over someone. But that did not bring true happiness. Now these words had touched a vulnerable and responsive spot in me. How could this speaker know? No, it was something that he could not possibly know.

My thoughts were now intensely preoccupied with the possibility that seemed to be offered. Was it really possible to feel joy? I did not immediately understand the sentence that followed:

"Let everyone see that you love one another and are kind to each other!"

I'm afraid that my idea of "love" and "kindness" had become proverbial among those people, across Europe and the world, who were unfortunate enough to fall into my clutches. Anybody who came near me felt afraid of me and feared for their life, sensing intuitively the hatred lurking behind my mask. So I was unreceptive to the idea of mutual love. Then I heard the following words:

"The Lord is near!"

BANG! At that point something exploded in my head. Still under the influence of Maurice's encouraging words, I actually turned my head round to see on which seat the Lord was sitting. I would not have been surprised if I had seen Jesus Himself sitting in the row behind me. The speaker had just pronounced those extra-ordinary words, so . . . He *had* to be near me. But I did not see Him sitting anywhere, neither behind me nor in front of me. Where was He?

So, I told myself, He is not immediately present after all. But how could this be? He was "near" . . . but He was not quite "here".

This was very strange indeed. Hardly had I begun to search for Him and yet He was already "near". Everything was happening so quickly. Hundreds of thoughts were assailing my mind, when my ears suddenly heard something else:

"Be anxious for nothing."

This time I was really hit on the head with a hammer. Had not the whole of my life until now consisted of fear and worry? Again, many thoughts flooded back: fear of the wickedness of people, of adults who never understood me, of the meanness of those around me, of the sanctimonious morality of the judges, of the police-machine. I relived a feeling of despair, disappointment, fleeing, being pursued – the whole course of my miserable life. This short verse, *"Be anxious for nothing"*, sounded like a fantastic promise, concrete and so necessary for my life. How wonderful that would be! Meanwhile the speaker went on:

"But in everything by prayer and supplication with thanksgiving let your requests be made known to God."

This bit I did not of course understand, because my mind was still preoccupied with the fear and misery of my life up to that moment. In any case, I was probably incapable of understanding that verse, because all Christian vocabulary was still foreign to me. Today, I understand its meaning much more clearly: I know that God hears us in any situation we might find ourselves, no matter how bad it may be. We can "beseech" and "thank" Him beforehand, because He has saved us and makes the best out of any circumstance, no matter how critical it may be. For "in everything God works for good with those that love Him" (Rom. 8:28). After that moment of puzzlement I once more became attentive and heard what was probably the key word:

"and the peace of God …"

At that point I stopped listening to the sermon, because I had some thinking to do. Yes . . . Peace! That is what I had been searching for all my life and had never found. Inner peace, something promised by all those gurus and teachers, but never found in any of them. At that moment in the cathedral, the unattainable suddenly seemed attainable. But as I sensed even then, this peace, called "the peace of the Lord", was probably not the same peace which politicians, philosophers, psychologists, "esoterics", and leaders of sects promise the people. "Peace" in this new sense was both something entirely fundamental to human existence and a very specific promise to me personally – that is what I understood the speaker to be saying. Even so, it was an offer I did not dare accept, for fear of being disappointed yet again. In the event of failure I would not have had the strength to start afresh – I really couldn't. I swore to myself once more, with a pounding heart, that I would not leave the city of Lausanne until I had made it "through the tunnel" and had gained some certainty about these new prospects.

"The peace of God which passeth all understanding," the speaker continued, touching yet again my vulnerable spot. I was sure that this man was still looking towards me when he spoke these words. This was the sixth time his words had hit me. "Understanding", "mind", "thought", "intellect", "analysis" – I had used all these notions to destroy myself as well as other people. The mind, this proud intellectual trap, could become an obstacle, a poison bringing discord to the world. Therefore, it was worth asking, this "peace of the Lord", does it truly transcend human understanding? I began to think of Maharishi's book about transcendental meditation, *The Science of Existence*, and remembered how much that book had seduced me with its apparent intelligence. In fact it had deluded and deceived me, and a whole generation, with its "human" wisdom. Indeed, those gurus and founders of sects are quite often highly eloquent theologians who idolize the cult of academic intelligence and catch all manner of those intellectually-addicted wise guys in their net. But Satan is more cunning than the whole lot put together. He uses intellectual vanity, along with many other tricks, to deceive people. The mind, divorced from the heart, can lead us to bad places. Now my heart was beating with much emotion as the last words of the speaker resounded in the church:

"[The peace of God] ... will guard your hearts and minds through Christ Jesus."

These words didn't immediately penetrate my mind, because my mind was still caught up in the fever of my hyper-active thoughts and occupied by the idea of purely human "intelligence".

Although there were some things that I was not ready to accept, I had been so moved and touched by the speaker's words – which were really the words of the Bible – that after his speech was finished, I spontaneously went up to him.

"Sir, tell me, were you speaking to me in particular just a moment ago?"

He looked amazed.

"No. I only recited a passage from the Holy Scriptures."

Maurice, who was sitting near him, heard my question and approached us saying:

"Of course, if you have taken everything that was said so *personally*, then indeed it was for you. Yes, my dear friend, God is near."

Then an ingenious idea came to Maurice's mind.

"Would you like to see where these words are printed?"

Even at that moment I had not imagined that those words, which seemed so personally addressed to me, might be printed somewhere.

"Yes please, I certainly would", I replied.

"Well then come with me."

The surprises continued. The next one awaited me round the corner. We crossed the square near the cathedral and went into the parochial house. Maurice opened a cupboard, took out a Bible, and opened it at the page where I could read, in black and white, the text that I had heard. Maurice was looking at me and seemed to recognize that my resistance had just suffered an essential defeat. Suddenly, with a quick, ingenious movement, he held the Bible under my nose:

"Do you want it?"

This was quite a shock, a painful one. What should I do? My previous experiences with Christians had convinced me that this book had been an excuse for numberless wars, inquisitions, power struggles, intrigues and destruction. I felt that my personal story, and also the whole history of the Vatican, amounted to an indictment that spoke for itself. All that seemed sufficient for not wanting to have a Bible in my hand, even if it had been offered as a gift. I stood there, motionless, feeling rooted to the ground, and in a real dilemma. I thought of all those hypocritical people, loveless and lifeless, who were always quoting this book – people whom I despised and scorned. On the other hand, just a few minutes ago, a Gospel text had sounded as though it was addressed to me directly and personally. A text from this very book had touched me powerfully. This made it almost impossible to say "no", but I still did not know what to do. The thought of taking this book in my hands made me feel dizzy. Darkness engulfed my field of vision, as though I was losing consciousness.

With extreme embarrassment and hesitation I stretched out my hand. Actually, I didn't know what kind of force was pushing my elbow forwards and prompting me to open my palm. I took hold of the book only by a corner, as if Maurice was about to put burning coals in my hand, and I felt ready to drop it at any moment. My face felt as though it was on fire – I was ashamed of myself. Had my soul recognized its "Master" and blushed? The unpleasant thought occurred to me that, when I left this room, perhaps someone I knew would see me with a Bible in my hand. My old friends would lose all respect for me. Had I seen my face in a mirror at that moment, I would undoubtedly have sneered at myself, as I had sneered at those pitiful "baby-face" Christians, who always carried a Bible around with them. Most intensely annoying to me was the thought that anyone might consider me to be part of that group of "chocolate-pudding-like" Christians. I left the parochial house disquieted. People would think that I was one of those priests, if they saw me walking along holding a Bible! It was very uncomfortable, and on leaving the building I hid the Bible under my jacket. Oh Lord! What had happened to me?

Before parting from Maurice, I threw out another "bombshell", shouting rebelliously:

"Whatever is merely printed is 'not valid', do you understand? It does not mean that Jesus has spoken to me!" Maurice knew I had asked Jesus to speak to me *personally* and not through His word in print.

Maurice only smiled. That was the end of Saturday. On Sunday morning at 9 o'clock, I had another meeting with him.

"Well, how goes it today?" he asked, walking towards me.

"Look, I don't know what is happening here, but Jesus has not spoken to me yet. He takes His time, doesn't He! Half a day has gone by since you promised me this."

Maurice replied that I must have patience. "I am sure He will come", he said.

But I still could not imagine how somebody who had lived 2,000 years ago in Palestine might actually come to Lausanne and speak to a person who in his eyes was a worthless ass, like me. I just could not get my head round that possibility. Suddenly I had an idea.

"Maurice, what would you say if you were to release me once more? Twice is better, and maybe He will hurry up then."

As I have already said, throughout my life every important message has had to be told to me twice before I could respond. I still had doubts about the things Maurice had been saying to me.

"Tell me, what do you say to my proposition?"

"With pleasure, if that's what you really want", he said, laughing in his deep bass voice full of fatherly kindness. We repeated the previous day's procedure. In the name of Jesus, Maurice bound, for the second time, the powers of the occult which had been preying on my body and soul, casting them out once and for all. After this, he said:

"Now everything is very secure. You will now be able to hear Jesus."

That morning I was a bit more open and more "willing" to be persuaded, but there was still some scepticism in my mind. Perhaps I was expecting spectacular experiences, or to be raised up on some sort of rosy cloud, but in the absence of any of that reality set in for the second time. During and after the second exorcism, I was just sitting on my chair. Perhaps my heart began to beat faster, but that was all. No Hollywood scene? Nothing sensational? Was it that simple? But hold on a moment, something was to come. At 10 o'clock there was a religious service in the cathedral. Edmée Cottier – whom I later dubbed "the midwife of my re-birth" – invited me to attend. At first I did not want to.

"I am not a Christian. I do not belong to you, so I have nothing to look for there."

"I am certain that you will find something", she insisted stubbornly. "Come on, it's important. You will see." She insisted and finally I followed her in. I walked slowly, sullenly. My only concern was to do Edmée a favour, because she was such a dear person. Still, I was pleasantly surprised by the pretty girls that I saw entering the cathedral, and I wondered what such attractive creatures could find in an old building such as this. Anyway, I told myself, I would at least have something to look at till the service ended.

CHAPTER TEN

ENTERING THE CATHEDRAL

I GOT ANOTHER SURPRISE when I went into the cathedral. I had
expected to see at the very most some gloomy-looking, elderly
women dressed in black, or to find some arrogant gossips mocking
the dresses of their neighbours. I had anticipated finding a forlorn
priest celebrating in a church that was more than half empty, and
a congregation who looked more like mummies in a museum
than faithful believers. That was the kind of half-dead scene I had
observed in churches in Italy and Spain, which I had visited for
cultural reasons. Instead, I saw a mixture of old and young people.
Their dresses were modern, some were even in jeans. There were
so many of them, the church was hardly capable of holding them
all. There were about 800 seats for a congregation of nearly 2,500.
In front there was a band playing with guitars, synthesizers and
electronic bass, which gave a pleasant atmosphere. Boys and girls
were sitting on the floor in small groups, because there were not
enough chairs. I was astonished! From the moment I had left
the Church, I thought that religious services were antiquated,
attracting few followers except for some traditionalists or those
who live eternally in the past. I had assumed that spending time
in a gloomy church was impossible, senseless and unimaginable for
most of my contemporaries.

Edmée and I filtered in and we went forward together,
through a vast crowd until we found two seats near the front. Then

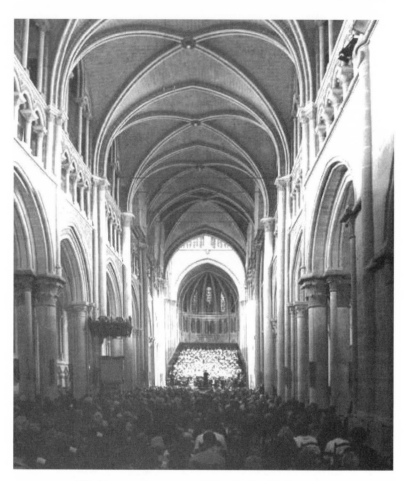

The big surprise – an overfull cathederal in Lausanne

the service began. There were five Protestant pastors and two Catholic priests celebrating this ecumenical service, because, as Edmée told me, "These days of Repentance and Prayer are a very important thing." As I could not really understand what was going on, I started to count the windows, to study the architecture of the pillars, to listen to the band and look at the pretty girls. Various thoughts were running through my mind, but they had nothing to do with what was happening at the altar. Towards the end of the service, when one of the priests turned towards the people, I heard the following verse:

"Blessed are those who are invited to the Lord's Supper."

At that moment silence reigned. Edmée turned towards me discreetly and whispered something in my ear. What was to follow can be described as *the most crushing moment in my whole life*.

"Hey Klaus, you come as well", Edmée whispered in my ear. All at once, I felt rebellious towards her. What had I to do with the Lord's Supper? This was for her – for Christians. The others were probably invited. In any case, no one had ever "invited" me to a party or feast. Whenever I wanted to go somewhere, I had to make myself invisible, so as to slip in unannounced, if necessary through the back door. With me the opposite was the case. All my life I had been disinvited, chased away, thrown out. Even from the womb of my mother, who made it clear she did not want me. I had been rejected, unwanted, whether it was at home, school, church, or anywhere else. Therefore, how could I belong with those who had been "invited", with the "blessed" ones?

Edmée understands nothing, I thought, so immediately I whispered back:

"No, this invitation is not for me. It is for you, for you Christians."

"That's not true, it is for you, too. Come on now." She did not give in, being convinced that "my moment" had arrived.

"No, I cannot and will not go there; leave me in peace!" I replied somewhat sharply. "I am not a Christian."

My goodness, how she disturbed me with her persistence!

"I have lost nothing here and I am not looking for anything! Understand me, once and for all, this is not for me. I am not one of you."

"Even so, Klaus, come", she insisted. "I am sure it's what you need right now."

How stubborn this Edmée was! Why is she so obstinate? I asked myself. Now she was really getting on my nerves!

In any case, I sensed that the majority of those sitting around me did not really want to take the meal that was on offer either. They might have "accepted the invitation", in the sense of going to church, but they did not want to participate fully. Why had they come to church, then? It didn't make sense. If I were invited to eat with someone, I would hardly go to his house and say, "No, I won't eat, thank you, but I've only come just to be here, not to receive your hospitality." Given that so many of the congregation were indifferent or lukewarm, it didn't seem to make any difference whether or not I participated at this "supper". So, *why* should I go just for the sake of pleasing Edmée?

In my view, she was demanding a bit too much of me. I felt pressured by her attitude and thought it would drive me mad. Not respecting the moment of silence and holiness, I exploded at Edmée, in a loud voice:

"Shut up, you're talking nonsense! You can't decide this thing for me, can you? Leave me in peace!"

The people around us jumped; but this left me cold. Edmée became silent. She was too wise a teacher to continue insisting. But suddenly all this tense exchange began to make me feel unsure as to what to do. Should I stand up and participate in the "meal" or not? I then started pondering. Actually, I realized Edmée could not decide this issue for me. I had to make up my own mind. And again I found myself in a dilemma (resembling the moment when Maurice wanted to put the Bible in my hand), until an ingenious idea occurred to me.

I had heard somewhere that the bread and the wine, which they were about to distribute there at the front of the cathedral, was in truth the Body and Blood of Jesus Christ. If this were not just pure sophistry or symbolism, then here and now was the time for Him to show himself. He could – no, *must* – prove it. *He Himself* had to decide whether He wished to offer Himself to me or not. *He Himself* had to invite me in person.

But despite all my deliberations over whether to come forward, I simply could not find the answer. It seemed that the answer lay outside myself. Perhaps I should ask Him, I thought. As there was nothing else in my mind, I bowed my head spontaneously and without any further thoughts I closed my eyes, so as not to be distracted by anything, and simply asked Him:

"Jesus, do you want me to come?"

In that split second, as if He had been waiting for a long time for this moment, He was there and spoke to me! Not in my thoughts, but I heard the following words in a loud and clear voice:

"Yes, come! I have forgiven you everything."

I was so startled and taken aback that it is almost impossible to describe everything that unfolded. I was simultaneously conscious of the past, the present, and the future. Since I had often heard voices from the other world in former times, I was less surprised by the mere fact of hearing disembodied words spoken in a clear and distinct way. What amazed me was the sense of *knowing* that it was HIM – His presence! I still cannot find the words to express the unimaginable love and happiness that embraced me. To this day, I feel enveloped in a joy that words cannot describe. It is like a man who had become stiff with cold and on the point of freezing, who suddenly finds himself under the warm water of a shower. As wax melts in the sun, I was melting with the heat and love that came from Him and was seeking to set my heart alight for Him.

A mere crumb of such an inconceivable love was what I had felt when I met Mother Theresa of Calcutta. And some years later, God again guided me to another holy person, a man who had even more of that kind of love and altruism, so impossible to put into words – these things can only be lived. But at that instant in the cathedral, the love I felt was more than anything I had ever experienced. It surpassed my understanding. I could not take it in. I was led from my head to my heart. Whatever had touched me was far too deep to try understanding it with my mind.

But at that same moment came the attack.

I could still discern the words of Jesus echoing in my ears, when all of a sudden I heard a terrifying whistle or hiss, which came down from the cupola of the cathedral and was moving faster and faster towards me. Instinctively, I sensed the danger of death and wanted to jump aside before the "wild beast" could hit me. But too late! In a fraction of a second a "two-handed sword" fell upon me like a flash and seemed to split my head and body down the middle before dashing out from between my legs. It felt like a fatal blow. I had the feeling of being destroyed and divided into two pieces.

Everything was crushed with that one blow. Where was the love? Where was the peace? A moment ago I had both love and peace, but they had been swept away in an instant, as though in a hurricane. My disappointment was too great, because my greatest fear from the beginning had come true – of being betrayed again! I could not bear it any more. In a flash, I was blinded by hatred, engulfed in anger, fury, aggression, disillusionment and violence towards everything and everyone around me, and the whole world.

I could have killed everyone there. I had a superhuman strength and thought of strangling Edmée with one hand, of throttling her till she fell. I don't know what kept me from doing this. In my fury I wanted to massacre all the people in the church, to spit in their faces and grind them into the ground. Deeply wounded, a profound feeling of contempt overtook my soul. Now this very same force was turning against me. Panic took hold of me and I felt I was on the point of being stifled to death. The blood was swirling round in my head as if it were a roaring cascade of water. The light in the cathedral became reddish-purple. My ears were bursting, as though a buzzing electric current was going through them. All the people around me suddenly mutated into liars and accursed Pharisees. "Cursed band of false saints!" said a shouting, screaming voice within me. Gripped by panic and short of breath, I darted out of the church, feeling as though I was running towards death.

The invigorating air sharpened my spirits once more. So everything I had heard had been nothing but a lie. There I was, standing alone again, deprived even of my last hope. There and then in front of the cathedral, overlooking the city of Lausanne, I was ready to die. In my whole life, that was the moment of the utmost loneliness and absolute abandonment. I was totally crushed, standing in front of a mound of broken pieces. I could no longer understand anything. Had not Jesus spoken to me? Had I not reached my objective? That is what I had believed and suddenly – BANG! – nothing. I was overwhelmed by a deep bitterness and powerfully convinced that I had lost all reason for my existence. Thoughts of death were now rapidly invading me, becoming more intense and quickly mastering my will, which in this state lacked all defence against destructive thoughts. Within a short distance of the cathedral, which is built on a hill, there is a precipice and I felt an overwhelming urge to throw myself down. It was ten steps, maximum, to the small wall in front of the precipice. Then, I heard another, very sinister voice.

Just a short distance now separated me from the place where I would cast myself onto the roofs of the old city below. How many times could I have easily died already, because of war, drugs, criminal acts, negligence, fire, desire for adventure, provocation, drowning, starving, being stoned – twenty-five times, or even more? Even though I had survived each time, of one thing I was now certain: in a few seconds, definitely, everything would be ended. In the next moment the unbearable tragedy of my life would be finished.

I was approaching the wall. And then, as if out of nowhere, an ice-cold voice, which I could hear clearly and distinctly, was worming its way into my ear and sniggering: "Ha, ha, ha – you are feeling miserable, then? You are not well, is that not so? Are you completely finished?"

Staggered, I stopped in my tracks. What was that? Where was it coming from? It sounded just as clear as the former voice. No matter – it didn't make a difference anymore. I went on. But again the voice starting putting on the pressure: "Do just what you have always done when things went badly! Use your old tricks again and start manipulating people. Ha, ha, ha!" You should have heard the mean and gloating tone of that voice.

Someone obviously didn't want me to take the last step over the wall. The fact is that Satan did not want to lose me. I had done so much useful work for him. So I found myself remembering that each time I had been down and out, I went hunting for prey. Like a vampire, I attacked my victims and seized hold of their life-energy, because I no longer had any of my own. Just like those who were dependent on heroin, who injected themselves, I dug my spiritual vampire's teeth into the victims' psyche and sucked out and lived on their power. In order to play these tricks, I wore a kind of "magic cap". I was a master of mime and movement and could present myself convincingly as a guru, priest or prophet. People unquestioningly swallowed my bait. I had learned my lessons from watching all those gurus, in many different countries, year after year. After observing them, I found it easy to penetrate, by visual contact, the soul of a victim. I inserted there the seed of passion, pride or hatred. I encouraged people to embark on the path of self-destruction. If I could not finish the job myself, I merely put my victims in a dangerous situation and let the terrible consequences unfold. In other words, I attached the "fish" to Satan's "hook" and he would take care of the rest.

At the same time, I had discovered, to my frustration, that this destructive type of activity would not work on people who truly believed in Jesus Christ, because they were under His protection. But I had not met many people of this sort. With almost every person I had met and influenced before, my time was successfully spent in a battle to take control. It was "having power" over others, especially girls, that pleased me – this was *my* drug. It seemed that "the voice" knew this too, and here it was again. Clearly and distinctly I heard: "Look behind you! Turn round and look!"

Indeed, the voice obviously knew me well and had something prepared for me. I turned round to see three pretty girls passing in front of the cathedral. I "smelled" prey immediately. If I wanted to find something to make life worth living, from my selfish point of view, there was not a moment to be lost. I quickly put on my "magic cap" and made my way towards them. My old game of "cat and mouse" began – a game that usually ended with satisfaction for the cat. I would let them wriggle for a while, then take their lives – deal a strong bite and throw them away afterwards. But this time it was no longer a game; it was a question of life and death. If I was to survive physically, one of them had to die spiritually. I intercepted them, and when I found myself facing the one who was the best looking, I spoke to her in order to have a chance to gaze into her eyes and in this way penetrate her soul. But here I had a shock!

It was a revelation – what I saw in her eyes. A curtain suddenly lifted, and probably by God's grace I could see with utter clarity into her soul. What I was allowed to perceive was no longer the beautifully dressed girl in front of me. Behind the mask of make-up, I saw sadness, discontent and frustration, and, to my utter amazement, I felt pity instead of opportunistic sadism, which would have been my old reaction. How was this possible? Had Jesus left some traces in me after all? Did I still have any destructive power over this human being, or any other person I chose? I suddenly realized that I did not. I was quite incapable of doing anything bad to this young woman – and that was a very painful discovery. I sensed that I had lost a whole array of negative abilities – qualities with which I had been identified for my entire life, powers that I regarded as being "Me", my defining characteristic. It seemed almost pointless to continue living. Who was I without all these powers? What did I possess? To preserve and refine those dark powers, I had sacrificed my whole existence. Now I had lost everything!

Now I began making an ice-cold calculation in my mind. The dark voice I had just heard promised success, satisfaction, and happiness if I went back to my bad old ways. But how could I find happiness in preying on unhappy people like that young woman? How could I find satisfaction in exploiting people who were anxious and discontented? How could I find any joy in or from these unfortunate sorts? There was no logic there. Then, all of a sudden, I understood that the voice I had heard came from the "father of lies", having heard this name from Edmée and Maurice. From that dark voice had been emitted the kind of impulse which had guided my entire life: "Do this, do that" . . . always with the promise of happiness and fulfilment, but never keeping true to its word. Each time there was bitter disappointment.

The immediate effect of this terrible revelation was to make me fall psychologically into a bottomless black hole. I kept on falling. My heartbeat seemed on the point of stopping. I actually fainted and crashed on the hard pavement like a stone. I thought I was dying. Something had indeed come to an end. My old life, in which I had served Satan, was over. God was calling me to a new life. He too was discarding my old existence.

How long I was on the ground I can't remember. I presume the young women must have thought that I was mentally ill and so went on their way. To my good fortune, the service soon ended and Edmée, Maurice, Ursula and my other friends came to look for me. What they found was a wretched heap of misery unable to speak. On my face was genuine despair. So everyone was very sensitive with me. It was important though for Maurice to clarify the events that had taken place.

"Klaus, you don't seem very cheerful. What has happened?" he asked me directly and without deviation, so that he could help me back to life.

I tried to tell him as best I could.

"It's truly horrific." But it did not seem as if Maurice felt any pity for me.

"To some extent you are yourself responsible for what has taken place."

"What? How?"

"Klaus, what has just happened was – how shall I put it – a counterattack from Satan. He has tried to get you back for himself. The devil doesn't let go of anyone very easily; this is his true nature. He is categorically evil and shifty.

"You must also realize that what happened is an answer to your prayer. You called on Jesus to make it clear when He was speaking. You have now heard Jesus, and you have also heard the voice of the enemy. You can now tell the difference, you can tell who is the liar.

"But nevertheless, from now on and for the rest of your life, you must be very careful, because he will keep on trying to hit back and tempt you to return to his fold. Until now, you have been one of his most efficient collaborators. Satan is like a 'roaring lion seeking whom he may devour'."

"So next time Satan comes, I will put on a huge pair of boxing gloves and fight him off", I said, still in shock from my experience. Maurice answered solemnly.

"You can't beat the adversary. No human being can beat him definitively. There is only One person who can beat him, and that is Christ. When you are in Christ, the adversary has already been beaten."

Oh, how I hated Satan now, my onetime "partner". At the same time I had a kind of "shivering respect" for him and his incalculable power. Which human being could boast of being more cunning than the devil? Only some benighted dreamers might think they were more powerful or even superior to him. Or even worse, they do not believe that he exists. What is written in the Bible about spiritual warfare had been lived out in the previous few hours of my life. It could hardly have been experienced more directly. To this day, I am utterly convinced that I would have physically died, had not Jesus entered my body and soul a short time before the meeting with Satan. Evidently, I was already under the protection of Christ. The enemy had spoken to me, but so had Jesus. This was exactly what I had desired. Laughingly, Maurice reminded me of my first prayer when we were together.

"You wanted to be *sure* that it was Jesus Who was speaking to you, didn't you?"

"It's true", I confirmed. In this way, that fatal meeting had been an answer to my prayer. Mind you, that is not the most pleasant way of receiving an answer to prayer.

"You have overcome the worst attack of all", he explained. "The first is usually the most terrible", the others confirmed, calming me and then inviting me to dine.

Only towards the evening did I calm down and my state of mind began to improve. Despite all this, I had *not yet* become a Christian and I certainly had not been "born again". A terrible panic was once again to overwhelm me.

Monday arrived. The festivities had not yet finished. From 9:00 a.m. the cathedral was invaded by more than a thousand people. I met Edmée in front of the cathedral doors. This time we both knew that I would enter with her into the church. She and I both felt that I was now one of the "blessed" ones invited to the Lord's Supper. A couple of days earlier, the idea of a long service would have bored or horrified me.

Now, for the first time, I really wished to participate in this Supper. Fascinated by the liturgical drama, I paid great attention to what was unfolding before me. Yesterday, Maurice had warned me quite clearly of the danger of a counterattack and strongly advised me to concentrate fully on the service. Of course, as the moment for Holy Communion approached, when the bread and wine, the Body and Blood of Christ, would be offered, my fear grew because I could still feel the shock in my bones from the experience of the day before. Merely bringing to mind what had happened made my knees feel weak.

On the one hand, I was filled with joyful expectancy, whereas on the other, my well-justified fear grew, because I anticipated that the devil would certainly make another attempt to stop me partaking of the "Supper". I was afraid, not without reason, that he was hidden somewhere waiting for the unexpected moment when he could charge like lightning and take hold of me. Because of this fear, I was twisting nervously to and fro in my chair, I really felt very tiny. Horrible thoughts penetrated my mind and I could not get rid of them. I was sure Satan would appear using any evil trick he was capable of. No, I surely could not withstand a second attack. My concentration wandered from what was happening at the altar to the fear of Satan, and back again to the altar.

All I could do was to arm myself with giant spiritual boxing gloves. "Let him come then!" I was saying to myself. I wanted to deal him one blow with all the wrath, fury and hatred that I could muster, because of the destruction he had caused. But deep down I knew for certain that these thoughts were simply a way of giving myself courage. Yesterday's experience had shown me very forcibly how incredibly quick and subtle the adversary can be compared to me or indeed to any other human being. The moment for Communion drew near and suddenly I heard Maurice Ray pronouncing once again the verse I had heard the day before:

"Blessed are they who are invited to the Lord's Supper!"

I felt a tension of two thousand volts going through me. Just at the moment that I was ready to get up and go forward, panic took hold of me, because I was convinced that the devil was waiting for this moment to act again. He *had* to do this! Because as soon as I partook of "the body of Jesus", like a protective medicine, it was presumed that I would become immune to his attacks. I reckoned that Satan could not allow this to happen.

In the midst of this intense fear which was turning into panic, He came! Not Satan, but JESUS. Surprisingly, and without my having called Him, He was there speaking loudly and clearly to me. I heard words of eternal life, words whose significance I grasped only after many years; words that I later read over and over again in the Bible. Oh, what grace and how much love did I experience – so difficult to describe! God *IS*. God is presence itself. This presence – so hard to convey – I felt for the second time. The presence of this pure love and warmth is not easy to put into words. One has to experience it. God was now inside me and HE had seen this unequal battle in my soul.

It was a fight beyond my own strength. That is why He came to my aid in His immense love, which He poured again over me so as to chase away all disappointment, doubts and fear. This was as true then as in the years to follow and for the rest of my life. To this day, I have never again experienced fear or doubt, and certainly no real despair. These words were erased from my vocabulary in the moment when HIS words transformed my fear into the fullness of joy and bliss. I heard:

"Do not fear!" "In My Name you will always be stronger!"

As I sat beside Edmée, waiting for the moment to get up and receive Communion, I burst into tears. It felt as if a dam, which had held back the tears for thirty-six years, had collapsed as a result of some tremendous force. The tears were pouring fast, rivers and rivers, free and without hindrance. They were tears of baptism, tears of rebirth. I was not at all embarrassed in front of all the other people taking part in the liturgy. Let them all see! I was weeping because of an onrush of joy and strength! With those tears I sealed the pledge I had just established with Jesus. From that moment on I belonged to Him, and in exchange for this He would give me His strength – this I knew for sure. What a wonderful, eternal assurance!

Power was something I had striven for all my life, and I had sacrificed everything to obtain it. But from now on I would receive strength, and much more, in His Name. This "agreement" came easily to me. To this I could say, "Yes" and "Amen", without hesitation.

When I stood up and went forward towards the altar with knees trembling, tears of joy were still pouring down my cheeks. Maurice was serving with six other priests. When he saw me coming, he spontaneously abandoned his official functions and ran towards me, his face shining with joy. In front of the whole church and its thousand worshippers, he embraced me, gave me a brotherly kiss on both cheeks, lifted up his arms towards heaven and shouted out loudly with obvious emotion, "Hallelujah! Klaus has made it! Praise the Lord!"

The entire event was much too overwhelming for mind and heart to take in. Every gift seemed to shower down on me at once. I did not look for any explanation. There was a vital new fact, which I now knew was of the greatest importance: that I had a "heart", a heart that could feel, could love others and could suffer alongside them. The whole of my life was completely renewed, miraculously touched through this encounter.

With a face soaked in tears, I went up the few steps towards the altar and stood with the first group in a semi-circle, and for the first time received this mystical "Bread", which is the Body of Jesus, and the "Wine", His Blood. Somehow the mysteries of this ancient rite were easy for me to understand at that moment. This was "Food" which gave life to a starving soul. It was a gift of immeasurable value, especially with regard to my future. This was the real heaven-sent Presence, a genuine gift of grace from God. Not the sort of thunderbolt which killed you, but one which restored life from the realm of death. At last, I was on the road leading back to paradise. Now, through and in Jesus, I had finally conquered the terror of death! I no longer feared death because I knew Jesus had vanquished it. As long as He was in me, there was no reason to dread death any more.

There I stood, reborn and actually crying like a newborn baby. Passing on the breadbasket and chalice, I noticed that the lady (about my age) on my right also began crying. I had good reason for my tears. But what, I wondered, had happened to her? When I returned to my seat, that lady followed me and addressed me. Both of us still seemed to be under the influence of something which had just taken place – because we were both crying. But with God there are no coincidences. The lady looked at me and said:

"I do not know you, Sir. But when I was standing next to you up there, behind the altar, something extraordinary and marvellous must have happened to you."

I wasn't sure what she was talking about. "What do you mean?"

"At the precise moment when you offered me the chalice with the wine I had a vision. I saw the heavens wide open. The heavenly hosts were announcing a very great victory, the angels were singing most wonderfully, something so beautiful that I have never heard anything like it in all my life. The joy in heaven was indescribably great, so much so – and please excuse me here – that I cannot stop crying. What has happened to you?"

You could see how deeply she was moved. I looked at her in amazement and still with tears in my eyes, like herself, I answered:

"I think I have just . . . become a *Christian!*"

Later on, Edmée, Maurice and several others, confirmed that this lady named, Madame Grosjean, was from Lausanne and was well known for her gift of vision. These visions always turned out to be true. This was the first evidence I had received. Afterwards there came a long list of other proofs, that I hadn't fallen prey again to some flight of the imagination or elegant illusion. No, because

My first photo after my conversion

before me was a person who was a total stranger, who could not have known anything of what I had gone through just before.

It was not long before the scales fell from my eyes and I understood that the name of JESUS does not represent a technique and has no resemblance to a "mantra", which is always linked to a Hindu god. I also learnt that every word spoken by Jesus is a message for the whole world. As He speaks to the people through every good work, every kindness, every positive thought, so are the personal words that I heard from His own mouth truly the words of eternal life destined for all humanity – as I read later in the Acts of the Apostles.

From this point in my life, I can now testify that Jesus Himself provided ample answers to two crucial questions about the nature of humanity, which had always troubled me. The first of these was the problem of forgiveness of sins, which in Buddhist and Hindu teaching means release from the drudgery of the karma and the long chain of reincarnations. In Hindu tradition this chain can be as long as 8,400,000 times. "Come, I have *forgiven* you everything." From this statement comes the real freedom that everyone craves: a freedom which is only fulfilled in a personal meeting with and acceptance of Jesus.

The second issue which had always preoccupied me was the discovery of some technique that would offer a way to salvation or freedom, however you defined it. Now Jesus had told me: "In My name you will always be stronger." This implies that we have no need of any particular *technique* for salvation, like mantras, yoga, Asian meditation, or any other esoteric practice, in order to find balance and inner peace.

I have met some so-called spiritual Christians (including Catholic priests) who dare to teach that, in order to become a good Christian, you'd better accept the help of yoga, Zen and other such techniques. These people are not pastors, but wolves. They are not only naïve, but also co-workers for the destruction of the divine revelation. For such spiritual leaders it is not sufficient to have the name of Jesus: they need Zen or yoga at any price, because they have never known a personal relationship with Jesus. Instead, they have studied theology for a few terms and have assimilated information from books. It is not that book-learning is wrong, for a certain amount of knowledge is needful, but mere study is *not* the final goal. One must endeavour to meet Jesus in one's heart, as a Person, face to face.

We have been created in the image of God. God is love and love requires two persons, otherwise it does not make sense. Human striving towards harmony and love is inspired by God and it makes sense only in Him. It cannot be an activity cut off from the "other" and concentrating on one's self, as in Buddhist meditation. "To become yourself", to become what you "are", means nothing less than to turn towards God, to become one with God. Each Christian does this in his or her own way, with a particular starting-point and a particular route. But all journeys are made with Christ as our companion.

After having this personal encounter with Jesus, I was able to ask Him about financial, spiritual, bodily, and even practical problems. Nothing is too small or too great for Him. Anything can be used to draw us closer to Christ. I will relate much more in the second part of this book, describing some of these miracles I experienced, for which I praise Him. But when I compare them with the miracle that took place in my heart, all those other miraculous events and gifts I regard as but small things, small way-stations on my journey towards Him.

Previously, my heart was the place where darkness dwelt. It was a place where I devised plans to dominate and destroy. Now through His grace there had appeared love, understanding, compassion, and Christian mercy. My longing to be "important" gave way rather to humility, which was the most efficient antidote against pride.

My whole way of looking at things was changed in a single stroke. That this could have happened at all, and so quickly, is even today a continuous miracle for me. Hatred and revenge were replaced by understanding and forgiveness. Not long after, I met the paedophile priest who had abused me for seven years, and I stretched out my hand to him as a sign of reconciliation. I must admit it was not the easiest thing for me to do, but absolutely necessary. I often travelled

Reconciliation with my mother soon after my conversion

to Germany, to my mother, and later on I found my father in Stuttgart. I forgave them both unconditionally before their deaths.

As time went on and I discovered the true value of life, I could feel how the eyes of my heart were opening. God had replaced my heart of stone with one of flesh. My old teacher, Satan, had taken my life and made of it a ruin gnawed by time: filthy, dark, covered in weeds, without a roof, with holes in the floor, putrid, stinking, without windows. When I accepted Christ as my new Master, as the "Landlord" of my "old" house, nothing very much altered to begin with, only the proprietor had changed. The new owner, though, loves His house, cares for it, keeps it clean and adorns it: the roof is repaired, the water is pumped out of the cellar. He puts new windows in, carpets everywhere, and arranges everything until the house becomes habitable once more. In short, He has love because He is love. This cleansing is brought about through the Holy Spirit and is in opposition to Eastern meditation, whose stupefying work actively impedes us from seeing the destructive power of sin, of the passions. It merely offers the soul something enticing but meaningless, to divert it from the truth. The "enlightenment" I had searched for in Asian religiosity found its true fulfilment in the *painful* recognition that all my earlier battles against vice and the passions had been lost. Once such a recognition has been made, it clears the way for the grace and forgiveness of Jesus to work. It was to give us this grace – always on the condition that we are ready to accept it – that Christ poured out His Blood on the Cross: for humanity as a whole, and for Klaus personally. Who could have thought such a thing possible?

Many of life's mysteries will remain in essence hidden to us, because they are not meant to be "understood" in an intellectual way. Only one who is ready to take the risk of faith will really learn how to live, only the person who is ready and willing to go on the long journey from head to heart. This does not mean forsaking one's own intelligence, but it does mean trusting one's experience. A believer will meet God, in himself or herself, in the beauty of nature, in others and everywhere else, and one day perhaps, by God's grace, even in people viewed as enemies.

But to know things more deeply, we first have to acknowledge how little we know. We need courage, like Socrates, who said, "I know that I know nothing". We have to detach ourselves from all the passions, prejudice, narrow wordly knowledge, professional pride, and all the other things that stand between us and God. He can administer and channel our energies much better than we can.

"Whoever has ears to hear, let him hear", so the Gospel says. These are the ears and eyes of the heart. Whosoever has courage and patience to open those spiritual senses through *pure* prayer, will "see things which no [ordinary] eye has seen nor ear heard".

The Gospel also tells us: "It is easier for a camel to go through the eye of a needle than for a rich man to enter the Kingdom of God." Only when we renounce our own riches, our worldly wisdom, our selfishness, self-will, the passion for money, lust for power and dissipation, and our old habits, does the door to LOVE and heaven on earth open up for us. At that moment we will be able to stop and marvel at the greatness of God's freedom and peace. Many miraculous and inexplicable things happened to me in the second part of my life, which I shall try to describe in the following pages of this book.

Ursula, my beloved fellow-fighter

CHAPTER ELEVEN

A NEW MANNER OF LIFE

AFTER ALL THESE EVENTS, all the searching and running away of my first thirty-six years, of course I thought that my journey had come to an end. It is true that over the next couple of decades the material circumstances of my life would remain fairly stable, at least in comparison with the peculiar wandering existence which had gone before. I continued to live in Fribourg and to make my living as a teacher. But after my encounter with Christ, my eyes quickly opened to a new reality, and paradoxically I saw that the real journey of my life was only just beginning. All the adventures I had lived through until that moment in the jungles and cities of this planet were not, spiritually speaking, anything more than superficial experiences. They were trivial compared to the proofs of forgiveness, the miracles and new spiritual battles that were to come. My early wanderings can hardly be compared with the great adventure of discovering who I was. Such a discovery is only possible when we start walking hand in hand with God, that is to say, when we allow Him to take us by the hand. But what prevents us from doing this is the problem of pride. Which of us can recognize well enough the hidden pride which we all carry within ourselves? Which of us can learn to distrust the messages we receive from our proud selves? Who has sufficient faith, humility or wisdom to accept being led by the hand? Who has the courage to "become a child" and see and accept his own limitations? However banal this may sound, he who dares to discard pride and become humble is the one who eventually wins. He gains faith, hope, love – he regains himself.

Signs, answered prayers and true miracles were to be an especially visible part of my daily life during the ensuing five years. The signs were so extraordinary that other Christians often asked themselves how it was possible. People often came to me at the end of a conference to ask why it was that they could not also have such experiences. As a new-born Christian, sadly, I could give them no definite answer to this mystery. My experiences seemed to be something "normal" for me, because I was living with such intense grace.

It took time for me to realize that I would have to pay something back for the miraculous gifts I was receiving. God expected something in return. What I had to give up was my ego, my selfishness. In the past the devil had asked for my soul, my true self, as the price for lending me his inexplicable gifts of power. In other words, my authentic self was buried and ruined, because the devil demanded this. Now God was asking me to participate in a vastly greater bargain. He was waiting for me to give up my selfishness, my worst self – my falseness, my fallen nature – so that he could help and heal. *"He who does not hate his own life, cannot be My disciple . . . and whoever does not bear his cross and come after me cannot be My disciple."* Why is this practised by only a few so-called Christians? What has gone wrong? Why do they lament and say that so little happens and that they experience no miracles? The answer, I feel, is closely linked to the degeneration of the traditions in which they have grown up and from which they receive their spiritual food. Why are the fundamental questions of the "mystery of life" hardly discussed in today's Christian West? The road from mind to heart seems closed to so many.

Precisely because organized Christianity in the Western world so often seems indifferent to any real, life-transforming experience of God, people in the West are easily attracted by Asian religiosity. They are fascinated by various esoteric cults, by Buddhist meditation, by the mystical side of yoga. Many mainstream priests, pastors, leaders of communities, spiritual teachers, are unable to impart to their flock very much of the mystery of life, because they themselves lack the necessary experience. Instead of experiencing the effects of a living faith, in humility and fear of God, parishioners are fobbed off with a form of soft marsh-mallow Christianity that tastes like a sickly pudding: sweet, easily digestible, and malleable like the wobbly double-chin of many clerics. Please forgive my sarcasm! But people instinctively feel that their thirst for God, for true and sincere knowledge and experience, cannot be quenched by a dried up theology. True seekers cannot accept being led by intellectual preaching alone. To understand the Bible, man has need of guidance in prayer and most of all of living models. When those things are lacking, the prince of this world, called Lucifer, steps into the gap and colludes in the production of false substitutes for real Christianity. At all times in history there have existed wolves in sheep's clothing. But in our era, this kind of false guidance has become a particularly acute problem, especially since the youth protests and hippie movements of the late 1960s.

I believe the revolt against authority, the sexual shamelessness, the anthems glorifying the use of drugs, raging rock music, wholly perverted and reckless lyrics, and the fight against the Church, has destroyed more souls than the first and second world wars in total. Families are falling apart. The family is an atom of society, its very nucleus. When that atom breaks apart a nuclear explosion is produced, certainly easy to recognize with a divorce rate of fifty percent and homosexual marriages. I speak here of my experiences as a teacher of some 200 pupils every year. This breaking up of the family-nucleus in society is more destructive than the atom bomb – where "only" physical bodies are being killed – because of the *souls* that might be lost for eternity.

We must not forget that the Maharishi, and through him Asian religiosity, became popular and gained influence in the West through the Beatles. The youth, having lost much of their true Christian beliefs during the years of the hippie revolution, were cheated by its substitute with a false exotic faith without anyone having grasped the immensity of the fraud. When unbridled rock music, the consumption of drugs, and the mass media with all its structures, began to drive out religion, God was at that time replaced by man. God was no longer of any use. Lucifer, the author of this change, laughed and seated himself on the throne. As an example, the praise that heavy metal and hard-rock music grants to Satan today would have been condemned forty years ago and banned as being of the occult. The more that Christian values are destroyed, especially through advertising, the more vulnerable will the people become, the more easily infected by trendy mysticism. But not only the young! Asian cults started to become fashionable in the West when the Beatles went to India on a pilgrimage to the fashionable guru Maharishi Mahesh, and their journey was enthusiastically covered by the media. The battle for souls is as old as the conflict between good and evil. All esotericism, with its New-Age baggage, Rosicrucianism, Freemasonry, white and black magic, Buddhism, in short, the whole esoteric self-service supermarket, has only one aim – to overthrow the One to Whom our hearts properly belong, in other words, Jesus Christ. These cults set out to usurp His throne. I believe that God's opponent is also helped by lukewarm Christians with little authority, homosexual priests, lesbian bishops, lifeless communities eaten up by internal struggles for power, and where all energy has fizzled out through years of administrative disputes, instead of the dedication to the healing of people's souls and the spreading of the message of Jesus.

People are not stupid; they will not accept shop-soiled goods. Disappointed with Christianity in its current form, they turn to a system like Buddhism that, externally, appears close to Christianity. I do *not* want to affirm that Buddhist philosophy is the same as esoteric beliefs or even occultism. That would be a mistake and would mean that I did not understand the Buddhist tradition. The positive side of Buddhism lies in its aim to cast off the "negative works" of the passions and suffering. What is missing, though, is that it does not sufficiently highlight the "positive works" or virtues of charity and compassion. In this perspective, Christ can be understood as the fulfilment looked for by Siddharta Gautama, or Buddha. By freeing the spirit of any visual or intellectual form, that is by creating a total inner "void", the Buddhist aspires to be free of all suffering, whereas the Christian strives to achieve a different sort of "fullness". He aims for inward perfection with, through and in Christ – by learning to "pray without ceasing" – until he arrives at the One who has promised: *"I am the way, the truth and the life; whoever comes to Me shall live and not die."* Life in Christ is not something static; it implies a life of sharing Christ's love for the world, of feeding the hungry, freeing the captive, healing the broken-hearted.

To attain union with Christ, as a great Christian teacher helped me to see, it is necessary to have much patience. We should avoid the mistake made by many contemporaries who, in great haste and with no proper preparation, want to find freedom, peace and all other spiritual gifts, even to the point of seeing God. These sorts of people often liken prayer to the Eastern practice of yoga, saying that both are techniques that make it possible to pass more easily and quickly on to the path leading directly to unity with God. My Christian teacher said this was a big mistake. Whoever desires simply to free his mind of all those things which he considers "relative" or "transient", in order to find his primordial origin, will find himself running into a dead end. These mental techniques have to be combined with a real spirit of self-sacrifice, of taking up the Cross and serving others.

What the Buddhist discovers, at most, is human beauty – and this is something real, in the sense that God created man after his own likeness. But something dangerous is happening when man simply contemplates himself, a self which is vainly mistaken for God or regarded as divine.

This can have tragic results because man, in contemplating his own self, can become fixated on a false image which he wrongly believes to be a refuge in the storms and confusion of life. He is thus distracted from the search for the really safe Harbour, which is Christ. This can lead to a tragic death of thirst, a kind of self-disintegration.

I can testify from my own experience (and that of other people I know) that meditation through inner emptying has led to the filling of the void by the enemy, the demons. In this way, all the doors to the heart and soul are opened up, unwittingly or wittingly, to the enemy of God, Satan.

One of the most powerful experiences I had during my days of experimentation with Buddhism was reaching a state of pure consciousness, which was somehow disconnected from the human brain. In this state, I seemed to experience, in a single instant, my entire life from the moment I was conceived in the womb of my mother.

I did not understand the full significance of this experience until I became a Christian. After my personal encounter with Christ, I began to see what Christ wanted to say by the words, *"Even the hairs of your head are numbered"* and, *"Nothing will stay hidden, which will not be revealed"*. There is a perspective from which all the barriers of time and space are transcended, where, so to speak, everything happens at once, and in the same place. That is God's perspective. From His point of view, nothing is too remote – in time or space – to be discerned. It follows that we will be held responsible for everything that we do and have done. The Book of life inscribes everything, down to the smallest detail, and we shall be held to account for every thought, word and deed.

If we recognize and admit our shortcomings, sins and mistakes, and condemn them during our lifetime, the *Judge* will justify us. If we try to justify *ourselves*, the Judge will accuse and condemn us. I repeat emphatically and with all vigour: yoga and Eastern meditation make us blind towards the failing of our inner self. Through yoga we all too easily avoid seeing the true fallen self, that is, the sinner, and instead we enter a process of self-deification. There is a delicate but important point here. Even though we have been created in the image of God, we are never God in His essence. But we can become *"gods by adoption"*, adopted by God; and until we get there, we need to seek His grace with our whole heart, soul and spirit. I set out on this journey on that famous Monday in Lausanne, and in this sense I was again at the beginning.

Put on your safety belts now and hold tight, because a new journey is about to start, full of the most incredible and inexplicable experiences.

Immediately after my return home, from Lausanne to Fribourg, I was to have an experience which revealed the presence of my newly acknowledged heavenly Father. A couple of months previously I had been fired from the private school, known as the "Institute of La Gruyere", where I had been teaching for the past year. The headmaster had told me curtly, "Mr. Kenneth, you are not suited to our school", and I had to agree with him. Rich and snobbish pupils came there and the school had to protect its image. I was something of a hippie, an intruder, a black sheep and, in all sincerity, I didn't care very much for the school rules. By taking this attitude, I contributed to my eventual dismissal from the school, although my relationship with my pupils had been really fine. To be unemployed meant, in my situation, that I would have to leave Switzerland. Was this to be a painful new beginning in life, coinciding with my spiritual rebirth? When I was born in 1945, my family was literally on the road, fleeing. I now had the sense that my rebirth might take place in equally turbulent circumstances. But in contrast to my earthly father, my new Father did not desert me. On the contrary, he stood by me.

Before I left Lausanne, Maurice had introduced me to a man called Georges Rapin. He was the leader of an ecumenical prayer group in Fribourg, my home town. Maurice indicated that I "would be in the best hands" if I joined this group; this would be important, especially if the enemy attacked again. Maurice then said good-bye, with a friendly warning. "On your own", he added, "you cannot continue to grow: a community is indispensable."

Still wary and determined not to fall into the hands of "those baby-faces", I went the following Thursday to a meeting of the ecumenical group which was called, "Maranatha". When I arrived, I said to the Christians there, quite openly, that if anyone dared to try and change me into a "baby-face", I would kill them. Their reaction was a burst of laughter. Then they prayed for me, and for the solution of my most urgent problem which was getting a job.

On Friday morning the phone rang. It was Mr. V., the headmaster of the Gruyere Institute.

"Mr. Kenneth?"

"Yes."

"I have been trying to contact you for a few days."

"Yes? Why?"

"Well, we have given you your job back! You should have been here already on Monday for lessons, but we couldn't contact you. Please come as soon as possible. We shall expect you even today, this afternoon, to give lessons."

I was thunderstruck. This was not possible. How could the same headmaster, who had so recently fired me, because I was not suited to the school, re-engage me? A verse that I heard that Saturday in Lausanne, from the preacher in the cathedral, went through my mind: "The peace of the Lord that passeth all *understanding*." I was impatient to find out how Mr. V. had justified to himself this "re-engagement". I waited a few weeks, because I was still feeling a bit insecure after my dismissal, followed by an incredible offer of re-employment.

When after some time had passed, I realized that I was indeed fully employed again, so I asked him:

"Mr. V., how is it that you are re-employing me?"

"You know, Mr. Kenneth, we on the board decided to take you into consideration after all." That was his terse and enigmatic answer.

In my mind, I was thinking: if only you knew, dear friend, Who it really was that was considering me ... But perhaps I'd better not say it out loud. In this way, the first of my problems was solved and I now had a "stable" job, essential for my development.

However, before long I realized that there was no future in this work, as it gave me no opportunity for growth. So I decided to finish my studies, which had been interrupted just before my second final exam at the university in Hamburg. I wanted to re-start the course from the very beginning, as I had forgotten too much of my subject since then. So I enrolled at the University of Fribourg, and went into the Dean's office, where at the same time a form was put under my nose, which I was supposed to sign. I was being asked to confirm that I was agreeing to the Swiss law, which stated that after the termination of my studies I had *no right* to any work in Switzerland. Hence, I would have to leave the country. But

I was so convinced that, at the right time, my Father would find a solution to this problem that I did not think about it for too long and signed the form.

Working and studying at the same time involved some difficult calculations. On the one hand, I needed to earn money to pay for my studies; on the other, I realized that the daily journey to the school in Greyerz (also known as Gruyere, and famous for its cheese) was taking too much time. Each morning and evening, I had to drive 30 km. I also needed some more permanent accommodation, ideally in the centre of Fribourg. I had been living in a village just outside the town. So I decided to apply simultaneously for a scholarship and for some lodgings. Soon I found a newspaper advertisement for an apartment – for only 180 francs per month! (The usual charge for such an apartment in Switzerland at that time would have been more than double that amount.)

When I first went to look for the apartment, I could not even find the building, and was about to return home, thinking it must have been taken already. Whilst waiting at the first traffic lights, I heard an amazingly distinct inner voice saying: "Klaus, go and look *well* please, do it properly!"

I was perplexed. Had I been negligent? Had "someone" else put negative thoughts in my mind, in order to make me despair? Was this a countervailing voice, offering encouragement? In any case, I understood. I went back once again along the same road, but further up this time, and indeed, there was the house hidden behind some trees, in the middle of a meadow of flowers. What a dream! As if all this had been waiting for me, I signed the contract not long after. For the few years that followed, my new home proved to be a true paradise.

Now the next step was to find a scholarship. A few days later, I went to see the inspectorate of schools for that canton.

"Good morning, Mr. B." I said. I had read the name on the door.

"Yes, what can I do for you?"

"I would like to apply for a grant."

He opened a drawer and handed me an application form. I filled it in there and then and returned it to him. He looked at it and said:

"I am sorry Mr. Kenneth, but we cannot offer you a grant. Sadly you do not fulfil the conditions that are required. You are not Swiss."

That was a blow. I went home. What could I do? Travel daily to Greyerz and waste all that time? During those days I had begun to recognize Jesus Christ as my true Father, Friend and Counsellor. He would, of course, have a solution. Of that I was convinced.

"Jesus, what do You suggest I should do now?" I asked Him sitting at my desk and without any ideas of my own.

"Go there again!" I heard this short and complete statement. That was all.

"What do You mean? Did I understand correctly?"

He did not answer. So, I went there a second time.

"Excuse me troubling you again, Mr. B." I said, "but I felt I had to ask you once more. Could it be that there was something not clear about my case? Please, could you find out? Or perhaps there is another source from which I could obtain a grant?" I couldn't explain any more. I was simply obedient to Jesus. But this I couldn't reveal to the public official.

"I have already told you that it is not possible. But you could apply for a loan, which would have to be reimbursed once things have settled down. I'm sorry, but that's as much as I can do for you." Evidently, this was not what I really wanted.

I returned home full of doubts and the following dialogue took place:

"Hello, Jesus. Are You there?"

"Yes."

"Is it possible *You* could have been mistaken? I don't understand why I had to go there again today. I didn't get anything! Were *You* wrong?"

"No."

"Please tell me what to do next to receive a grant."

"Go there *again*."

"What!!! You can't be asking that of me again. He will think I'm an idiot. Then they definitely won't give me anything. This is impossible!"

"Do you not trust me?"

"Well, yes, if that is how You see it. I'll go there once more!"

It seemed incredible that I was asked to repeat something which evidently did not make sense, and that the command was given in such a dry tone of voice. Feeling somewhat confused and with a huge question mark hovering above my common sense, I went for a third time to Mr. B.'s office:

"Forgive me for coming again. But, tell me, are you absolutely sure that I have no right to a grant? There must be a way. I have reason to believe that I am eligible for a grant, but I cannot go into the details as to why."

"You are a rare bird", he said, leaning on one side, pulling the drawer of his bureau open. After taking out a thick reference book relating to legal matters, he opened it up and began searching. He pointed to a paragraph which I read with my own eyes saying that because I was foreign I had *no right* to a grant. There was no need for any other explanation.

"But even so I can help you", he went on. "Ask at DAAD (Deutscher Akademischer Auslandsdienst). This is the German academic service for foreign students. They give grants."

"Where do I find them? Do you have an address?"

He did and wrote it down on a piece of paper. Feeling happy, I went to Stuttgart in Germany. I found the building, went into the office, explained my situation, and was given an application form.

"Yes, we can help you. As a German citizen abroad you have the right to a grant. Please fill in this form."

Happy with this, I then completed the form and was about to leave the office. Everything seemed to be in order.

"Oh, please ... just a moment".

"Yes, what is it?"

"On reading the form, I see your age. We give grants up to the age of 30, and in special cases up to 35. But *you* are 36. I am sorry. We cannot give you a grant."

What a blow! My dream was shattered. What did all this mean? Was this God's caring? He let me travel 700 kilometres for nothing? When I returned home I was bitter and disappointed. My old dialogue began again.

"Jesus, I am very angry! Why are You playing games with me? Where are you?"

"Yes. I am here. What do you want?"

"You know *exactly* what I am thinking, is that not so? You understand me, don't You? And You know what I want!"

"Yes."

I lost patience. Why was Jesus always so direct and why at the same time did he seem so unmoved and uncooperative? I had every right to be furious. He had disappointed me. But as I had no one else to advise me, the only thing I could do was to cool down and ask Him to help me again.

"Please tell me – what do You want me to do now? Have You any ideas?"

"Yes. Go again to the inspectorate."

I thought I had not heard correctly. Perhaps I had been mistaken.

"Jesus, You are joking. I am sorry . . . but You are wrong. You know that they won't give me a grant."

"Do you want to believe in Me or not?" came the teasing answer.

"Oh Lord, Lord, how much You ask of me. It is impossible. How will they deal with me? How they will laugh at me! All right, I shall go there, but this time You come, too. Do You agree?"

No answer. Do I need to describe how I felt when I entered that office? Probably God was not interested too much in how *others* saw me, because *He* saw me in His own way. On opening the door I said to myself, "Jesus, please, You enter first, I will follow You".

"Good morning, Mr. B. I know you will think me crazy, but I still have the feeling that I will receive a grant from you." I explained what had happened in Stuttgart, then continued:

"I don't know what else to say . . . Do you have to tell the commission which decides these matters that I am a foreigner, or perhaps you can find another solution? Please excuse my insistence." There was nothing else I could think of, and with these words I left the room.

Back to studies

A few days later, I received a letter confirming that I had been officially given a grant! Because of my lesson in *obedience,* I had come to understand a bit more clearly that the peace which "*passeth* all understanding" (Phil. 4:7) is not just a biblical phrase, but a statement about life itself.

Not long after that, my new Father helped me to rebuild my broken life in various other ways. I was able to study subjects that had been a real problem for me ever since primary school, but which, as a sports teacher, I could not avoid. Chemistry, physics and especially abstract mathematics had always been dreaded subjects for me during my school years. Now I was to study physiology for a whole year, but God managed (or rather, "God knew how") to make this unattractive subject quite enjoyable. The unimaginable happened, when I successfully passed the exam. At the same time, another exam had made me more nervous than any other subject: anatomy. It was not that I disliked it; on the contrary, I found anatomy very interesting. But God used the subjects of anatomy and physiology to test anew my obedience and my faith. This did not prove as easy as the learning of the subjects themselves. And this is how it all happened.

After teaching us for a year, Professor Papadatos, a Greek, gave us students a series of lists covering eighty anatomical subject areas. Each little topic was summarized in the form of questions that needed answering, and this material was meant to be used for exam preparation. Out of these eighty possibilities, six questions would be asked in the exam, with one point going to each. To pass the exam, one had to answer at least four questions correctly, six points being the highest mark. Soon after getting the lists, the students received, by post, an invitation to sit the exam at a certain date, time and place. The heavy period of revision arrived and I spent whole nights poring over my notes, text-books and exercises. At a certain point, I suddenly realized that only two days remained till the appointed Saturday. By then I had thoroughly prepared fifty topics out of the eighty. It all began on Thursday evening, when I went to my desk ready to start on the last thirty themes. Whilst studying, I heard in my mind:

"Seek ye first the Kingdom of God, and all these things shall be added unto you".

I continued concentrating on anatomy and tried to ignore what I had just heard. This was not a time to be distracted from studying. Again the "voice" came: "Seek ye *first* the Kingdom of God and all these things shall be added unto you." This time it sounded more emphatic and I stopped working. It became clear that once again something was going on "up there".

I faked deafness and sank back into my books. But it was not possible to carry on. Here it was again, that "voice" insisted on being heard: "Seek ye *first* . . ." Evidently, it was no use resisting it.

I gave up. "Well, Jesus, I understand it is You. But please, will you leave me in peace. You see how much I have to learn."

He did not cease. "Seek ye . . ." Now the accent was put on "all these things" and on the word "added". I needed some time before I understood that this meant something more than just anatomy and concentration.

"Jesus, You can be quite annoying with Your insistence, therefore what do You wish me to do?"

Silence. No answer. It was typical of Him. So I began to think. The words "first" and "all these things" seemed to be His message, and I interpreted this as meaning that before anything else I was to seek His Kingdom – here and now, tonight, *before* my anatomy revision. Where was the heavenly kingdom to be found at that particular moment? Oh, yes! Thursday evening was always the prayer meeting for the "Maranatha" group, which I had joined after my conversion. I decided, despite the shortage of time, to go there for at least an hour, and then to quickly recover the "lost time" and continue with my studying. I hurried downtown, got there a little before the start of the prayers in St Joseph's chapel, and greeted George Rapin:

"Hello, as you can see I have come."

He looked at me surprised and replied:

"Why this strange greeting?"

I told him what had happened half an hour earlier, then George said:

"If I understand you correctly, you should stay here not only for an hour but to the end. I think we are talking about a step called an *'act of faith'*."

"What does that mean? What's that – an 'act of faith'?"

"This means that you will do no more studying this evening but put all your trust in God – blindly. Do not try to fathom it out; it won't work. This is an act of faith."

"But my exam preparation?"

"Leave it all to God and put your trust in Him."

To my horror, George reminded me of the following evening's gathering at the little town of Payerne where he lived, and where he had organized an "evening of testimony" for me. I could not revise during the day, because I was standing in for somebody at school and had no time for studies before the evening. Consequently, I would lose this time too! With all the goodwill in the world I could not permit this to happen.

"George, you must cancel the meeting tomorrow night."

"That is impossible, Klaus. There are a lot of people coming, I received positive replies from friends in Neuchâtel, Berne, and all around; people who are coming especially to hear you. No, Klaus, this is an act of faith, I see this very clearly."

Obviously I had no choice. All the escape routes were closed and I knew my Father too well not to recognize that He arranges everything in such a way that there are no doubts.

"All right, but promise me that Saturday morning, while I am taking my exam, you will all pray for me, okay?

"We promise."

That evening I remained there until 11 o'clock. I held my talk on Friday evening and then did not arrive home until after midnight. On Saturday morning I was at the university at 9:00 a.m. My heart was beating fast when I entered the room. Facing me was my examiner, an elderly professor, who spoke German. Next to him was Professor Papadatos, a Greek, who had taught anatomy in French that year. (Fribourg is bilingual.) On a table to my right, there were about twenty leaflets face down, each with six questions on it. Each set of questions was different. Before pulling one of them out, I turned my back in such a way that I could change the leaflet unobserved, should I happen to pick one with a question on it I had not studied. Unfortunately, that is just what happened! At a glance I skimmed through the questions and I had a shock. I had imagined that God would take care of things, and that I would pull out a paper with questions I had revised. Sadly my assumption did not prove to be correct. So I had to find refuge by being crafty. At the very moment when I was trying to put the first leaflet quietly back, I heard behind me the very severe tone of Professor Papadatos:

"Mr. Kenneth!" I jumped. "What are you doing, that's cheating! How dare you try to pass the exam in this way!"

My heart fell to my ankles – no, it reached Australia. I was thinking of many things, but none of them were of God. Throughout his life, the "old Klaus" had learnt only to cheat and lie. An exam was an opportunity to cheat. But this time being caught would mean cancelling my right to participate in this year's exam and waiting at least a year to resit the paper. Damn! I was convinced that I had failed, and my hopes of a successful exam had ended before I had even begun. At least I could not reproach myself that this had happened because of laziness. But the atmosphere in that room was now ice-cold. With a thunderous expression, Professor Papadatos ordered me:

"Give the leaflet that you are holding in your hand to Professor G!"

Phew! At least he had not disqualified me on the spot. But what should I do now? On the leaflet I had certainly seen questions I had not prepared for. The fear that gripped me while I took those few steps towards the desk, where the two professors were sitting, was overwhelming. It was the sort of fear that could easily send me back into Satan's hands. And indeed, the "old Klaus" was not easily defeated, so I prepared another lie. I reckoned as follows: My professor, the Greek, had taught us in French. So he almost certainly doesn't speak German. On the other hand, the person about to examine me is German-speaking, so I handed him the paper and lied:

"Sir, I can see on that paper questions which have never been taught in our course. They must be questions from last year."

Now all hell was let loose! Unfortunately Professor Papadatos had understood every word very well, and now exploded:

"Mr. Kenneth! How dare you say such a thing! It is sheer impudence. I taught every question scrupulously!"

The ground was disappearing beneath me now. I wished I had studied the other thirty questions. I felt dizzy and my senses began seizing up. I couldn't hear anything and everything went black before my eyes. I could now forget about the exam. The temperature seemed to have dropped even further – call it 15 degrees below zero – and the room felt icy. Only then did I remember that I had – obediently – *first* sought the Kingdom of God, rather than swat up on my anatomy. Now that my clumsy attempt to cheat had failed, I had no choice but to leave things to God. It would be up to God – *"and all these things shall be added unto you"* – and I had to leave everything to Him. Besides this, I had been promised that prayers were being said for me. With these thoughts, I suddenly had a feeling of inner peace and was again calm. The professor looked at the paper and asked the first question. I could answer it without hesitation, because I had studied the topic.

But already the second question was causing me problems. On the paper in front of the professor was the drawing of a human brain with the central part indicated by numbers. The examiner pointed his pencil to a certain number:

"Please tell me, what you *know* about this part of the brain, here?"

In fact, all I *knew* was that this question was amongst the thirty I had not revised. So it was hardly worth replying to. But at exactly that moment help from God was at hand. Professor Papadatos, who just before had been so upset, now seemed completely changed. He made a sudden movement forward with his head, so as to attract my attention. I looked at him and saw how he was rather obviously putting his left hand to his left ear – he was trying to tell me something. But his colleague, the other examiner, could not see what he was doing. He repeated this gesture several times. In addition, he said in an expressive voice:

"*Listen* to the question Mr. Kenneth, *listen* well!"

I understood the message. I gave a short answer:

"What you are pointing to is the hearing centre of the brain."

"Good", confirmed the examiner, who then pointed to the next number:

"Here, what have we got here?"

The "game" continued. My professor pointed at his eyes several times with his index finger, then blinked one eye and said: "*Look* at the question. *Look* well!" The message was clear.

I gave a clipped, dry answer: "Sir, this is the visual centre."

"Yes, good, you are well prepared", he praised me.

From that moment on, my professor helped me each time we came across one of the thirty questions I had not revised, and in the end I passed the exam with 5.5 out of a possible 6 marks. I breathed a sigh of relief as I left the room. How much nervous tension had I expended over these insoluble problems, and how God had "tortured" me up to the last minute! It would have been much easier, of course, had I studied the topics and "counted on myself" through conscientious preparation. On the other hand, many things would have been hidden from me, if I had not made my act of faith: the rich possibilities offered by a living belief in God, the negative effect of trusting purely in one's self, and the true Presence of God in all circumstances of life. How can we know Him except by obedience to His word?

After the university state exam, I received fresh signs of the importance of obedience to God. I mentioned earlier that when I enrolled at my college, I received a form from the dean's office specifying that I would have no right to practise my profession in Switzerland. This official rule would have, under normal circumstances, rendered useless all the effort of my studies, and destroyed any future prospects of employment in the country which was now my permanent home.

I knew that God would challenge me over my professional plans and prospects, and that to question Him would only lead to despair. But I was still perplexed about the future. At least in worldly terms, what mattered most to me at the time were my studies and my career as a teacher. That outlook now looked doubtful. But I did not allow myself to worry excessively. I obeyed my Father.

I pressed on with my studies, and I was a rather unusual student. Being nearly 40 years old, I was bold enough to question some of my professors, of literature for example, and tell them that my life experience might be worth more than their book-learning. Once I had gained a certain reputation as a forthright character, I was sometimes allowed to give lectures myself, in the professor's place. But I was diligent enough to get through my studies. After a few years, I obtained a teacher's qualification and sought employment, even though I knew that I had no "right" to a job. Fortunately, the act of seeking a job wasn't forbidden. At the end of my studies I heard that there were sixty-four graduates and only four teaching posts available, so it seemed that I had no chance. Still, I kept my inner peace. God would know what to do with my degree. He always had something up His sleeve. Anyhow, my faith had greatly increased by then.

It was the beginning of the holidays, and the schools and universities were closing. I was on the point of packing my bags to go on an evangelical tour of Sicily, when the telephone rang:

"Mr. Kenneth?"

"Yes, it's me. What is it?"

"Can you come to see me as soon as possible?"

"Who are you and where should I come?"

The name and address were supplied.

"What is it about?"

"That I cannot tell you over the phone, please come here quickly."

After a few minutes, I was in the office of the director of a secondary school, of whose existence I was unaware.

"I am very pleased you have come. Please sit down. I must say that what I am about to tell you is to be treated in the strictest confidence."

It all seemed very strange, if not mysterious. I was tense, because I suspected that it was a typical trick – in the best possible sense – of the sort my Father liked to play.

"Our German teacher has *disappeared*." Disappeared? God was working here, that is what I immediately thought.

"How? Have I understood you properly? What does this mean?"

"The problem is this: Mr. S. has not attended classes for quite a while. I rang his home, but not even his family could enlighten me as to his whereabouts, and he has been gone some time."

It was a real mystery.

"The reason I have asked you to come is this. If Mr. S. does not appear after the holidays, would you, Mr. Kenneth, be willing to take his classes?"

"But of course, with pleasure." A gleam of hope!

"Good. I will take you on as his substitute to begin with. You must understand that if he does appear during or after the holidays, I will have to give up the idea of employing you. Mr. S. is a state teacher, with a permanent teaching post, and as such cannot be dismissed."

I felt I should instantly accept this proposal, knowing that a few weeks of income would be better than none. So I agreed and signed the contract.

The next day I left for Sicily, with my musician friend Gaby, where we worked on the beach with young people who had fallen prey to drugs. We talked to them about Jesus and the Bible as the only solid basis for their lives. About the middle of August, I received a telephone message that I was expected at the school and so left for Fribourg. Something dreadful had happened. For some reason, Mr. S. had killed himself by jumping off a bridge. His body had been found. My first reaction was one of horror over this personal tragedy, and pity for the dead man's family. May God have mercy on his soul!

But the fact is that any dramatic human event has multiple side-effects, often completely unanticipated by the people immediately involved in the drama. In this case, the death of Mr. S. had left the school in desperate need of a teacher. Although I had no wish to benefit from another human being's misfortune, I was relieved at the prospect of being able to establish myself, after all, in Switzerland. I told myself by staying in Switzerland I could progress in my faith and afterwards take up God's work again: work in school, work among my fellow believers, and evangelising. I tried to make good use of this opportunity. After three years, I received a permanent post as a teacher in the Swiss state school system. This status was hardly ever accorded to people who were not Swiss citizens. It would be a mistake to think that I earned this reward by being a better-than-average teacher. I simply accepted it gratefully as part of God's plan for my life. "What He opens no one can shut, and what He shuts no one can open" (Rev. 3:7–8).

God has never abandoned me. During this period of my life, I got into the habit of going every Sunday to the city of Basel, about 140 kilometres north of my home town. I would take part in charismatic services for the youth. The worship there was lively and captivating, and the "Elisabeth-Church" was generally full of vibrant youngsters. But on some occasions, I had a strong sense that I was still an imperfect person, given that both my heart and mind were still badly in need of cleansing. On one such evening, in the middle of the sermon by Johannes Czwalina, a pastor in charge of the Basel church, my heart felt really weighed down: I was on the verge of losing all courage, because of the burden I was still carrying from the past. A strong feeling of sadness came over me and I wanted to leave the church, when Johannes suddenly stopped in mid-flow. I heard his voice echoing through the microphone:

"There is a man here tonight who feels so tied to his past that it is suffocating him. Jesus is telling him now to look fearlessly forward to his future, and that he has definitely been freed."

When I heard these words, I had a strong physical sensation: I felt that great thick chains surrounding my heart had suddenly loosened and fallen noisily onto the floor. I felt so much at ease, as if I were floating. I remember wondering with amazement how those huge, thick chains had room enough to fit around my heart. They were the kind of giant clanking chains which might be used for the anchors of ocean liners. The incident left me with a deep sense of gratitude, a feeling that God not only created me but continues to love me.

Another series of events, around the same time, brought home to me the power of the Holy Spirit. Before Jesus ascended, He promised man that He would pray to His Father for "another Comforter" to be sent to mankind. We are talking about the life-giving breath of the Holy Spirit, which in the words of an ancient prayer, "is present everywhere and fills all things." The life-giving Spirit is absent in oriental religions, because through Eastern meditation every thought and energy is anaesthetized, and this can easily result in an inner void. Christian friends kept asking me if I had received the Holy Spirit. How could I know that? And Who was the Holy Spirit anyway? I could not give a clear answer. But God already had a plan for me. What awaited me was not easy to bear – to tell the truth, it was downright difficult. Here is what happened.

Our charismatic Fribourg-based prayer group, "Maranatha", asked me to join them in the French city of Strasbourg. We were due to attend an event called "Operation Pentecost throughout Europe", which attracted about 30,000 people from across the world, from cardinals to small evangelical groups. It was a difficult journey, mainly because it was exceptionally hot. When we arrived, the long wait to be assigned accommodation was exhausting for the older members of our group. But I soon felt a fresh wave of energy coursing through me and the people around me. It seemed to penetrate my very limbs. But this was not yet Pentecost.

The story of my life had spread rapidly, because it had been told many times on "Radio Luxembourg", "Radio Monte Carlo", and other international broadcasters. The response from listeners was so strong that a booklet with my testimony was published and sold by the thousand. So I was often invited by the organizers of big events to give my testimony. These organizers seemed ready to serve me in every way and even revere me, to an extent that swelled my pride. Without realizing it, I began to put myself above others. After all, I asked myself in foolish moments, what were the others? – Jesus had spoken to me personally! Such vanity had stealthily crept up on me unobserved. I regarded myself as a very important person and took it for granted that I would take the place of honour on the rostrum with all the dignitaries at any religious gathering.

In other words, I always expected to be among the main speakers, along with hierarchs like Cardinal Suenens and famous charismatic figures, like Thomas Roberts and Daniel Ange.

Along with this pride, there came a highly questionable state of mind, into which I had often fallen in the bad old days. It was a sense that I had never belonged to the great mass of humanity. I had always been more cunning and intelligent than most of my fellow countrymen. What's more, I was important! Therefore it was beneath me to queue up here in Strasbourg, like a nobody, with all the other thousands of people, in order to be fed.

At previous conferences, I had worked out a trick to make sure I avoided the queue for food. I would leave five minutes before the end in order to seat myself at the table while the other "poor" people melted in the heat of the sun as they waited their turn. That was pretty clever, wasn't it? On the Friday and Saturday of the Strasbourg gathering, my trick worked brilliantly. But by Pentecost Sunday, the Holy Spirit had had enough of this "Klaus full of pride".

On waking, the warmth of the sun lit my face and as I was saying morning prayers I was surprised to find myself full of proud thoughts. I was convinced that I was great, a natural leader. That may sound odd, very odd, but that is how my thoughts were running. However it was clear, at least to one part of me, that this was not the kind of thought or behaviour expected from a Christian. So on this day my *firm* decision was that I would queue up for food, and when speeches were in progress I would sit in the conference hall together with all the "ordinary" people. I wouldn't try to sneak into the area reserved for VIPs, as I usually managed to do. This new thought rather pleased me. How could I have behaved so badly, in my pride? From that day forward, I resolved to be a truly kind, thoughtful and humble young man – a real Christian.

But theory and reality don't always coincide. Entering the main conference hall, I noticed the platform reserved for honoured speakers, and the barriers that were intended to keep ordinary folk away. As I approached, an irresistible force pulled me in the "wrong" direction. My mind was filled with self-justifying thoughts. Yes, you really are better than most of them, you are important, you have suffered a lot, so you deserve the best place. There in the middle of the crowd you will be squashed, it smells horrible and it is so hot – you will faint.

Before realizing that this was a temptation, I played a familiar trick and brandished my guitar so as to suggest that I was due to perform and therefore needed a place of honour. (In fact, I had not been asked to perform.) Relieved to have escaped the crowd, I sat down on my undeserved seat of honour. I was still unsure of what was happening. I recalled my earlier vow to take meals with everyone else and not to leave the hall before the conference was finished, and it was still fresh in my mind. I had failed in my first resolution – to sit through the speeches with the crowd – but I was determined to keep my second vow, to queue and dine like everybody else.

Then the surprise came. One of the speakers addressed the very subject that I was pondering myself. I heard him say:

"Beloved brothers and sisters, it is somewhat unpleasant for a speaker to see people leaving the conference hall before the end, stepping over others, making a noise and thus distracting their attention. The Holy Spirit cannot work in that way. Do you agree that we should all sit together until the blessing is given?"

Loud clapping indicated people's hearty affirmation. My amazement grew as I realized how close to my own self-correcting resolution his words had been. I remained there listening attentively until five minutes to twelve. Then my stomach began to rumble, very quietly at first.

All the same, I was resolved! I would not move. Three minutes before midday, the rumble became even more powerful. Ooh, I began to sweat, to feel dizzy ... and minute later the lead weight feeling in my stomach became unbearable; it gnawed at me powerfully and my thoughts were balefully influenced by this strange spiritual attack. I was totally convinced that I would die of hunger in the next two minutes if I didn't eat something *immediately*. If I had to queue up for any length of time, I would surely get sunstroke, because of the burning heat outside – oh no! I visualised this happening on top of all my other travails. It was all so unbearable. The fear of death from starvation and sunstroke finally made me get up from my chair.

I tried to filter through the rows, walking on tiptoe, bending down so I could not be seen at my full height – how absurd – but it was my guitar that was attracting more attention than myself. With a very red face, because of my anxiety, I made for the exit hoping for mercy from the thousands of people in the hall. After all, I was on the point of death, wasn't I? Halfway between the platform and the side exit, the multitude began to hiss and whistle, because I was the only one not respecting the rules. There were five thousand people or so on my side of the conference hall, and another 25,000 people in the remaining area. I was the only one who had dared to break the rule which had just been made! My shame became insupportable. If only the earth had opened and swallowed me up! Feeling delirious, I stumbled out into a "void".

When I sat down to eat, my food became indigestible, tasteless and as heavy as stone. The sight must have looked so surreal. I was sitting totally alone, in a giant dining hall, faced by thousands of empty seats, trembling inwardly.

Satan came to accuse me:

"Go away from here you wretch, you are a good-for-nothing!" I had to agree with him. I was good-for-nothing. Three times I had failed. My good intentions were to no avail. I felt like screaming. I was a "nonentity". Everything within me had fallen apart. Bang! I was shattered.

"You are not claiming to be a Christian, are you?"

Satan was on the mark again.

"You are not worthy of these people!" he continued to accuse me. How right he was!

"Go back to Fribourg and distance yourself from these good and pure people. *You* don't belong to them."

His wish became my command and I started on my way home. I was running away from these Christians, because I was not one of them. As I had neither money nor a car, nor knew the way out of the town, all I could do was leave the dining hall and roam through the streets of the city. My guitar, always my consolation during lonely times, was for the first time silent – it couldn't console me. I felt unable to play. I spent the next four hours in torment, desperately looking for a place where I could find some peace and comfort. No such place was to be found. Music, alcohol, drugs, fornication, travel, philosophy . . . my experience told me none of these things offered any real respite. I had already tried them and they only led me to emptiness. I was utterly broken and torn up within.

Then the unexpected happened! Perhaps it was the baptism of the Holy Spirit. The awareness struck me in a split second. I realized that outside of Christianity, in the world that I had left behind, neither peace nor consolation nor stillness could be found. A single alternative remained, to turn back! I had to return from where I had run away. This thought came to me with a flood of tears, making me feel small, so very small. Confronted by my own weakness I learned much more from this moment of suffering than from all possible lessons on morality or the rules of social behaviour. This truth became evident only through the Holy Spirit. It is true, Christians *are not* any better than other people, but they *do have* something better – *they have the protection of the Holy Spirit*. Satan was on the point of destroying me – yes, and using truths to do it! With the help of the Holy Spirit, through what had just occurred, God initiated a real change in my consciousness. By the Holy Spirit's presence, self-destruction became the rebuilding of a true self. That is how my new Master, the One Who teaches and consoles, appeared. The Holy Spirit is the most efficient teacher of all, and He charges less than any psychologist, therapist or social worker.

After those burdensome few hours I knew what to do. I had to ask for forgiveness, and return. In the end, it was not difficult to tell Jesus that I was worthless and to ask Him to receive me once again to Himself, despite all that had happened. And that is exactly what I did. I returned to the gathering and lived through the following surprise. At the exact moment I turned the handle to open the door to the huge assembly hall and entered, I heard (from a German speaker) the following words: "To know the Holy Spirit means to recognize your sins." Unbelievable! I jumped for joy, I had just received confirmation that the Holy Spirit had come down on me! A loud "Hallelujah" came from the depths of my heart! Pentecost was real. "Blessed are they that mourn for they shall be comforted" (Matt. 5:4).

Let no one believe that everything was now solved. On the contrary, the practical side, the application of these new insights to my everyday life, was clearly lacking. As you will recall, everything significant in my life has had to be demonstrated twice over. My toughest lesson came on the day after my return.

The next morning, after my return to Fribourg, I found an old document issued by a local garage in my car. It was an awkward reminder of a little trick that I was in the habit of playing. The document, which was designed to be shown to an insurance company, said the car door had been broken and the cost of repairs would be approximately 600 Swiss francs. This was an over-statement of the damage to the car, one that I had quietly encouraged the garage to make. My usual tactic in such cases was to present the estimate to the insurance company, who would duly reimburse me, and then I would do the repair myself. Being in perpetual need of money, the "old Klaus" did not worry about the fact that this trick amounted to a lie. Such things did not even occur to my fallen, cunning self. When I found the latest estimate, I initially thought that it was time to go through the familiar procedure once again. So I went to my insurance office the following day.

"Good morning. I have got here an estimate for some damage. My car was broken into and I had to renew the lock. Here is the repair invoice from the garage."

"Let me see it."

I placed the invoice on the counter and the lady clerk looked at it.

"It is all in good order. We will transfer the sum."

"Thank you. Goodbye."

I turned to go towards the door and was about to leave the room, when the clerk called me back.

"Hello, excuse me please. Come back here again."

I began to feel afraid; why, I did not know.

"Yes, what is it?"

"I need to know the date of the damage."

I was afraid that I would not receive this money if this had happened some time back. At that moment Satan came like lightning and I lied, saying:

"Er … this was a few days ago."

"Good", she said, and noted the date on the damage form.

"So, goodbye."

"Goodbye."

Once again, I started for the door and was on the point of disappearing when I heard her voice again:

"Sir!"

I froze. What now?

"Please come back here once more."

As I approached she looked me straight in the eye and said:

"Can you tell me please how it is that you gave me such a recent date for the damage when on the invoice I read that the harm was done a few months ago?"

I felt rooted to the spot. A bomb had exploded in my mind; I was totally dumb-struck. I went as red as a tomato and I hoped that the ground would open and swallow me up. I went hot all over, dizzy, and could say nothing, nor could I move. I was visibly and deeply embarrassed as the clerk waited for my explanation looking straight at me. I could think of nothing to say to her, absolutely nothing. No one could have made the lie I had told any clearer than I myself had made it.

The silence became embarrassing and painful even for the secretary, so she said:

"I see that you are somewhat confused. Please take the form home with you and post it back to us."

I left the office staggering. Once home, I fell on my knees in front of Jesus, and wept bitterly.

"Jesus, I am unredeemable. I am full of sin. I deserve to be despised by you."

"But I do not despise you."

"Jesus, you saw what happened! It was painful. How can I sort this out?"

"You don't need to sort it out. Truth cannot be manipulated."

"But what shall I do? I have no idea."

"Tell the truth."

"What?! You can't ask this of me. I will never succeed. I know."

I could accept the idea of going to a pastor to confess, yes of course, but to go and confess to a secretary, that was unimaginable.

"Do you love truth? Do you love Me?"

"You know this …"

"Then you know what you must do."

I felt as if I had a stone pressing on my heart. I had to come to an understanding with Jesus. So I proposed:

"All right. I will do it, but You must come with me."

"I promise."

Nearly all week my heart burned within me, and I kept trying to make different excuses and explanations, but it was no use. Truth is always truth. I delayed my "judgment" to the very last minute. By Friday afternoon when I ran out of excuses, I returned to the insurance agency. Before entering, I said again: "Please Lord, You go in first – I'll follow You."

The secretary was seated at her desk and came to the counter, when suddenly her gaze met mine:

"Good afternoon. Ah, you have come in person."

I was certain that she knew from previous experience that people tried regularly to cheat on their insurance. It may be that this very thought had inspired me to act "differently" from those who tried to cheat, thus behaving like a Christian. Not beating about the bush, I handed over the form saying:

"You can believe what you like about me, but this claim was a lie. I have no right to any of it. I am sorry and I ask you to forgive me. You can destroy the paper."

Phew, I'd said it, and felt several kilos lighter. On hearing these words, I could see that the person facing me was so taken aback that she found it difficult to hide her amazement. Perhaps nothing like this had ever happened to her before. But in a way, that was her problem. I breathed freely again, after this unusual confession. Literally, everything is possible with Jesus. Throughout all those long years I had been taken to task for my pride, selfishness, prejudgments, anger and suffering: one after the other, they had taken control and turned a free man into a slave. Wrestling with these temptations is a process that will continue to the end of my life.

The Holy Spirit often comes unexpectedly and alights on the "erstwhile" in us, our past lives, which still need to be purified. When I was blinded by the influence of past experiences, and bad old habits, He clearly showed me that I had strayed from the Lord's path. When Ursula and I had a problem with our car while travelling back from the Camargue in France to Switzerland, once more something special happened. We were in a hurry because Maurice Ray was expecting us that evening. We were halfway through our journey, in between two villages in the south of France, when the accelerator cable broke and the car stopped with a rattle. We were towed and brought to a garage in the next village, where there was only one car mechanic. Surrounded by other broken-down vehicles and waiting clients who all wanted to be first in line, the mechanic gave us an angry look, as if to say, "That's all I needed now". In a subdued voice, I explained our situation and urged him to see to our broken cable "quickly" and take us on before all the others. The furious explosion that followed was accompanied by much swearing. "The devil take you!" he said.

"Go to hell!" I thought. "That is where you belong, you vulgar, wretched person."

Of course, I was very frustrated, because I could not have what I wanted, and because I was afraid we would not reach Lausanne the same day, when suddenly the Holy Spirit descended on me and made me understand exactly what I had been thinking of. My attitude could be called by whatever name one wanted, but it certainly was not a Christian one, and so I corrected myself. This poor man was already in hell, through the work he did, and the fact that everyone wanted to be first made his life even more hellish. When I saw this more clearly, I changed my attitude to the hapless mechanic. "May you be in paradise", I prayed for him. "May it come about that you will find the peace and calm of paradise." Then the miracle happened.

A few minutes later, he came to our car and asked me to lift up the hood. We worked, grumbling and snorting with irritation. We felt angry with the car manufacturers, who had made such complex couplings for the cables that it needed two of us working for an hour and a half to replace a simple cable, which was linked to the gas pedal. With oily hands and black faces, we finished, sweating and laughing as we came out from under the hood, but happy to have been successful at last.

The mechanic had totally changed and amazingly we heard him say:

"Rarely have I met such a complex piece of work. It has been a real challenge for me, but I have wasted so much time with you that I am past caring. My time is a gift to you. It is done for free."

That was not all.

"Wait a second", he said.

He disappeared behind the workshop and returned in a few minutes holding a large plastic bag and gave it to us. From within some delicious red cherries smiled at us.

"Now take these to munch on during your journey to Switzerland", he said with a shining face. "These are from my wife, from our garden."

Lord, how great You are! *"Ask and it shall be given unto you...."* The Bible is a book that lives. How long will it be before I stop having such little faith, and fear no more! Our parting could not have been friendlier, and of course we arrived in time at Maurice Ray's.

CHAPTER TWELVE

GIFTS

A NEWBORN BABY receives many presents. In my case the joy of infancy – and the sense that life brought one gift after another – continued for quite a long time, several years in fact, after my rebirth in Christ. I dare to think that I may have been showered with an unusual number of divine gifts precisely because Satan had kept me so firmly in hell for the first half of my life. I was in dire need of God's grace, and I received it. I only hope and pray that I will be worthy of that grace.

Certainly what I received was more than I deserved, but I can only describe things as they were. Later on, I would see the reason behind God's providence and dispensation. In order to change "the old Adam", God guides each one of us with heavenly wisdom, assuming we are ready to receive his guidance. Even if He withdraws His Grace after some time, He does so because He wants us to set about regaining it, with ascetic pain, obedience and patience. Why, I sometimes wondered, did so many Christians complain to me and say how painful it was that the grace of God never manifested itself to them? Perhaps, I suggested to them, it was because they had not given themselves entirely to Christ; some little part of them was holding back. In my case, the surrender to Satan had produced such terrible results that I felt I had no choice but to try surrendering my whole being to Christ. Whether I could be worthy of this conversion every day of my life was another matter.

As I was beginning to realize, it is not enough to be converted "once", and then to come to church twice a year, at Christmas and Easter, and say you are a Christian. Every day of our life, we have to experience anew the teaching, "Ask and you shall receive". I have seen this to be true in my own life, and I sometimes think that if those words had not been in the Bible already, I would have written them myself. God became known to me in small as well as big ways. He was there each day and at every moment, so it seemed normal to want to share this great, inexplicable joy with others. As I strongly felt, it is not enough to know God just for one's self: I wanted to be active and testify to all that he had done for me. Because I was a singer, I wanted to sing for Him and make an album. However, my guitar was not good enough for that, so I asked Jesus to help me. A short time afterwards, someone called at my door. I was quite amazed.

"Hey, Diane, where have you come from?" I was overjoyed. Diane was a vivacious young Hawaiian woman, whom I had befriended on a journey through the jungle in northern Thailand. For a long time I had dreamt of living permanently in Hawaii, until my conversion changed all those plans. But now, here she was at my door!

After entering my living room and making herself comfortable, she began to explain:

"I was thinking of you quite often, and I really wanted to come and visit you." It's true we had liked each other from the very first moment we met. "And as I remember also that you like to sing and play the guitar, I have brought you this one. You mentioned once that you would need a good instrument. Please take it as a gift." This left me open-mouthed. She then handed me a solid brown case, which contained a guitar.

"Open it." She didn't need to ask twice.

My heart was pounding as I took the guitar out. It was an *Ovation Classic* – a very expensive instrument and one I would never have been able to afford. I suddenly had the feeling that paradise was not inaccessible; here I was holding in my hands "the answer to my prayer", received from Diane's hands. "Hallelujah". That was how my first journey to the recording studio became possible. I asked the best musicians I knew, from all backgrounds, if they would be prepared to sacrifice some of their time for God. No one refused. Piece after piece, month after month my dream came true: the dream of giving Jesus my voice and musical talent. The cassettes we made were very well received, especially in Switzerland. Our concerts were broadcast by many radio stations and reached far beyond the usual audience for Christian music.

The expense of hiring a studio and sound technician would normally be very high in Switzerland, but the technician we dealt with always gave us a good price – he would only charge for about a third of the time we actually took up. This was one of the many mysterious and providential ways in which our activities were helped along.

To take another example, a lady called Maria B., invited me one day to go for a walk with her in a stretch of woodland which she owned, near Zurich. While discussing spiritual themes, she suddenly took out a packet of cigarettes:

"Help yourself Klaus." She tapped the packet lightly with one finger, sliding out something that resembled a cigarette. I did not pay much attention to it and put the object in my pocket. We continued our walk, talking and praying. Only when I was on the train back to Fribourg did I put my hand in my pocket and found four Swiss banknotes of 500 Swiss francs each, rolled very carefully to the size of a cigarette and tied with elastic. Other sums I found in letters without the sender's name in my mail box. I was thus able to pay all my recent studio expenses to the last cent. With this enormous help from God my first album of twelve songs came out. From the beginning it was clear what the title would have to be. The subject was my long journey of two million kilometres, "from head to heart", as told in verse and put to music. "From Head to Heart" describes the difficult road out of hell, from the darkness of suffering and hatred to the light of hope, peace and love. After the album was made, it wasn't very long before I was invited to perform some of the songs on stage.

A fellow student from university had organized a large music festival in Sion, in the south of Switzerland, and invited me to participate. Taking turns on the stage there were hundreds of musicians, composers, dancers, organizers, and a ballet troupe. This was to be recorded live and broadcast on Swiss Radio on New Year's Eve, 1982.

There were more than one thousand spectators filling the hall. One of my compositions describes my long journey towards Jesus and I wanted to transmit its message to an audience, which was for the most part non-Christian, without being pitied or viewed with contempt for being naïve enough to follow Christ. The song had been rehearsed with the radio orchestra from Geneva. Unfortunately, at the main rehearsal everything was rather creaky: my guitar would not tune up, the sound apparatus was faulty, the loudspeakers were dead ... I was nervous and impatient and the rehearsals were interrupted. My stress level was rising visibly and in the evening I ran up a temperature. I was about to begin a special moment of prayer before appearing on stage, when all of a sudden the principal organizer pushed a camera into my hands asking me to take photos during the performance. That was all I needed. With this double load I was simply not going to cope, and half an hour before my appearance I felt at a total loss. I handed over the camera with a brief explanation to Diane, who was with me, and then ran to the dressing room. I just wanted to run over my lyrics quickly and in a stupor realized that I could not remember one word of them – my mind was ablank. I felt sick, my hands were shaking, and I was unable to strike a clear chord.

In my despair, I hid in a dark and empty room and prayed to Jesus, crying:

"Jesus, I cannot appear on stage. You see how nervous and closed up I am."

Then a miracle happened. Suddenly, Jesus was there with me in the room and answered very calmly:

"Yes, I know."

There was something totally reassuring in His presence and answer. I felt deep down in my soul that He knew all things: He understood me and was not going to leave me to myself. Still I continued to complain:

"Jesus, it isn't going to work. I cannot sing. I don't have the courage to appear on stage in front of one thousand people."

"For *whom* are you singing?"

That short question unleashed an avalanche of feelings, and the scales fell from my eyes. It was *I* who wanted to be the star of the show, to enjoy all the honours, me, Klaus Kenneth – yes!"

"Have you not given Me your life! Or have you decided otherwise?"

Oh My Lord and God! Was all the honour for me? I had to ask myself. Was I being a liar, then, when I sang "Hallelujah?" Clearly, God did not want me to become a liar. But there was another problem.

"But Jesus, I can't remember the lyrics."

How can I best explain this? Jesus seemed now to be standing in front of me, asking me to recite the text. With knees trembling from fear, I was to recite every word in front of the King of Kings, and to justify the contents of the text before Him. Once I started, it felt as if every word was etched on the fibres of my brain, just like the needle that scrapes along the grooves of an old gramophone record. When I had finished, I got up and climbed the stairs into the glare of the blinding spotlights, with my guitar under my arm. I must have looked like a creature sleepwalking through a dream. The ballet girls had just finished and they shouted to me as they were descending the steps:

"Hi Klaus, wake up, it's your turn. You've just been announced!" I might have seemed half asleep, but in my heart and soul I was completely awake. The man on stage was no longer "me". The one who was singing, blinded by the spotlights, in front of a giant dark wall of people, was totally calm and sang "His message", without hearing the applause. He then retreated from stage as if in a trance, convinced that this "message of love" was not just public entertainment, but something the audience could take home – a fragment of hope. Here are the words:

I tried it

I tried with whisky and I tried with rum –

I had confusion and I had some fun
I tried with music and I tried with speed –
Excitement all over was just rising my greed.

I tried revolution and I tried to steal –
I went through 'morality' still I wasn't 'real'
I tried with girls, I tried all I can –
I just found strangers and was raped by some men.

Now I tried with money but I found myself poor –
Then I tried an 'insurance' to make myself 'sure'
I left my country to find me a home –
I lived on the road and I was alone
I lived with the devil and I gave him my soul
exploring the hell I understood to be my rôle
I tried with Mohammed, I tried with 'Shiring' –
I lost all my money in 'yoga' and 'yang-yin'
I tried with Krishna, with Buddha, and with 'Greens' –
But their millions of rules made me a fool, as it seems.

Searching for love I was provoking as a punk –
Seeking for love I meditated as a monk
I crowned myself 'king', but still I had to run
Until I came across these seven gangsters
And was reborn through their guns.

Then I met Jesus and He made it all clear
He covered me with His love and said He loved me so dear
He blessed me with joy, satisfaction and surprise
He cut through my chains and His Spirit made me wise.

O thank you, my Lord, I say 'thank you' to Thee
I say 'alleluia' – because you set me free
O Father, O Father, you cannot deceive
You give us everything freely, if we just do believe.

It seemed to me that through this and other manifestations God wanted to show me that I had lost nothing by having changed my spiritual camp through conversion. In my new situation, the company was far better and the cultural level was even higher. Now the angels were ministering instead of the demons, and God was the One who decided what event should take place and when. If this was what He truly intended, then all the doors and paths

"On tour" – immediately after my conversion

were open to me, even state frontiers, to the point of making me invisible. In fact this happened twice.

I was giving the testimony of my conversion in Porrentruy, a town near to the French border, when a group of French people came from neighbouring Belfort and Montbéilard to meet me. They had read and heard about me and wanted me to speak the next day at their assembly in France. Not having my passport with me, I told them I was unable to cross the border and fulfil their wishes. However they insisted, saying that this was quite an important event with lots of people waiting for me.

"Well, at least we can try", one of my new French friends insisted. "Let us travel the fifteen kilometres to the border. It's not that much of a detour."

It did seem worth trying. No sooner said than done. My friends took me in their car, with my guitar, and around midnight we arrived at the frontier. We got out of the car, and I went to the customs officer.

"Good evening. I have a question and a plea."

"What are you talking about?"

"Are you working here tomorrow afternoon?"

"Yes. Why?"

"Listen please, this is my situation. These people very much want me to hold a conference tomorrow morning for their community in Belfort, but I do not have my passport with me. And because you are seeing me now and would recognize me again, would it be possible for me to re-enter Switzerland tomorrow afternoon? You can see that I am not doing anything illegal."

"I am sorry, I cannot do that. Without a passport, I cannot allow you to re-enter Switzerland." His face became very stern.

"But please, what is the problem?"

Any further discussion of this was clearly of no use, because it would lead nowhere. This was a conscientious Swiss worker.

"I would like to make a bet with you", I continued. "I will leave Switzerland, and with the help of God, I will return." I felt that God was allowing me to speak in this bold manner. I was neither rude nor arrogant. It was a test for me.

"Well, I cannot stop you from leaving Switzerland, but be assured that if I see you tomorrow, I will not let you re-enter the country. Besides, the French border customs may not allow you in without a passport."

"I wish you goodnight. See you soon."

I must admit, I was surprised at my own boldness and was wondering where all of a sudden that power and firm conviction, that confidence to act the way I did, had come from. After a minute, the officer on the French side signalled with his hand for us to proceed into France. We didn't have to stop the car.

Sunday was a day full of grace. There were about six hundred people in the hall. God worked wonderfully and many people were blessed. Many hearts opened that morning to receive the Gospel message. I was invited to lunch and later my friends took me back to the French border. My heart began to pound when, as we approached the Swiss border, there he was, the officer from the night before. He stopped us and came up to the driver.

"Your passports, please."

He looked at us in silence. I was sitting at the back between two of my companions. He then ordered them to get out of the car. When I was left alone, a distinctive Voice said to me:

"Stay where you are!" So I did.

What happened next is truly unbelievable. The officer checked the passports belonging to the others and came back towards the car, looked inside through the window – but saw nothing! The windows were not steamed up, nor was the visibility impaired by the reflection of the light. I was truly invisible to the customs officer. During this time, I was sitting normally on the back seat of the car. It was as if I were behind a mirror, from where I could see his head moving to and fro ... perhaps because he was not finding answers to his questions. After a few moments, my four friends climbed back in and we drove on to Porrentruy where I had left my car. Everything is simplified when God decides on the action to be taken. My only contribution to this mission was to put all my trust in Him. And He *knew* that I would trust Him. Whilst He made me invisible to other eyes, He was "visible" to me.

It was not much different when I met Mother Theresa again, some time later. She had come to hold a conference in the cathedral in Lausanne. I need hardly underline the reasons why this was a special occasion for me. First the cathedral, this House of God, was "my home", and also I had a special relationship with Mother Theresa. In Calcutta we had spoken at length about Mary, the Mother of Christ, and how much she protects us through her intercession with her Son. At the time, I did not understand exactly what she was trying to convey to me, but now I reckoned that it was appropriate to ask her some questions about this. Moreover, it was my great joy to tell her how I had become a Christian in the meantime. When I arrived in Lausanne, I found, not surprisingly, that Mother Theresa was totally surrounded by security guards. She was sitting in the room where, a couple of years earlier, Maurice had carried out my exorcism. My wish to meet her was something more than journalistic curiosity. What I really wanted to do was ask her some very specific questions. I had an intense desire to see "my mother", and there were two reasons in particular for this. She had been the first person in my life who had appeared as a sort of mother to me; and secondly, I thought she was also the one person who could help me find out if I really had a Mother interceding for me in heaven. She had told me in Calcutta that the Mother of Jesus would be my intercessor. When I saw how the security guards were positioned, not only in front of the garden-door, but also inside the garden and the entrance, I thought it impossible that I would reach her. But again, God opened the door for me.

"Just go to her", more than that I did not hear, but I obeyed. The guards did not seem to see me, although I was walking normally and straight on. There was no move to stop me, not a question as to who I was, not a single barrier all along the way, as if I were invisible. Thus, I passed through three or four prohibited zones and suddenly found myself face to face with Mother Theresa. She stopped her conversation with the person in front of her and turned towards me.

"Good day, Mother."

"Good day, I am glad you've come. What can I do for you?"

"Do you remember me?"

"Oh yes, of course." I was stunned. And this after so many years!

"Look, I have prepared this for you." I gave her my written testimony. She looked at it attentively.

"I will read it later. I have no time now; soon I must appear."

"Thank you. I am so glad that I have met you again. God bless your speech."

I left the room and went into the cathedral, which of course was crammed full of people who had come to hear Mother Theresa speak. Suddenly, I remembered that I had forgotten to ask her the most important question. I left the cathedral again – and seemingly invisible – I went a second time through the security zones, passing by the guards who were like dumb statues. I was once more facing her and asking for a clarification:

"Remember back then in Calcutta, you talked to me about Mary, that she is my and every Christian's Mother, that she will protect me; that all I have to do is to ask her? Please can you explain this to me in more detail? I have never understood what you said to me."

"Oh, Klaus, this is not something that one can 'understand' – it is a mystery. You cannot comprehend this with your mind. You simply have to do it. Pray with your heart."

"What do you mean by that?"

"Well, just pray to her."

"How and what do I say? And" – I hesitated – "is it not dangerous? The Bible doesn't recommend such a thing."

Again she was laughing, she must have thought, "What a child this Klaus is".

"Of course it is biblical, but this is a mystery and is not written literally. By the way, in the Scripture you can read about her: '*All generations will bless Thee . . .*' Do the Protestants bless her? You have to understand the Bible through the Holy Ghost, and not with mental study; only then will you find out. Now just do as I do. I will tell you how I pray daily. You will see and experience much love and strength emanating from her intercession. My personal prayer is very short. It is, '*Mary, Mother of God, be my*

Mother and lead me to Your Son.' Don't think about it with your rational mind – just say it."

"And if I don't succeed? Is it not enough to have only Jesus in my heart? Many Protestants say that Mary is not important and we must not pray to her – that that would be idolatry."

She started laughing heartily, for whatever reason. …

"Don't worry, I take it upon myself to pray for you every day."

My heart was full of joy that I had received such help. I had the feeling that I had "opened an account in heaven", to which we would both contribute regularly – even if I didn't rationally understand. Once again, I saw how God gives us His whole strength when it is a matter of finding our way to Him – even the power to become invisible to others.

In general, this cathedral seemed to be a place destined to play a role in my life. It is no surprise that over time God took me to all the people who had played an important role in my journey towards Him. In that cathedral in Lausanne I met, on my birthday, someone who had a powerful influence in my opening towards Christianity. Before I left for South America, Ursula had given me a book called, *The Cross and the Switchblade*, to read on the way.

In reading this, I was greatly surprised that these tough guys had become Christians. The hero in that amazing story was a gang leader called Nicky Cruz, and he was anything other than a "baby-face"; and now I was here in the cathedral with Nicky sitting beside me, exchanging the experiences we had both lived through. Our missions were similar, as we had both realized from the beginning. As brothers in faith we prayed together for our work.

This was a time of mission, not only in words, but also through music. I was again invited to Lausanne to arrange a weekend together with Leon Patillo, keyboard accompanist of the renowned guitarist, Carlos Santana. Leon had also become a Christian and was certainly not among the "baby-faces". In Leon, I found a brother who had devoted his talents to the work of God in a remarkable way. I was happy to know that in my new family I had real brothers and sisters who worked together to the same end, giving hope and showing the way to those who lived without any good purpose in life. I considered it a great honour when, as a result of my music albums, I was asked to take part in the legendary *Jazz Festival* in the lakeside town of Montreux. I was asked to play in the "Gospel boat", which was an important feature of the festival.

I did not seek rational explanations for all this, but only the presence of God each hour of every day within my soul, in my thoughts and in my heart. I wanted to remember His presence like a "tooth-ache": when you walk, talk, work, eat, read . . . you always feel "it", feel Him. This I share even today with my brothers and sisters, so that they too may have a new beginning every day with Him – always by the grace of God. This is my answer when people ask me about these things. In the last few years, I have heard so often, "God has sent you" or "You have come at the right moment", even when sometimes it is obvious that I have only come by chance. In this way many people have felt the presence of God through me, a sinner, and certainly not a "good Christian", while I, too, often feel the presence of God through others. There is always an exchange of experiences and thoughts. The more I was humbled, the more powerfully God used me. I could see that Christ's saving grace embraced all things, every facet of life, on every level of society.

One day in Berne, I met Grete B. She invited me to her home for a prayer meeting. During our discussions she told me that her husband was the head of a government department in Berne. He was proud of the diplomatic honours he had acquired and the newspapers wrote much about his activities. But from his wife's point of view everything sounded completely different:

"Each time E. goes away on official business, I now know for certain that he enjoys himself with other women. His attitude is disgusting and he forgets that he has a wife and children at home! Often his travels are only a screen, so that he can visit a girlfriend in a particular country." How sad, to abuse his position in this way!

Consequently, we prayed frequently and at length to God, for Him to clarify this undignified situation. Some months later the papers wrote that this once acclaimed person had now been given the sack. After his shameful dismissal, disciplinary actions followed. God's wheels grind slowly.

In another case, different to the one I have just related, I had read a book written by a very influential Swiss diplomat of high standing, the ambassador Dr. S. I could not get away from the impression that this book gave me, namely that it represented an incomplete but at the same time very serious personal quest embarked upon in Tibet. I understood that what was missing were the decisive elements of truth which, evidently, the author had not yet found. His search had given him no answers but, as I knew, the answers he wanted could easily be discerned in the presence of Jesus.

I was burning with impatience to discuss these things with him, and such a conversation did take place after I had an invitation, through some friends who were diplomats, to certain festivities at the Swiss embassy in China, on August 1st, the Swiss national holiday. (I was passing through China after visiting a friend in Seoul.) In a short time I was sitting beside Dr. S. at a table and together we began a deep conversation, such that within twenty minutes he seemed to have forgotten all about his guests, even the honoured ones. Amazingly, we became so absorbed in our discussions that, as his guests were leaving, he only half raised himself, threw a glance at them, and nodded his head as a "good-bye".

Our spiritual talk, in a spirit of unity, lasted until one o'clock in the morning, after which I heard him say, word for word:

"Heaven has sent you!"

I was happy to hear that.

"For some time now I have been searching for an answer to *this* specific problem and never found it."

Through our discussion, God had answered him. For very personal reasons he had embarked on a spiritual quest, and I was able at least to point him in the right direction. God is truly great!

God also solved, in a wonderful way, another unresolved problem from my past. Once during my youth, when I was in the south of France, in the Carmargue, I had had an extremely unpleasant experience. During a very turbulent period, which I spent in the remote, water-logged area known as the Etang de Vaccarès, I had completely destroyed my girlfriend's trailer. This had happened as a result of a strong mistral wind, at a time when I was under the influence of Satan and behaving recklessly. (It was an old model and no spare wheels were to be found.) One of the wheels plus the brake drum had broken down, and thus this huge vehicle was unfortunately blocking the small road in the midst of the wilderness. All cars in the area had to do a fifty kilometre detour because of the blockage. For an entire day, no one had been able to move the monstrous thing off that narrow road, and night was drawing in. Here I sat, alone on this winding road, next to this broken monster trailer. It was a bad situation to be in, first, because I was posing a danger to other traffic, and secondly, there was no obvious place where I could spend the night. Looking around me, I spotted a small light far away on the other side of a swamp. An arid path took me several kilometres through marshland and bushes, at the end of which there was an ornithological institute. Thanks be to God that the dim light of a small bulb in front of the house helped me to see the entrance. There was no bell, so I stepped into the house and found myself in a kitchen. Voices could be heard coming from there. Something incredible happened then.

"Hello Klaus. Where are *you* coming from?" I heard.

It was inconceivable. Seated at a table was Aude, an old girlfriend from Fribourg, and she was just serving supper. She had been working in this remote ornithological station for a year! A heavy weight fell from me. But the second miracle came after supper. I had searched all the scrap yards and garages between Nîmes and Arles to find a spare wheel for the trailer, but it was such an old model that no one could help. But here, in this wild place where the foxes and rabbits are almost the only inhabitants, just at the back of the house, there was a rusty old 1949 vehicle – and what do you know – the wheels fitted the caravan! I felt a ton lighter and was able to continue on my odyssey through the dark night, thanks to the help of my ornithologist friend. But where should I leave the wrecked caravan? After ten kilometres, I found a farmhouse, completely in the middle of nowhere, with its lights on.

"Good evening. Please forgive my troubling you at this late hour." I explained my unfortunate situation. The young woman was welcoming and perhaps rather too friendly, when she suggested that

I put the object in the giant barn near the farm and leave it there for as long as was needed. After that, everything she said sounded somewhat provocative – much too sweet for my taste, in fact, "You can spend the night here with me, if you want to." How awful!

I pressed the retreat button. I did not want to stay there. I was right in thinking that here, in the middle of nowhere, there was a house where the world's oldest profession was practised. I left the wreck there and hastened away from that sinister spot.

However, ten years later when I was spending some time in Ars (near Lyons in France), I experienced the miraculous continuation of this weird story. I was participating in a Roman Catholic meeting with five thousand people at a gathering, in honour of John Vianney, "the priest of Ars" (*le curé d'Ars*), a saintly Catholic preacher of the 19th century. I witnessed a miraculous healing of seven people, who in the name of the Lord Jesus Christ were able to leave their wheelchairs and walk. It is incredibly impressive to see this with one's own eyes. But this was not the miracle that impressed me most. I had always had the dream of playing music with gypsies, whose outcast status somehow appealed to me. Now I delighted to be invited into a gypsy caravan and asked to perform on the guitar. My hosts were among the vast and diverse crowd of people which the Lyons gathering had attracted. The miracle happened when a gypsy woman entered the crowded caravan to listen to me singing and strumming. She had a very expressive face. I liked her, and after I took a break, we started talking.

"Greetings. Hello."

"Bonjour – I heard good music being played, so I came in to listen. I hope you don't mind."

"No problem." A little later: "What is your name?"

"Nerthe."

"That is an unusual name. Where is it from?"

"It is not so rare for a gypsy. Where are you from?"

"Originally from Hamburg, but I live mainly in Switzerland."

"Oh, from Hamburg? Many years ago, I met a man who came from Hamburg."

"Really. But you, Nerthe, where do you live?"

"In the south."

I knew the south of France well, so I asked more details.

"In the Camargue", she continued. "I had a farm there once, a "night shelter". Now I live in Nîmes."

"Where was your farm?"

"I can't explain that. It is in the middle of nowhere. Even people who live in the area won't be able to tell you where it is."

"But tell me, nevertheless. I know the area of Camargue pretty well." I insisted on this because my memory of Camargue was still very much alive. Was this just a simple conversation, I asked myself? It was not usual for me to ask such inquisitive questions. She explained:

"I lived for a long time in the nature park area of the marshes of Vaccarès, between Gacholle and Le Paradis south of Tour de Valat. These are not localities but just farms. It is impossible to find them – even on a map." Suddenly, I became very attentive and had a certain presentiment:

"Tour du Valat is an ornithological study centre, is that not so?"

"How do you know that?"

I told her about the mishap I had had in that region with my caravan and how, miraculously, someone found a spare wheel so that I could continue my journey; and how I then travelled a few kilometres in the pitch dark until I ..."

"... arrived at a farmhouse", she interrupted, "where a young woman allowed you to enter and at last to be rid of that wretched caravan."

Spontaneously, we embraced each other and praised God. We had both become Christians since then, and God had brought us together, here in Ars, among five thousand people, in a gypsy caravan, as brother and sister. Hallelujah! When we met, I had been a reckless, selfish, hippie and she had been a prostitute. But now Jesus wanted every detail of our past lives to be resolved in our minds, so that ghosts from the past would no longer trouble us with disturbing thoughts. What He has already begun, He will see through to the end.

Nerthe, gypsy woman (left, behind me)

CHAPTER THIRTEEN

MONEY AND OTHER MATTERS

As a teacher I was earning a regular wage for the first time in my life. It was not too late at the age of forty-two to begin work, and with my new income I was well off. But now it was time for God to teach me about *money*. Jesus began intervening in an area of life which I thought was comfortably under my control, and as a result, I would learn a necessary lesson in obedience. I knew Jesus well enough to recognize Him when, not for the first time, he stepped into a situation where I had not expected to discern his immediate presence. Maybe he took me off my guard on purpose. Yes, it became clear that every area of life had to be "sacrificed" to Him, and his method of teaching was a "crushing" one. He opened my eyes to some new facts on my next autumn holiday.

I decided to leave all my usual activities behind for a while and spend a week in Majorca. In Spain alcohol is cheap, and now and then I drank a glass of gin and tonic or whisky and soda – not to get drunk, of course, because I had had enough of such excesses in the past. Picture me early one afternoon. I had left my hotel room a few minutes earlier and was holding on to an empty lemonade bottle. I was walking along the seaside promenade to the nearby supermarket, to buy a bottle of gin. I was enjoying the sea breeze and the scenery, thinking of the glass of gin I would have the pleasure of drinking that evening. Out of the blue, He crossed my path and stopped me.

Very distinctly, I heard His voice within me:

"Where are you going?"

It was characteristic of Him to be brief and direct. Never a redundant word. This meant that you had to really think and not allow any ambiguity to get in. I myself was more prone to negotiation and bargaining.

"Well, as You can see, I am going to the supermarket to buy some gin", I replied, continuing on my way.

"Klaaaus!"

His voice sounded stronger and more expressive. I stopped, so that I could concentrate on the discussion.

"Am I doing something wrong?" I asked, somewhat embarrassed.

"No."

But still, it sounded as if He did not want me to carry on.

"Jesus", I continued, "Would You *not* drink gin?"

"That is not what is meant."

"But what then? Please tell me."

He was silent. Not a word. I raised my eyes to look up and see if He was following me from above. People were looking at me rather curiously, and I knew that they must have thought me "a strange sight", as they observed someone lost in thought, looking up at the sky, while standing in the middle of the sidewalk and with an empty bottle in his hand. One thing was clear, I could not continue on my way. So I put obedience before desire and went back. He will show me at some point what His purpose was. I had to demonstrate my faith as that is what He apparently wanted, and I duly obeyed. This "meeting" in the street only lasted a few minutes and I turned back to my hotel – without yet realizing what was happening – so as to accomplish His new plan, whatever it might be. I came back to my room, put my empty bottle on the bedside cabinet and went downstairs with the intention of walking once again along the sea front.

But things were about to change.

At the hotel bar I saw two pretty young women, who were having a drink. They turned out to be mother and daughter. We looked at each other and began a conversation – with me intending to talk to them about Jesus. After telling them how I had accepted Jesus into my life, a long and serious conversation followed with Mady, the mother. As there was a lot more to say, we decided to go and dine together in a restaurant and went into the village.

Mady and Nathalie – in Majorca

During the meal, Mady asked:

"Klaus, why don't you bring your guitar here and sing us something?"

"Oh, we are in a restaurant, I can't do that without permission."

"Ask the owner if he has anything against it."

I got up and suggested this to the proprietor. He was delighted and immediately ran to the jukebox and disconnected it.

"No, no", I exclaimed, "not now, only when we have finished our meal, then I will bring my guitar."

Half an hour later, I took the instrument out of its box and began singing. It was obvious that the landlord enjoyed it, as I sang some Spanish and Italian songs; not long afterwards, he came over holding a tray with glasses and placed it on our table.

"This is for you all and of course it is free of charge. This is *on the house*", he said smiling.

There were three tall glasses full of . . . gin! I had not said a word, so how did he know? I sang again and the people at the other tables were obviously enjoying it. Some came over to our table.

"We would like to join you. Can we put our tables together?" No sooner said than done.

Their high spirits were infectious and soon I was singing song after song, just as people requested, like a jukebox. After a time, an elderly gentleman arose – he was Hans V., a lawyer from Essen (a large city in Germany), and he went towards the bar. He came back with a bottle in his hand and placed it on the table. Its contents were . . . gin! I did not want to get drunk, so I poured gin in all the glasses. Meanwhile the joyful mood in the bar grew so intense that more and more people started coming in. The money in the landlord's till was growing and he was delighted. A little later his neighbour came to find out the reason for all the merrymaking and the ever-increasing flow of customers. He approached me and asked if I would go over to his restaurant when I had finished singing here, to sing for him too. I promised to go over and later on I duly changed venue. The same incredible, amazing things happened there also. Free gin was poured out in good measure. I had to be careful to see that no one became drunk, otherwise the festivities which He had organized would degenerate. God is not only kind but He gives abundantly. This I was to find out later the same night, when two Scottish girls came up to me in the midst of the merrymaking and asked if I would go over to *their* Scottish bar, once I had finished singing in that place. Even though the tips of my fingers were becoming painful I still went on, singing my last song at about 2:00 a.m., perpetually surrounded by "generous donors", who made sure their customer was well provided with . . . gin! I had never mentioned to anyone the word "gin"! The only One who knew was the One Who is above us.

On all these occasions His lessons were very clear. Of course, Jesus has nothing against gin. Nevertheless, He made me realize that my money belongs to Him. I was not the owner, only the administrator of the money that came by His mercy. Now I learnt to account for every penny spent – this has stayed with me until today. This was to be a very important lesson for later, when God wanted me to set up the "King Solomon Academy" in Kenya. In that country we built five new buildings for a school. At times those buildings had to accommodate about 200 kids. The academy is an association designed to help those who have had little or no opportunity in life, and to help women to learn about hygiene and how to avoid AIDS. When I saw the enormous poverty of the post war-torn Serbia and Montenegro, my heart was "wounded" once again, and I founded a second relief organization, called "St Sava", where, with my financial help, we would help to restore destroyed churches, feed poor families, give medical help; in short, support people living in dire straits. The money went also to Christians in Palestine, in Bethlehem in particular, and many other places where assistance was and still is needed.

Only when one learns to be honest in little things does God give responsibility for bigger projects. As I found, this also holds

King Solomon Academy – fruit of my foundation

good for the income from the sale of my books, cassettes, CDs, DVDs, etc. God always has a plan, because the poor have always been His friends.

Any alliance with the demon called mammon means distancing one's self from the place that God should have in our hearts. I would have brought destruction upon myself if I had allowed myself to let money build up in my bank account and then gloat over the ever-improving balance sheet, while knowing that there were people living in terrible poverty and even dying of starvation. I have never been rich, nor have I ever handled large sums of money. I was certainly not immune from the danger of wasting money without cause, just as many people do after winning money on the lottery. But here, also, God had prepared me well. In various ways, he taught me that there are more important things than gaining and spending money. The comical episode with the gin was one such lesson. I understood that He would only make me "rich" if I gave from the heart, and that I would remain "poor" if I kept the money for myself, or spent it on clothes and other vain things. How many times was I to thank Him for showing me that! Was I not myself a beggar before God, asking for His mercy? The generous gifts I received from God were not something I could keep to myself. The one who receives and the one who has the opportunity to give, both are indebted to God. Whether we give or receive it all comes from God. The fact is that we come into the world naked and leave it the same way. Everything we acquire during our lifetime is God-given. If we receive riches, it is only to test us – and the trial can be severe even for the one who is fully aware that he is being tested. Blessed is the one, in the midst of all these tests and temptations, who still counts the poor as his "family".

Many people say to themselves, "If I were rich I could do so much for others with my money." They only mislead themselves. A saint of the early church, John of the Ladder, said: "Love of money begins when you think you can do good with it and ends in hatred of the poor." I urge people to observe the rich and see how they behave: they are usually quite mean with their money. Wealth makes them hard-hearted, not generous. At the same time, we do not need to accumulate a lot of money in order to be charitable, because *the Kingdom of God can be bought with even two mites*. Each act of compassion we perform helps to pay the debts of our sins. I have known monks who refused large donations to their monasteries, usually with some strings attached. One monk replied to a financial offer by saying, "I do not want too many of these thorns, they sting horribly."

All banks promise us great rewards, if we place our money in shares and bonds. But we should remember that however much we try to have control over our investments, we cannot take any of them with us at the end of our life.

No, that is not quite true. Every pound, dollar, euro, every franc we have given to the poor becomes an investment in our own eternal life. This is the best income anyone can attain. And whoever understands this secret during his lifetime will gain a great deal. He has realized that one sort of money, at least, can be taken to eternity.

The next lesson I had to learn was about Easter. On Great and Holy Friday (Good Friday), Jesus gave His life on the Cross, for my sins, so that I could be free. Free from what? Free from my sinful past, from passions, unhealthy dependencies; from the three enemies of all human beings: the demons, our fallen nature, and our bad habits – in a word, from iniquity and its consequences. This has nothing to do with lists of moral rules. Sin simply means self-destruction, betraying the Love of God. In order to renew our faith, we have to fight against particular forms of self-destruction and betrayal, to which we are prone. One of my greatest passions is food. Without doubt my appetite was often my real lord and master, and I'm afraid it came even before Jesus. I only had to see good food and immediately my mouth watered. I had the excuse that in my childhood I nearly died of starvation several times, but that was no longer an acceptable justification. Jesus did not want me to remain in the *past*; he wanted to introduce me to the reality of the *present* (1 Cor. 9:27). I had to change my habits regarding food, before they changed me. If gluttony and overeating were included in the "Ten Commandments", the population of the Western world (especially the United States) might not be so excessively fat in body…and mind! Overweight persons will pay any price to lose weight, but often they will not do the most obvious thing, which is to restrain their appetite. Changing an "old habit" – that of gorging on food – goes beyond what they are willing to pay.

Although I did not at that time belong to a church which requires its members to fast as a spiritual discipline, the idea of fasting was on my mind when this story begins. It was the day before Good Friday. On that very evening, I was invited to dinner by an old girlfriend, who served me an excellent meal. Afterwards I felt that I had almost overeaten, as though I needed to stock up for some reason. Whatever impelled me to do this must have been deeply rooted in my subconscious. In my conscious mind, I had never even considered fasting, perhaps because I was still under the influence of childhood memories of food being short. But on Great and Holy Friday I decided, spontaneously and in His honour, to keep the fridge door closed, and to do without breakfast at least. The idea penetrated deeply into my mind, and then I decided to fast all that day. I wanted to be sure that I was not doing so for selfish reasons, in other words, for the sake of weight loss or a better appearance. For the first time in my life, as I resolved, I would not eat anything for twenty-four hours. This was unknown territory and one that provoked fear. Then a dilemma arose. I was invited to an Easter camp, lasting from Friday to Sunday, by a youth group in the town of Biel, which was half an hour's drive from my home. My hosts did not usually practise fasting. I hoped that I would be able to resist temptation.

On arrival at the camp's Bible group, I had a headache, was very tired, and experienced moments of fear. The hungrier I grew, the more intense my prayer became. I knew that I would not be dining, so I retreated discreetly while the group was enjoying a meal. Then a surprise. At the meeting that followed, I heard that on Great and Holy Saturday, the next day, a fast for the whole group was planned, beginning officially after breakfast. I had a slight shock, and then consoled myself by thinking that this did not apply to me: I would have successfully passed through my period of fasting by then. Nevertheless, after a good healthy breakfast . . . maybe I'll make it? All night long I feared Great and Holy Saturday, and felt the incredible force of hunger. I was being bombarded by thoughts that I would never succeed, and that soon I would pass out from starvation. I stayed strong and prayed a lot. "Oh Lord, may Your will be done, and please tell me if I should add another day to this one." It was breakfast time and there was no reply. So I sat myself at the dining table, quietly and hungry as a wolf. Mmm! The smell of cocoa penetrated my nostrils. I put butter on my bread and placed it on a plate. After thirty-six hours without food, I was going to enjoy this light meal.

Just then, Denise, one of the organizers, asked us to have another choir rehearsal before eating. We were to sing at a service that was starting in an hour's time. Oh well. I got up, not too willingly, and rehearsed. When at last I finished, I was first back at the table, so that I could finally "devour" my sandwich. At that moment, I was asked by Wally, a participant who was paralysed, to go to his bedside and discuss something. Because I was very fond of him, it came naturally to leave my place once again. Wally asked me to sing the song of my conversion, *"I tried it"*, to the whole community. This request took me aback somewhat, but I accepted out of love for him. Now I wanted nothing other than to return to the table, where everyone else was already eating. But what a shock! Someone was sitting in *my place*, in front of *my plate,* eating *my sandwich*. What a cheek! Who had dared? Whoever it was could not have seen that the place was already taken. All at once I saw that the person holding my buttered bread and touching it all over with his fingers, was a friend called Rudy, who was blind. He had come in later than the others, as he walked more slowly than everyone else. Now I began to understand. Then Lisi, who was on food duty that day, confirmed that she actually had miscounted the place settings. We were twenty-five people in camp and by mistake she had only set the table for twenty-four. This was why Rudy was placed there. She did not think she had done anything wrong.

In my mind there was something else going on. "Thank You, Jesus, for the sign You gave me." Everything was clear now. "I will only succeed with Your help, Jesus." All the same, I swallowed hard three times. Physical weakness and the fear that had suddenly come over me, with thoughts of dying of hunger, mingled with nervousness over having to sing in church in just a few minutes. As a result, my vocal chords were completely blocked. The devil attacked me, saying that I was too weak to sing, that I would never survive, and that I must eat as no one would know what I had done – I could at least drink a mug of that delicious cocoa, and so on. The more he attacked me, the more I hung on to the Holy Spirit. The more my stomach gurgled, the deeper my prayer to Jesus became. I had faith in Him. He had given me wisdom, and He would give the necessary strength to accomplish the mission.

What a temptation after breakfast! Everyone had left the room and pots of cocoa with bread, still on the tables, were staring up at me, and there was no one to see me indulge … I still waited to receive some sign "from above". Was I allowed to eat? But it did not come. Fear, anxiety and hunger kept me rooted to the spot. I took up my guitar to practise. Two things loomed ahead of me. We were supposed to sing in a big church within the next half hour. Because of my promise to Wally, I felt I must participate, and that "my song" – performed solo – must be part of the repertoire. I was feeling discouraged by the weakness in my muscles and felt too frail to play any chords, when Lisi appeared with a thick slice of bread and jam, excusing herself for having "stolen" my seat earlier. With my mouth watering strongly, I thanked her from my heart and said laughing:

"Maybe later." My smile must have been as "friendly" as one of those grotesque guard dogs at a Chinese temple. She left. My hope now lay in the permitted ration of fruit juice at lunchtime. Oh well, I did not think God would be against this, especially given that I had not drunk anything at all since the day before. What would we do without hope? Anyway, first we were to go to Bible study and thereafter to the church service where we would perform.

I was acutely uneasy, my stomach felt like lead, and I had stage fright. I left the assembly room for a while in order to practise the guitar. Phew! My muscles were aching so. The enemy had another go: "Klaus, you are too weak! Give up! You will never succeed!" But I returned and during the service I tried to master these attacks from the adversary. But Satan cornered me persisting, "Klaus, you are too unclean, give it up, you can't do this, you're too timid! The people here are not good for you, they are too old for your kind of music. They will not accept your music in their community. You are too weak to sing in front of them. You are much too unworthy. This is a sect and they want to monopolize you. ..." This hellish attack was let loose for forty-five minutes until, feeling small and frail, I knelt down in a corner and shouted within me: "Jesus, save me!" I hoped that the pastor would forget about me, or that something else would happen to get me off the hook. But Jesus, I knew well, would not leave me, even if I could not see or feel Him. I said to Him, "Yes, I know I am not worthy and can do nothing myself, but I want to sing in Your honour, and I am ready if necessary to faint from physical weakness in front of the whole community, yes, even to die for You, Jesus – at least I will have tried." At that moment, the victory was mine.

Like lightning, I felt at ease and the feeling of hunger was quashed. To begin with I couldn't believe it, and I started closely observing my body, to see if this suffering and torture would return. Nothing like that happened; everything was peaceful. The "blind Ruedi episode" now became a confirmation that I was in God's hands, and it even encouraged me. A few seconds later, my name was announced. Hallelujah! How easily everything went. I knew I could talk and sing about the love of God.

The day was not yet over and the battles not yet won. In fact, in the afternoon I was asked to leave Biel and drive 40 kilometres to Berne to pick up someone there. On the way, Satan tried again: "Klaus, you are too weak to concentrate on driving." Right! Passing by advertisements for food, groceries, pastry shops, supermarkets, bakeries enticing me to enter, was indeed not the easiest thing. "Go and buy something – just to make sure you don't die! Now, while nobody can see you. You're not in camp now, so you are not tied to the rules! Special missions give you the right to special exceptions! Klaus, there is nothing nice to eat tomorrow and moreover you did not even drink your "promised" juice earlier on. Instead they sent you to Berne to bring Fritz to the camp. They are only exploiting you. Come on! Stop the car, you have the right as long as the others are drinking juices!" I understand now why Satan is called the *beast*.

But I was under the protection of the One Who is greater than Satan. In the name of the Almighty, I rejected all temptations, to the extent that I was able to enter a supermarket and buy some things for Fritz. I prepared some tea for him later on, and besides that I entertained the whole group with my guitar, because hunger was no longer an impediment. Evidently, the suffering and chastening endured had been overcome; and now I was happily comparing my adventures with the travels of Odysseus – the supermarkets had become my Sirens. Obedience had given me the necessary strength. After fifty hours, my body felt calm – what a joyful heart I had! But God's most precious gift was still to come. Meanwhile, I neither ate nor drank a thing.

Because I had involved myself in this battle, I was hoping that God would bring me a big surprise for Easter, maybe a delicious breakfast on Easter Sunday, or something similar. Once again, I was salivating. Jesus would be risen from the dead, and Klaus would surely get a decent meal. Eventually, Easter morning came. Breakfast was served, but . . . what frustration! I had no appetite. The food was nothing special and I did not feel any particular joy or strong emotion. I went on eating, even when I wasn't hungry anymore, still hoping for something special. It had to be! But nothing happened! Absolutely distraught, I finished my meal. Such a shame, I thought.

After this frustrating breakfast our group left for the nearby village of Twann to participate in a service with Pastor David McKee, who was a friend of mine, and his community. I was a little anxious, because I had spontaneously proposed to him that our group should sing the "Hallelujah Chorus", which we had rehearsed earlier. David wanted the Holy Spirit to give him an answer to my suggestion. During his sermon from the pulpit, he told the congregation that he would indeed like us, the visitors, to sing the "Hallelujah Chorus". I had a feeling of refreshment and felt happy; but this was not "it", the moment I had been waiting for, yet. Just as we were about to take Communion, "the longed for" thing happened. In my mind, I went back to my conversion in Lausanne and asked – as I have always done since – whether I was still "invited" as the Lord's guest. In that moment came the good news. Suddenly, Jesus was present once again and said:

"I know you. I love you. Now you will receive the *true food* which I have prepared for you."

Only then did I understand that my expectations had been physical, instead of spiritual. I had placed all my hope in transitory things, whereas Jesus was offering me the food of eternity. I was overcome by weeping and powerfully moved by the joy and love with which Jesus always led me, allowing me to see His love more and more clearly. The tears poured down, just as they did that time in the cathedral in Lausanne. I stood up before everyone and went forward to receive the Body and Blood of the Lord Jesus Christ. I could hardly breathe from happiness! I do not think I have ever tasted such special food as that Easter communion. I had never felt so well fed, joyful, and at peace. To this was added, in great abundance, the overflowing presence of the Holy Spirit. Oh Jesus, You *are* wonderful! Whereas I am just a blind, scheming man with very little faith, who does not deserve Your presence. Forgive me, but I love You despite myself and all the miserable rubbish that is within me.

But Satan was not to be beaten. He tried *immediately* to crush the grace received. This is a familiar pattern, as I can see clearly now, looking back after many years. We may be warned: if Christ pours out His Grace on you, Satan is *always* waiting around the corner to take it away. It seems that this is the way we grow spiritually.

So, back in the camp, I found myself amidst much noise, glib discussions, stupid laughter, gossip. I heard prayers that seemed prearranged, learnt as if they had no meaning, cold and not at all as if they were the work of the Holy Spirit. All this in an atmosphere that was neither spiritual nor Paschal – whereas I was still under the influence of grace and had become used to living at a deeper level with "something" better. In fact, I felt "better" than the others, and this gave Satan his cue.

"Klaus, you really should not be here among these people, who are lacking in maturity and just ramble on." The voice became more resolute:

"Come on, *leave* this place! You have got something better to do at home, don't waste your time here with these immature people."

I believed this voice and felt suddenly, totally destroyed. I could not be sure of myself any more. I was suffering and was convinced that this group had contributed to my suffering. I no longer understood anything, so I began to pack my bag. Contrary to the peace I had been given in the morning I was now very upset! I felt alone, lost . . . I went round the house trying to find a quiet place to pray, in the cellar, in the attic . . . When the group gathered to pray, I was on the point of leaving. I did not want to hear again a string of words "imitating prayer". I felt terribly alone and lonely.

Finally, down in the kitchen, I found some friends who were on duty: Kongo, Patrizia, Franzi . . . and among them the atmosphere was peaceful. I complained about my suffering and "Kongo" (now Pastor Markus Flueckiger) responded as best he could and suggested:

"Hey, let us go and pray!"

I lost no time. Silently, I prayed to Jesus: "Please enlighten me. What has happened?"

And He showed me. Without a doubt, what I now saw shocked me deeply – *pride*! Jesus showed me my conceit. I was "too good" for other people. I was "something special". If I was bothered by the fact that they were not as I wanted them to be, was I really a Christian, a good servant of God? Did I really want to serve my neighbour, or did I condemn him instead? Had such an attitude not lead to separations and schisms within the Church throughout her history? My heart was very much frightened at such an ugly discovery in myself. I was shocked! May the Lord forgive this moment of shame . . . and improve my perception of the enemy's snares.

Christ did forgive me and moreover He gave me many genuine brothers and sisters to accompany me on my way. Hallelujah!

"What kind of a prostitute have you brought in here?" The pastor spoke in an excessively loud voice which rang out across the entire hall, so that Eliane, the person I had been looking after for a year with prayer and discussion, could not have helped hearing. It was not a very sensitive thing to use such words, and I would have expected better from him. The girl, whom I had brought to this pastor to find salvation and give her life to Jesus, trembled with shock. Even before getting to know the Church of Jesus Christ, she was being accused and cast out. But I too felt deep disappointment. It is true that "hot pants" might not be the most suitable attire for a religious centre, but this she would have come to understand later on. The pastor's accusation confirmed the revulsion she felt towards clergy of all sorts. It took another long year for Eliane, who had – together with her four sisters – endured sexual abuse from her father for many years, to have any kind of trust in the "religious types". I explained to her that all human beings – be they pastors or lay people, and certainly including myself – were weak and liable to sin at any time. But that incident with the sharp-tongued preacher was still a terrible setback. The little faith and confidence I had been instilling in her, step by step and with much effort, was now demolished in a single blow by this "servant of God". Even my own feelings about clerics were somewhat changed. *"Not every one that saith unto me, Lord, Lord, shall enter into the kingdom of heaven"* (Matt. 7:21). It was clear that we do not gain the Kingdom of Heaven just by saying beautiful words with our mouths, but through the heart. Our words and actions are directed from the heart. Everything depends on the heart, because that is where Jesus lives if we grant Him entrance, and a healthy heart cannot be false, hypocritical or judgmental.

People who turn to God with less than a full heart often find themselves asking: "Why does nothing happen for me when I pray?" The answer is that most people have only learnt to pray with their lips, and in their heart there is no fear of God. They have no sense of His holiness. They do not pray from the heart, and when they pray, their mind wanders. Clerics who fail in this respect can be likened to the Pharisees, who were "exceptionally good" in public and prayed ostentatiously, but once they were at home within their own four walls, their masks came down and they sinned; even worse, in their hearts they accused the "weak". In such conditions, of course, nothing much will happen when God is called upon. But the Pharisee hardly cares. It is much easier to hide behind the law and point a finger at those who do not obey it, than to look honestly and humbly into the mirror.

Soon after the unpleasant incident with Eliane, about five years after my conversion in Lausanne, I felt that trials were in store, and that the grace of God would take another form, perhaps a tougher one. "Blessed are those who do not see and yet believe." God's grace for the newly born is somehow "undeserved", almost "stolen" from God, or else it is a sort of "loan" from our Heavenly Father. But He does not allow us to keep it indefinitely. He wants His children to grow through patience and struggle against the "former man" and against his passions. He wants us to struggle out of love for Him. Consequently, God the Father lets go of his child's hand at a certain stage. I realized that it was time for Klaus to learn to walk by himself. As part of this learning process, I would have to follow the example of Jesus and serve others, instead of expecting people to admire my superior qualities. He had washed the feet of His disciples! I needed to learn this lesson, too. My old friend, Ursula, made this very clear one day, when I complained about a group of noisy, gossiping Christians, who had just enjoyed a hearty meal and left others to clear up. "Klaus", she said, "many people come here to engage in theological chitchat, which is not very useful spiritually. But you, on the other hand, in washing dishes are serving others, and this is a holy work." She convinced me and I continued with my work without grumbling. We will be judged according to how useful we have been in serving our neighbour with love, not by how much Holy Scripture we have learnt by heart.

Another difficulty which I learned to negotiate: During the period after my conversion, I lived on such a "high" that I could hardly believe there were Christians who had important responsibilities or were renowned theologians and . . . who had no faith.

But on a trip to Jerusalem I received the following "spiritual slap" from some of these so-called Christians. We were a group of pilgrims flying with El-Al towards Tel Aviv, on the way to a Pentecostal meeting.

"Watch out Claudine!" I shouted laughingly, as I pulled the ring on a soft drink can pointing at her. Claudine and Nathalie, who were sitting behind me, lowered their heads quickly to one side. I shook the can assiduously and the drink gushed out under the pressure, over Claudine's seat and – oh dear – it went straight onto the faces of two ladies who were sitting behind Nathalie. They were not part of the joke and they were not amused. Our burst of laughter quickly turned into embarrassment. It was clear that I had done something terrible, but the reaction from the two ladies still dumbfounded me.

"Christians don't do this kind of thing!" they shouted very indignantly. I thought I had misheard. What had this to do with being a Christian? Did Christians always have to put on a gloomy look and talk only of the sorrows and despair in the world? Were Christians not allowed to have fun and a good laugh?

Something worse happened the next day. I went through the old city of Jerusalem, on my way to a meeting place, with two "important" Christian ladies beside me. In the semi-darkness of a bazaar I saw a blind old man, just skin and bone, his body full of sores, sweating and unshaven, coming towards us with the help of a stick. In Jesus' time this would have been quite a familiar scene. Behind him was a donkey carrying on its back a bale of hay, almost a metre high.

Moved by the sight, my companions exclaimed:

"Look at him, poor thing!"

"Oh yes, how terrible! Awful! How can they let him, this poor…!" the other one joined in.

I wanted to confirm:

"Yes, it is terrible that in our days there are still such poor people as this poor creature."

"Who are you talking about?" the first lady asked.

I pointed to the blind man.

"We were talking of that poor donkey, who has to carry that big load."

I felt thunderstruck. Who was *more* blind, the two women or the blind man? Some people are much more loving towards *animals* than towards man!

One day I had a visit from Todd Burke, the author of the book *Anointed for Burial*. Todd was a person called by God, who had lived through an incredible experience working in Cambodia as a pioneer. At first we liked each other and felt that we had similar missions to fulfil. Todd asked me if I would become the pastor of a "branch" Church in Fribourg, affiliated to a large mother church in America. I was honoured and wanted to pray about this to find the answer. But how could I lead a community, when I myself was a newborn Christian, without much experience? Flattering as the offer was, it was clear that this could be a temptation which might result in a spiritual failure. The very fact that he made such an offer suggested that he was rather inexperienced. I sensed that I was being asked to engage in a kind of show business, with star performers and a clear commercial agenda. I felt very uneasy about it and I broke off the contact.

Further tests were in store. I soon found myself being vilified by people who maintained that I had made a girl pregnant and then forced her to have an abortion. I had the feeling that certain people wanted to skin me alive. Many untruths were spread about me and, what was worse, this was being done by Christians! At the Catholic university in Fribourg I was ridiculed in public, before the whole auditorium, when I confronted Raymond Abrezol, who was the main promoter and defender of a personal development method called "Sophrology". On one occasion, as he was praising the "liberating action" of "Sophrology", I stood up and insisted that the only real "liberating manifestation" is the presence of God in the heart of man. All I earned was scorn. How naïve I appeared to be in the eyes of several hundred students! But in the same Catholic university (one of the most prestigious Catholic institutions in the world) there were courses offered in the practice of yoga and Zen, based on the argument that this was a quicker way to becoming a better Christian. Scorn, calumny, ridicule, and misery were always my harvest, when I raised my voice against such untruths.

Equally painful was the experience I had to endure with the "Catholic Police", as I called them. I was forever in conflict with the guardians of Catholic purity when I participated in large Christian gatherings in places like Paray-le-Monial, Lisieux, and Ars. To those Christians, the essence of their belief seemed less important than the external framework. They were more concerned with keeping rules than with having a living faith. With many of them you could only communicate on a very superficial level. Trying to draw them into a deeper dialogue was like having a conversation with a machine.

The pettiness of the organizers of these events showed up in a number of small ways. At mealtimes, if I received a child's portion and asked for a little more dessert, I would be refused.

Once, inside a giant tent, I mistook the entrance for the exit. I took a step across the threshold of the entrance way, and I wouldn't have minded if I had then been asked to go back the other way. But instead, the security guard ordered me to continue and forced me to push my way through the crowd and leave by the entrance. I was deeply troubled by this kind of stupidity.

When I wanted to visit my really close and good friends, the gypsies, who had their own section at the gathering, I was prohibited from going anywhere near them, on the pretext that I was not a gypsy myself. This, curiously, was their absolute criterion, more important than anything else. A day earlier, one of the conference organizers had taken me to visit the gypsies, to talk to them about my experiences and give my testimony. With gypsy friends like Madoun, Nina and their sons and daughters, I had the closest relations – I was always received in their caravan as a son! Nearly all the gypsies knew me personally, because of my testimony or because we had played the guitar together in their trailers.

Another feature of these mainly Catholic gatherings that I did not like was the choir practices. The choirmaster made us go through endless rehearsals. But once the "real show" had begun, he would himself sing into the microphone so loudly that not a single voice of the choir could be heard. Moreover, when he began "his" singing he wouldn't give a sign or a note or even indicate which song it was. The orchestra was confused and remained silent. Even after the tenth time we singers had asked him to work *together* with the orchestra, this "important" leader remained deaf. It was grotesque to see how he exposed himself as a vain, self-important performer. If I needed to have a few minutes of quiet to be on my own, "Catholic spies" would suddenly appear who wanted to take me, almost by force, to one or other of the meetings. This method of dominating instead of serving, this heartless stupidity instead of love, were attitudes which drove me far away from these zealots, and I took refuge in the arms of God. I told Him about my disappointment as

I had done once before in Biel: "Lord, what does this mean? I know that sometimes Your Holy Spirit annihilates something in me for good reason. But I am not talking about my humility, is that not so? Jesus, these Catholics are destroying, crushing and trampling anything that is of Your Spirit. Should I remain here?"

But then I remembered. Had not Mother Theresa told me: "Don't strain . . . gain." These words helped me to endure the frustration I was experiencing. But I still complained to Jesus:

"Lord, why do You allow these monsters to devour people? Can You not see how they discredit and destroy us, not just me but You and everyone as well, in the name of Christianity?"

Because my heart was truly burning with pain, the answer came straightaway:

"Yes, I do see that."

"Therefore, the place for these people is in hell, because they crush all that is alive! We should get rid of them, because they induce so much suffering, and suffocate all love with their rules!"

"Klaus, would you like to see them in hell?"

"Yes."

"They have *not only* brought Me pain, they have even *killed* Me. And I love them still."

There was no need for any other words – Jesus had shut my mouth. I had goose pimples and tears were running down my cheeks, because I had seen my unreasonable reaction. Instead of forgiving and loving them, I wanted to destroy them. The content of the lesson I had just received was inexhaustible. I knew that a long, long way was still ahead of me.

Christ's message of forgiveness was a hard one for me to put into practice. For example, it meant forgiving the Catholic priest R., who had sexually abused and tormented me for all those years. This was not the easiest thing to do, but one day I found myself at his door with my hand outstretched as a sign of reconciliation. I cannot tell what effect this had on him. He took my hand and looked at me with indifference. But I, at least, felt free.

Equally hard, in some ways, was the question of reconciliation with my parents. Immediately after my conversion, I talked with my brother, Lothar, about Jesus and faith. In all our meetings, he always repeated the same sentence: "Mother's presence in my thoughts suffocates me!" And, indeed, he died from asphyxiation while diving in Greece. He had been a doctor at a university hospital. May the Lord have mercy upon his soul. Was it the power of my mother? Could she have wanted this? Certainly not consciously. His death was a warning for me.

I was sick and tired of the fact that my mother was perpetually under the influence of the occult, so much so that I used any occasion to visit her in Germany. She had aged, and I not only wanted to forgive her, but to help her open the gates of paradise. One day I rang the doorbell.

"Who is there?" a suspicious voice called from within.

"Your son, Klaus."

Once inside with her, I didn't lose any time but spoke rather quickly about the burden I carried in my soul.

"Mother, you are not getting any younger and one day you will find yourself in the presence of Christ and will need to account for your life. How does this thought strike you?"

"Oh, leave me in peace about such things. I am not afraid. I have been shut out of the parish for a long time, but I am still a Catholic and I believe in the Pope."

"But the Pope can't save you when you reach the next world."

"You're going on about these things again! Leave me to my faith. Do you think your faith is any better?"

I knew her (and Satan's) tactics well enough from long ago. I knew it was a mistake to be drawn in by an "adversary" to a theoretical discussion. And so I simply said:

"Come on, let's pray."

"You may do that. I don't know what to say."

I called on the name of Jesus and asked Him to open her heart so that He could free her. This I did for a period of three years, praying for her and also together with her, for the salvation of her soul. When we met, she would often rain horrible verbal attacks on me, swearing and blaspheming. She assaulted me on every level. In a matter of seconds, she would change the expression on her face in such a way that many people would have found frightening. When she didn't know what else to do, she screamed:

"Go away from here, leave me alone! Leave me at last in peace!"

She behaved as if she was being tortured by evil spirits, and it reminded me of how once, in the name of Jesus, I had been called to free a man possessed by such spirits. He was foaming at the mouth and groaning, crouched in a corner. I did not speak to him directly, but addressed myself to the spirits who were holding on to him – and Jesus came to my assistance. That experience helped me to deal with my mother. I noticed that when she "hit out" with ever more insulting words, she lost her balance and fell forwards: directly and literally into my arms, close to my *heart*. Little by little she began to feel something beating inside me. I let her find the love of Jesus through my heart.

Many years later I succeeded in persuading her to undergo exorcism, which was duly performed by Maurice Ray. I invited her to stay with me in Fribourg and rang Maurice to set up a meeting. He said he would be happy to meet my mother and we could talk in German. On the appointed day, my mother and I left for Lausanne by car. She sat silently beside me. To my mind she was somewhat too quiet. I felt a rather heavy silence. She seemed to be concentrating on something, with a hardened look on her face. Suddenly a bang was heard, the engine began to make alarming noises and was losing power. We were in the middle of the motorway, having just left the town of Bulle, some 35 kilometres from Lausanne. My mother sat beside me looking very stern, almost like a stone statue. Not a word came from her. If Jesus had not been close to me, I would have begun to panic at the sight of her face. With a struggle the car arrived at an exit from the motorway, but the engine was badly damaged. I rang Maurice from a nearby farm to cancel our meeting. From the look on my mother's face, I knew exactly what – or rather who – I was dealing with. Travelling slowly, with the car lurching to and fro on the country roads, we returned to Fribourg. I rented a car from the garage and we made another appointment with Maurice for the next day.

There was no need to talk to my mother about the forces that were acting within her. Even today, I cannot tell if she was aware of those forces or if she remembered her physical transformation when afterwards she returned to normality. It was not long before a fresh attack came. It was after 10 p.m. Just at the moment I wanted to go to bed, the phone rang. Strange!

"Klaus K., can you please come *urgently* to see me?"

"Who are you?"

I had no idea whatever who was speaking to me. He explained. He was a Colombian, called Hernan, the ex-husband of my friend Renaude, with whom we had prayed together for his salvation. Renaude had told me often about Hernan's involvement with transcendental meditation and the negative consequences, which finally included divorce. I had never met Hernan, who was a psychologist, and I felt it was rude of him to ring at such a late hour. On the other hand, this could be the long awaited opportunity to have a talk with him.

I asked him then:

"What do you mean? Is it really urgent?"

"I can't answer that on the telephone. But it is very important. Please come quickly."

It sounded as if a fire had broken out. On being given directions, I started on my way. I had great hopes. Perhaps he needed urgent spiritual support. It was mysterious. Imagine my surprise when being told, on arrival at his home which was in the centre of Fribourg, in a very simple and ordinary way:

"I have some technical texts here which I have to translate from Spanish into German. Please help me! It has to be ready in six weeks."

The texts were all about tractors and agricultural machinery and the matter was neither urgent nor important. I was upset and angry that it had not been something spiritual and, thinking of his misleading tactics, I now understood what Renaude had mentioned about his habit of using people in a cynical way. Nevertheless, I did not want to lose this opportunity of helping with the translation of the texts, hoping that "serving my brother" was a proof of love in Christ, and that maybe a door would open later on. I stayed with him and worked on his texts as late as after midnight until, totally fatigued, I finally returned home. Strange, strange indeed seemed all that had happened that day. As I was driving home from Hernan, a loud bang came from underneath the car. An incredible force was pushing the car, which I had hired the day before, to the ground. With a shattering noise the suspensions supporting the wheels broke loose. All four at the same time! The bottom of the car fell down onto the pavement, leaving behind it a trail of sparks and at the same time making the most horrendous noise. Now a second car was finished! It could not be real! Beyond any doubt, this was my mother's doing. When, at last, I reached home, utterly exhausted, the door was locked. I knocked.

"Who is there?" As if she did not know.

"What has happened? Why do you lock the door again?"

Although my mother spoke, it was not her voice. The voice I heard had a higher pitch than usual.

"I have been told that I am not allowed to let anyone enter."

"Who told you that?" I insisted, wanting to find out.

"I am not allowed to tell you", some whispering was then heard.

Then my mother disappeared and left me standing in front of the locked door. I banged it with my fists. Nothing. I felt surrounded by ghostly forces and was obliged to climb onto the roof, where I could let myself in to my apartment through an open window in the kitchen. Just unbelievable! When I tried to speak to her she behaved naïvely, as if she knew nothing of what had just happened. She relinquished every responsibility.

"Why didn't you open the door?"

"I was not allowed to."

"Who didn't permit you?"

"I've told you already, I am not to say who."

"Was someone here while I was away?"

"Yes. But I must not speak about that." Finished as always.

The next day, I bought two tickets for Lausanne and was justifiably afraid that the train would be derailed. I sensed an urgent need for my mother to be exorcised. We arrived by train at last, and were in the safe hands of Maurice who prayed, talked and explained at length what was to follow. Without any kind of participation, my mother accepted the whole ritual with a totally blank expression on her face. Maurice bound up, in the name of Jesus, the powers of darkness and destructive forces from her soul, while she remained unmoved. After an hour, it was all over, and after having lunch together we left in a good mood and took the train back to Fribourg. Suddenly a strange suffocating presence was there again. It became chilly and I could see my mother's face changing into an evil venomous mask – horrible!

"Ha, ha, ha", she sniggered. "Did you think you would triumph over me?"

It was truly frightening, what I was seeing. Cold shivers went through me. The person saying these words was not my mother. She had been a famous actress and, because of her experience and through the power of the spirits, she was still doing "very well" at acting. Both Maurice and I had fallen into her net. I thought I would go mad! Could she not be helped in the Name of Jesus?

"What is happening to you? Do you not want to be free, ever? Can you not see what it is we are talking about?"

"Indeed I do, very well." The tension lessened. "But Mr. Ray is a Protestant: Catholicism is the only true religion. Your Mr. Ray can't do anything to me, because he has no faith."

It was exasperating to see the destructive influence that obsessive "Vaticanism" could have on people.

"Would you accept exorcism from a Catholic priest", I went on asking. She agreed. Who could tell what other games she was going to play with me now? Nevertheless, a year after that moment, after a lot of pleading and prayer by me and my friends, she did say she was ready to try again. Maurice had obtained the address of a Catholic colleague in Feldkirch, Austria. So I drove to Germany to pick up my mother. No effort was too great in order to save her soul. During the journey we talked a lot and I felt in good form. Maybe a little too much, because I was feeling so well disposed that I nearly forgot Satan, while my mother was again playing a game with me. Incredible as it may seem, five kilometres before Feldkirch, once again, in the middle of the motorway, I heard a worrying noise and a rattling from one of the front wheels, which soon brought the car to a complete halt. I froze! I think I would have gone mad had not Jesus been with me. I got out of the car and began to repair the steering system, break discs and pipes – all this on the side of the motorway, and therefore risky – until at last we were able to continue on to our destination. We finally arrived and the Catholic priest opened the door. He stared at us in disbelief at first, but after a while he seemed convinced by our sincerity, and as soon as I conveyed Maurice's greetings to him he completely relaxed.

He brought out a series of objects: icons, holy water, incense, a stole, vestments, and then began to explain to my mother about Catholic exorcism. I watched her with great attention this time. She seemed less tense, more open and attentive – I could see this. She appeared to trust this priest and gave herself over to his will. She even repeated the prayers of "casting out", as he had asked her to do. Everything happened without any opposition from her side. Finally, a very great burden was lifted from my heart, and an incredibly long saga took another turn. It is true to say that when a tree has grown in a certain direction for more than seventy years, it could not simply just be straightened, because it would break. That is how it was with my mother. Her old behaviour kept returning, but had it not been so with me? At the same time, I saw more and more how she was changing inwardly. We could now pray together, leaving the rest in the hands of God.

Even so, our relationship during the rest of her days did not become very close. Perhaps it was not pure chance that I happened to be very far away from her – in fact the furthest possible place on this planet, in the Outback of Australia – when I heard of her death. This once so famous and applauded cinema and opera star, who earned over 1,500 Reichsmark (about $2,500) per night, had finished her life alone, died alone, and was buried alone. Except for me, there had been no one to accompany her on her last journey. Not even my older brother. What a life of suffering! My love is with her soul. May God have mercy on her.

All his life, my father would have nothing to do with the Church. Now I visited him in Stuttgart and spoke at length with him about Jesus and His grace. He told me curtly and concisely that it was enough for him to have been baptised Catholic and that he had no need of the Church. Nothing but nothing would remove his belief that after death everything was finished. I prayed ardently for him to recognize his sins before dying. How great was my joy when, on an Easter Sunday, he exchanged his attitude of "not caring" with one of happiness that his sins had been forgiven. This is how it happened. With all the depth of love and persuasion I could muster, I asked him to join me at the Easter service in the Catholic Church. He strongly opposed the idea and stayed home, and finally I went alone. When I returned home, some time around midday, the television was on, and my father stepped into the room exactly at the moment when the Pope was giving the Holy Easter blessing, *Urbi et Orbi,* from the Vatican. My father went on to say that this was just as valid on television as in Rome, and this was confirmed by the television commentator. Whatever that meant, my father had accepted the Pope's declaration of forgiveness of sin. Only God can tell the real value of that. From my heart came a "Hallelujah" full of thanks. But my father insisted, "You see! I don't need the Church! This does just as well."

In the years preceding his death, I found it impossible to establish a true friendship with him. He was much too imprisoned within himself and within his egocentricity. I forgave him and loved him, but this poor person could never really love. After a while, he died. I felt real pity for him. May his soul be in eternal rest!

CHAPTER FOURTEEN

THE HILL OF DIFFICULTY

My life in the "wilderness" – the period of trial and difficulty as a new Christian – reached a culminating point on another Pentecost vacation. Together with two believing sisters, Mady and Priska, we travelled, in Mady's big Peugeot, the one thousand kilometres to Lisieux and Bayeux in Normandy (France). Our destination was the "Pentecôte des Pauvres", that is, we wanted to spend Pentecost among the poor and homeless from all over France. Five thousand people came: vagabonds, drug addicts, and those who live on the fringe of society; all of them to receive a ray of hope from Jesus Christ, or a piece of cake and a bowl of soup. It was arranged that I would speak to them, and when I arrived I was told I would be informed in good time before my turn. Passing through the campus, I met Daniel Ange (author of many books), whose personality had already impressed me in Strasbourg, where I had heard him speak.

"Hello Daniel!" I greeted him on approach. "I am happy to meet you again. I think I have a lot to learn from you. For example, humility ..."

"No Klaus. If anyone is to learn, it is me, from you!"

His humility was disarming. We talked for a while longer and then the time came for us to put up the tents. The sky was blue and the sun blazed down. I was happy to be there and happy that I had the chance to speak to the "poor". Nevertheless, this feeling quickly changed. God is not a God of theory – at least, not for me. All my life, everything has been centred on living, on life and experience, never on theoretical knowledge. God was careful this time also to see that this "Pentecost for the poor" would not become an event in my honour. Just as we finished putting up the tents, Mady heard the devastating news that her father had died. In her state, she would not have been able to drive alone those one thousand kilometres back to Switzerland, so Priska took on the job. After they had left, I felt alone, very much alone. Black clouds were gathering in the sky and torrential rain began to fall. It did not take long for the whole field to become a swamp. Soon I was completely isolated from the others and those few words exchanged with Daniel Ange were all that was said until I left!

Daniel Ange – famous Catholic youth leader

My return would be a problem, too, as I had come with Mady in her car. Now I waited anxiously to be called on to the stage and hoped that in that way I would make some acquaintances. I was covered in mud, frozen in my wet clothes, trudging hither and thither and trying to make contact with other Christians, only to find they moved away as if I had the plague. I took no part in any of the talks over the next four days, no, not one. Bitterness engulfed me. I felt ignored and alone. To add to my misery, the organizers themselves seemed to have totally forgotten I existed. No one came to call me or asked about me, much less ask me to be an applauded speaker! I would have loved to free myself from this isolation. But when God is holding you in a certain place, you cannot come out by your own strength. I was too late even for the meal that day, so I remained hungry. In my wet tent there was a little milk in a pack, and whilst drinking it I felt something solid on my tongue. Being hungry, I bit into this something. It felt quite hard and had a dubious taste in my mouth ... I had just chewed three large sticky snails, which had drowned in the milk and swelled up. Ugh! I spat everything out. However, as I later realized, this perfectly suited the picture of "Pentecost for the poor", which I had come to discover. Now I had found out what it really meant to be alone, poor and rejected ... just like Jesus Christ had been.

When I understood the importance of this Pentecost lesson for me, I praised Him with all my heart. God did not want to turn me into an applauded theologian. No. He was leading me by the hand through life, through the wilderness, and at times towards suffering. He was always on the side of those who are rejected and alone. He did not ask the reasons for the situation they found themselves in, but simply loved them. Only at the last minute, not long before leaving, did the Lord show me the meaning of His lesson and free me from the isolation to which I seemed to have been condemned. Only then could I raise my arms, along with another five thousand tramps and poor souls, and bid my farewell with an exploding "Hallelujah" coming from the bottom of my heart. Ten thousand arms waved in the air like a wheatfield in the summer wind, praising God. There were waves of love: hippies, nuns, punks, monks, academicians, high born society ladies, handicapped, disabled, some hideously deformed, the sick ... in a word, Your people, Jesus! And at that moment I was part of them and the happiest of all.

Whenever things began to weigh me down and I felt somewhat "lost", He gave me signs that He was there. I would like to call them small miracles, because they were so inexplicable that my mind could not grasp them. For example, my incredible meeting with Graeme.

Graeme came from New Zealand and had joined the monastery at Wat Bung Wai in Thailand shortly after me. From the very beginning he had had trouble with the other monks, and in time I became his guru and the man he could trust. Whenever he had questions or was in sorrow, he came to speak to me. We had been like brothers in the Buddhist monastery, seeking God and a meaning to life. One day he came all the way from New Zealand to visit me in Switzerland. After that visit I didn't have any news from him for a long time – he had obviously lost my address. In the wake of that robbery in Colombia, my address book had disappeared as well, and so I also could not keep in touch with him.

Sixteen years later, I was on a world tour and had just arrived in the Fiji Islands. The next morning I was to leave Waya island for a neighbouring one by boat. But black clouds and rain obliged everyone to remain on the main island, because no boat would raise anchor in that kind of weather. But I had better leave the original diary entry of August 1996 to speak for itself:

Friday, 2. 08. 96 – Lantoka – Waya island, Fiji

"The rain has stopped and we are happy to be able to fulfil our desire to watch the sun set on the sea and walk the length of the beach. Apart from a young bearded man, who appeared to be meditating under a thatched umbrella, my companion and I are totally alone. There is really nothing to do here. We went to the beach hotel and drank a small "Fiji bitter" at the ocean side. Other than the bearded man, there was not a shadow of another human being as far as the eye could see. It was then that the idea of renting a room in this hotel came to us, as it was more conveniently placed than the first one, where we were around two hundred metres from the beach. If the price was acceptable, we could stay a few days more. After finishing the beer, I asked the proprietor the price of a room and if he could show us one. The rooms were bigger, had a kitchen, dishes, bathroom and were all-in-all far superior to the rooms in our hotel. In addition, they were even cheaper!

"When we descended the stairs with the hotelier, one of the guests who lived in that very room we had just 'examined', ran after the proprietor – it was the bearded man again – to complain that the ceiling fan was out of order. In fact, as this was none of my business, I did not listen, but when the boss said, 'All right I will see to it', and the bearded man said thank you, I whirled around…I was one hundred per cent sure and shouted into the semi-darkness, 'Graeme!'

"A split second later we were embracing each other – I lifted him up, spinning him in the air. We were overjoyed at meeting again after sixteen years . . . How often had I thought about him! Each time I met a New Zealander on my travels, which was quite often, and even in Australia two years previously, I remembered Graeme and longed to see him again and find out his news.

"It was incredible that we should meet at that moment, at the other end of the world, in the dark, and just before his return to New Zealand. No one can say that this was just a coincidence. We sat together on the beach, under a thatched umbrella, and relived the last sixteen years. I was eager to hear his news. What Graeme told me about searching for the light made me immediately understand why we had been brought together. He had given himself the name *"Shining"* and searched relentlessly for the "light" since leaving the monastery. He did not seem happy and quite openly admitted he was less and less capable of living or even working. He had bought thirty-five hectares of land in New Zealand, but could not cultivate it. He told me that he could not work longer than about an hour a day on his kiwi plantation. He felt paralysed.

"The last three weeks he had spent on a nearby island here in Fiji, at the house of an old committed Christian who, to his annoyance, kept telling him about Jesus and became very insistent two days before his departure. When I spoke to him *again* about Jesus, and about how many things He had changed in my life from the moment I left the monastery, Graeme laughed loudly . . . He was profoundly touched.

"We ended our conversation after about three hours, because Graeme had to get up very early, and I helped him with some money (he was penniless) for the return journey. Then I understood why we had had such bad weather, because if it hadn't been so, we would have left for Waya Island before meeting Graeme. Man proposes and God disposes. Farewell!"

I could relate a whole series of such meetings in Bulgaria, Greece, the Canary Islands, in Rome...but I will close this chapter with just one more. Here again it was a matter of one second. When God unfolds His plan it is with great precision.

A young Swiss Christian called Beat Liesch from Zizers, near Chur in Switzerland, had enjoyed seeing a television broadcast about me. By letter, he proposed organizing a conference in the Graubünden canton. As I happened to be in that area every now and then, I suggested to Beat I come and see him the next time I found myself near his house and then we could discuss his idea. Only nine months later, I was on business in eastern Switzerland, and my wife Nikica and I realized that we had plenty of spare time. In the morning we went for a little sightseeing tour of the city of Chur. As we left the motorway at the exit, which apparently led to Chur, I was surprised to find that I still had thirteen kilometres to go. What had the road builders been thinking of?

"Oh no", said Nikica, who was sitting beside me. "You have left the motorway at the wrong exit – this one leads to Davos." That had never happened to me before.

We passed through several villages and suddenly I remembered. In this neighbourhood, there should be a village which was the home of somebody who once invited me to a conference. But I only vaguely remembered. What a pity I did not have the address with me. I had promised that person that I would let them know when I was in the area, in order to prepare things. How stupid of me not to have remembered the name of that person nor his address. Just now I would have had time for such a meeting.

A few kilometres on, I spotted a board with the name of the village, which was "Zizers". It sounded somewhat funny and I said:

"I think this could be it. I am truly sorry that I have forgotten the address and name of the person. But I remember the place-name sounded something similar to this village."

I went on thinking, but could not find any clue. On entering the place I read on a board, "The Foundation *God helps*" (*Gott Hilft*). What if that was it? No, this sort of name certainly did not figure on the letterhead I got nine months ago. Never mind. Speedily, I drove passed it. Then suddenly, in my heart, I felt an order: "Turn around!" I had already gone a couple of hundred metres. At the first opportunity to turn the car around, we went back to where the notice board was. The establishment "God Helps" was made up of several buildings, some of which were offices and others, homes. I leaned out of the car and studied a plan of the area. The whole terrain with so many different structures was bigger than I imagined my young correspondent's organization to be. While I was perusing the board, I realized I was blocking the exit for a car that was just about to leave the car park. The driver seemed to realize that I was hesitating and searching for something, and he got out.

"Are you looking for something?"

"In fact, yes."

I wasn't sure how to explain it to him. I just continued awkwardly:

"In fact, I am looking for someone whose exact name I don't remember and for whom I don't have any address. I don't know the place where he lives or his name. There's not much more I can add to that, is there?"

The young man looked at me for a second. He probably thought I was crazy, and I was thinking the same. After this he said:

"Are you Klaus Kenneth?"

I thought I'd been hit by thunder.

"You are looking for me!" It was Beat Liesch! The placard on the road said, "God Helps!"

Could I have found a better guide in the town of Chur? Everything that followed later was blessed by the grace of the Holy Spirit. I eventually addressed three meetings organized by Beat with up to a thousand people present at each one.

I feel inclined to stop my list of incidents here, in this place, although the list of such events is in reality a much longer one. It is possible that some weaker-minded person may not believe these things and in this way I might be misunderstood. When will we learn to listen less to the head and more to the heart? That is when God will be everywhere present and miraculously visible, and we will receive signs, which could not be recognized if we only used our head. It takes courage to cross over from head to heart.

For a long time He carried me through His house, allowing me to have glimpses into His Kingdom, but there was only one thing that I wished for now and that was to remain close to Him always. There were still moments when my old self took hold of me again. It was then that I felt truly far from paradise. This brought about great suffering, and the pain of being severed from God drove me back into His arms. Without Him there is no life, no love, no real joy…nothing.

But in those early years after my conversion at the cathedral in Lausanne, I was helped by the sensation of having stepped onto a conveyor belt that virtually carried me forward most of the time. When I fell back into my old self, the "old Adam", it felt as though I was turning backwards on the conveyor belt. It was an unnatural sort of movement, and fortunately, these regressions never went disastrously far. As soon as I made a sincere effort to stop moving backwards – by entering into quietness, prayer and repentance – the conveyor belt would transport me back into His arms.

But gradually there came a time when instead of simply being carried, I yearned to carry others who for some reason could not go forward. This would require a total commitment of body and soul. I found an outlet for this yearning in my frequent appearances at conferences, concerts and church events. This way of life became exhausting. Even if 95 per cent of my activities were accomplished successfully in the Name of Jesus, there were wicked attacks from Satan. My life as a preacher and teacher was marred by mysterious obstructions, illnesses, misunderstandings, and temptations. There were spiritual disturbances, practical problems, moments of intense physical pain and anger. One thing in particular I found draining: the discussions that would begin after I gave a lecture. People would question me until the small hours, and afterwards I felt I had used up my last drop of energy. I felt as though I had given part of my life-blood. In some tiny way, I began to understand what is meant by saying that Christ gave his blood for the life of the world.

In many of the Christian communities I visited, I couldn't help noticing certain pathologies which cast a shadow over any real life of the Spirit. In some places, ambitious individuals were concerned with promoting their own name or "brand". In others, there was too much emphasis on intellectual study and book-learning, at the expense of any real movement of the heart.

I remember having a friend at the time, an Irishman as it happens, who gave up his theological studies in Switzerland after nine terms. I asked him why. One reason, he said, was this: "When I saw those learned but naïve students and future priests, who had no experience of life and who were let loose on the souls of people with only their intellectual school-knowledge, it made me tremble for those souls. I wouldn't even place my cat in their pastoral care!"

An excessively intellectual approach to "thinking about Scripture" had led to a cerebral sort of theology, and ultimately to heresy. As my friend realized, his fellow students were like children, but not in a good way. Our Lord's invitation to enter the Kingdom "as little children" is not an excuse for foolish *naïveté*, but an appeal to surrender ourselves, with child-like trust, and then let our Father carry us to the place where He knows we can best serve Him. It will not necessarily be a comfortable place. Anyway, that place is what I half-consciously desired, but had not quite found.

Despairing at times of people who were formally pious, I began to go and see convicts. I went regularly to the prisons to tell the inmates about my experiences and give them hope. Several times I met murderers; some of them were even allowed to come to my lectures, under police guard, of course. I felt very close to them, having been in prison myself. Once I told a group of prisoners who had heard me lecturing, "there is no guarantee that I won't be joining you as a fellow-inmate one day". My point was that even a person who is leading an outwardly pious life can fall into sin. A snake which has apparently ceased biting is still carrying poison inside, with the potential to be unleashed whenever the provocation becomes intense. Weirdly, my less-than-serious intimation of returning to jail myself almost came true. The Swiss police caught me using French number-plates on my Swiss-registered car, and I was prosecuted. The police said it was a serious offence which might lead to a prison sentence. Fortunately the judge let me off with a fine.

At that stage of my life I had no hesitation in travelling thousands of kilometres to share my story. It seemed worthwhile if I could bring one single person a ray of hope through Jesus. I received countless visitors at my home in Switzerland; and then there were phone calls from spiritual seekers, which could last for hours. I was invited several times to visit East Germany, at a time when the Communist regime still seemed unassailable. My hosts were Protestant pastors who would warn me to be careful of the Stasi secret police agents who were present everywhere. I ignored these warnings and on one occasion was barred from entering the Communist state, because I was on the black list. I felt sorry for the people who lived under Communism, an ideology which attracted me at one point. First, they were deprived of their hoped-for paradise on earth, which failed to materialize; and secondly, they had no access to paradise in heaven.

But as I found myself in ever-greater demand, I discovered that Satan kept inventing new tricks. If he didn't succeed in stopping my activities through illness or other cunning acts of chicanery, then he would try to fool me by overloading me with work. I found that I could only devote a relatively small amount of time and energy to each person who sought my help; and perpetual exhaustion gave me a false sense of virtue. Things reached the point where I could neither attend to my own needs nor to those of other people.

I realized that it was time to find a home, a parish, a community, where I could receive advice and support and grow spiritually. Since my conversion, my faith had only seen moderate growth, and this growth was mainly the result of meetings with some well-known Christians. I had tasted some rich spiritual food in my encounters with great living Christians of many confessions: they included Mother Theresa, Thomas Roberts, Daniel Ange, Kim Collins, John Stott, Ulrich Shaffer, Nicky Cruz, John Griffith, Edouard Glottin, Dave Parson, Olivier Clement. But whatever I had received, it had not proved enough to bring about any deep-rooted and *permanent* spiritual growth.

I had received some useful lessons, but I needed a spiritual leader or father, who could answer all the burning questions in my heart when needed. And I had plenty of questions. I read the Bible from cover to cover and it seemed to offer more questions than answers. I was conscious of being on the receiving end of an unhealthy personality cult. I felt that a good number of communities I visited, especially what I call "do-it-yourself churches", with no tradition to fall back on, were treating me as a "star" for their own purposes. By receiving and showcasing me, they were advertising the importance of their own little groups. This kind of treatment was only flattering my ego, while in my spiritual development it became a real hindrance. "Therefore let him who thinks he stands take heed lest he fall" (1 Cor. 10:12). No sooner was I cured of one sin than another was already at the door: if greed were overcome, vanity got the better of me, along with self-praise. If I showed mercy, pride became my downfall. If I learnt, to some extent, to pray, I would accuse others of not having reached my "high state". As soon as I felt the Holy Spirit guiding me, I suddenly considered myself to be "master of the world", although in truth I was driving the Holy Spirit away from me faster than lightning!

In the course of my short meetings with famous Christians, none of them got to know me well enough to say I needed to *humble* myself. In so many Christian communities I came across, I could see the same power-seeking game going on. The game was being played within parish councils, by band-leaders and singers, and between stubborn priests. The result was invariably splits and separations. This, I felt of a surety, couldn't be the true teaching of Christ.

After having had quite close relations with dozens of Christian denominations, I have became convinced that all the scandals and separations in the history of the Church were produced by a single root cause. This is the fact that no one is able to accept "injustice" by following Christ down the path of self-abasement. Everyone wants to preserve his personal dignity and status. Nobody is willing to accept blame and a little injustice. Whereas Christ tells us "not to resist evil" (cf. Matt. 5:39) and Paul says, to "accept wrong" (1 Cor. 6:7), instead of perpetually fighting and going to court against one another.

Back in those early days, I was amazed to notice that many different denominations were striving to win me over to their side. They regarded me as a potential "trophy" or "advertisement". In fact, I felt at home in all places where there was prayer. But I often had the impression that in each of these many communities I detected only parts or a fraction of the teaching of Jesus Christ. There was no common "roof" or connecting Head between each self-made-church. Each one of them focused itself on a Bible interpretation of its own. For some, the mystery of baptism was the most important thing, for others, it was the spreading of the Gospel, for a third group, the focal point was the Second Coming of Jesus, and for others still, serving the Vatican seemed to be all that mattered, based on the conviction that salvation was possible only through the Roman Catholic Church. For the Pentecostalists, baptism in the Holy Spirit was the "one and only" important thing. At every street-corner, a different recipe was on offer. Fribourg, my home town, is extremely Roman Catholic. The priests there suddenly made friends with me and they liked to remind me that I had been baptized a Catholic and of course belonged *to them*. Meanwhile, the Evangelicals pointed out that I had become a real Christian through them. Various kinds of Protestants kept inviting me to be *with them* – about twenty different denominations wanted me. But *to whom* did I really belong? To my taste, too much came from my friends' brains and worldly ambitions and too little from their heart. One day, this piece of advice came to me: "Why don't you pray that God guide you to where *He* wants you to be and not to where *you* would like to be?"

CHAPTER FIFTEEN

A NEW DOOR OPENS

SOMEHOW, THESE PRAYERS WERE HEARD. Christ had already led me a certain distance, and now he would open new doors which would usher me directly into His presence! And this I mean quite literally. One day, I was driving through Lausanne with my old friend Ursula. Suddenly, we almost ran into an unusual looking figure, as he was crossing the street: a slightly stooped and elderly man, with a white beard, who wore a long black robe. A similar but somewhat younger man in the same garb was beside him.

Ursula knew the older man. She asked me to brake quickly so we could stop and talk. We got out of the car. The older gentleman and I greeted each another and he invited us to follow him to a room in a nearby building. Ursula whispered in my ears, "He is a very famous *staretz*."

"What's that?" I hissed back.

"He is an elder, a spiritual father, and his writings have had a tremendous influence on our whole generation – world-wide."

"Is he a guru?"

"No, of course not. He is much more – he is someone like the Apostle Paul or Peter!"

"You must be kidding!" I said. But as I looked at him, I sensed that some mystical power was emanating from this man. We sat down in a nondescript room – seemingly an office or workplace of some sort – and to bring the atmosphere down to earth, I tried a bantering line of conversation.

"Life is so beautiful and colourful – why for God's sake are you wearing such long black apparel?"

Instead of answering, he made a sign with his hand, to follow him to the window. "Look carefully down at the road", he said.

I saw all sorts of cars passing by. Let's say, a blue Ford, a silver Honda, a grey or red Volkswagen, a black Mercedes taxi, a yellow Fiat, and so on. We stared down for a short while. Then he looked at me: "Which car did you like most?"

"Well", I replied, "for me, the most elegant car was the black Mercedes."

"This is why we are dressed in black", he gave back with a playful smile and soft laugh. I liked that kind of humour.

Ursula explained that she wanted to stay and do some work with the mysterious gentleman. I had to go on to the nearby town of Neuchâtel to give a talk, and I said as much.

He responded in a tone that was still playful.

"You know", he went on, "I have some experience in giving talks. May I give you a piece of advice?"

"Please do, I beg you."

"When you start a public lecture, it is always good to begin with a little joke, so that people can laugh. Once they laugh, you will have them 'in your pocket', and they will gladly follow you anywhere. Try it now and tell me afterwards, when you come back, how it worked."

I could see that he was laughing; and as his whole body shook, once more something mysterious was emanating from him. There was a great sweetness about him, and it came from somewhere very deep.

And so, after my return from Neuchâtel, I duly reported that I had followed his suggestion, and that he had been absolutely right.

From the moment of our meeting, my heart and soul informed me with absolute certainty that I had met a saint. As with Mother Theresa, I felt that in front of me was a model Christian. In a split second, he made the deepest and most powerful impression on me – not by theories or lofty theology, nor through his high rank, but through his humour, unlimited warmth, total frankness and, most of all, his overwhelming love for me and respect for my person. All my life I had searched for such a person. This much you could tell for sure: he was love incarnate. I thought that such "wise men" existed only in films or children's fiction – as in *The Lord of the Rings* or *Narnia* – but never in reality.

I was overwhelmed by this 87-year-old man with his kind regard that seemed to see through you in such a loving way, by his understanding smile and long white beard. More than anybody I had ever met, he represented perfection. He was a living icon of Christ Himself. Instinctively, I had no doubt that he was the latest *apostle* to emerge from a 2,000-year tradition. What he represented was a Christian tradition which had never changed one iota of the teaching of Christ. His freedom, simplicity, humility and inner peace were all palpable, and I felt as if I had been embraced by the mystery of life itself. The doors of my heart flung wide open from the very beginning of this unexpected meeting. One thing I knew as an absolute certainty, he was the "one" I had been longing to find. I had found something I desperately wanted. I realized that I had seen pieces of the jigsaw in various churches and communities; all these were now united and combined in the saintly priest-monk, whose name was Father Sophrony.

I sensed that this person was a representative of the True Church, just as Jesus had founded it. A Church which had somehow escaped the effects of deviations, schisms, interruptions, scandals, outbreaks of envy, competitive proselytizing. Of course, as I later learned, these things are by no means absent from the history of Orthodox peoples; but somehow the Church of Father Sophrony, the Orthodox Church, in its essence, had remained pure and intact – that is what I understood. This man was a true incarnation of the Church of Christ with all her saints, elders and fathers, stretching from the dawn of the Christian era as far as our modern age – a living image of Christ. Especially during that second brief encounter, when I reported on my talk in Neuchâtel, my heart leapt for joy and tears poured forth, simply because I was so moved. I must admit that this meeting was indescribably richer than the one I had five years earlier, when I met Mother Theresa. The nun in Calcutta gave me a first intimation that there might be such a thing as unconditional love. Meeting this monk felt like God's direct gift to me. My heavenly father had led me to my spiritual father.

Before I left, I asked permission to take a photo of him.

Elder Sophrony – the picture I took of him

"No!" he said with a stern voice. I was taken aback. What kind of tone was that? Fortunately, he did not leave me in confusion for long.

"You know, dear Klaus, everybody has tried to take pictures of me, so there are hundreds of photos. But they all depict who I am *not*. It's simply enough now. Perhaps you will understand."

I felt a bit sad, because I liked him so much already.

He must have felt my sadness, because he immediately seemed to change his mind.

"All right, I give you permission now. Take some photographs of me. The problem is that I am not yet humble enough."

Humble? I was flabbergasted. Why did such a great and respected soul need to feel humble? Anyway, he took off his glasses and "posed" for me. My heart was overflowing with joy. Somehow or other, this snap had a lasting effect. More than twenty years later, my wife visited a monastery in the Balkans and spoke about Father Sophrony. The nuns showed her a photograph of him and my wife immediately recognized it. She told the astonished abbess that this was the picture I had taken of the saintly teacher on the first day of our acquaintance.

A few months later, I had another meeting with Father Sophrony. By this time I had learned some of the bare facts of my new friend's life. He was born in 1896 and grew up in the intelligentsia of Tsarist Russia. A talented artist with a deep spiritual calling, he had moved to Paris after the Bolshevik Revolution, and then to Greece, where he spent many years on Mount Athos – a peninsula which has been a bastion of monastic life and prayer for the last millennium. He was already considered one of the great spiritual teachers of the Orthodox Christian Church. This was a form of Christianity of which I was only dimly aware for most of my early life. I had suffered no dark experiences with it (as I had endured with Catholicism), but I had no reason to think of it positively either. On my visits to Jerusalem, I had observed Orthodoxy as one among many Christian denominations. It seemed rather exotic, but it did not concern me very much.

So my mind was more or less open when I headed for the monastery east of London, where Father Sophrony had founded a small community, including both monks and nuns, in 1959. The very word "monastery" had a somewhat negative connotation for me, because I associated it with Catholic seminaries, where some very un-Christian things would take place, behind high walls. But I hoped that this Orthodox establishment would be something different, and my immediate impressions were positive.

I found myself in the flat but pleasant countryside in the county of Essex, near the border with Suffolk. The North Sea was not too far away. Father Sophrony had built up his community around an old Anglican church and rectory. The modern buildings, including a newly built chapel, were plain on the outside, but at the very moment I arrived the interiors were being superbly decorated. As I walked into the chapel, I saw scaffolding up to the roof. Father Sophrony himself was working on the ceiling and directing others, creating a pleasant buzz of activity. To this day, the iconography at the Essex monastery is a wonderful example of traditional styles depicted with great freshness and luminosity.

Other surprises were to follow. I was given a pleasant room in the rectory with a large Georgian window. On this and several subsequent visits, Father Sophrony devoted an extraordinary amount of time to a deep and loving dialogue with me. As he walked down the path from his little white cabin and spotted me outside the rectory where I was staying, he would open his arms wide and I would feel a tsunami of love rolling over me. To the amazement of the community, he would sit in my room and talk as though there were no other urgent calls on his time.

Among his gifts was the ability to meet people in the place where they were, even if that place was far from the formal structures of the Orthodox Church. One of my enthusiasms, at that time, was playing the guitar. Sensing this, he invited me to play some of my rock compositions in the refectory, before an audience of bemused monks and nuns. Orthodoxy has a rich musical tradition, but it is based almost entirely on the human voice, with little place for instruments. I still don't know what the community thought of my strumming, but this gesture made me feel profoundly welcome and appreciated.

I had a deeply ingrained habit of acting as a spiritual teacher myself, and I initially had the foolish idea that I would teach Father Sophrony at least as much as he taught me. I shared with him some of my ideas about the Bible, and some of my life-experiences in Asia and Latin America. I must have sounded very naïve, but he always listened attentively. My life had made me wary of formal religious structures, rules and hierarchies. With Father Sophrony, I felt a warmth which transcended all structures.

So strong was the effect on me of visiting the monastery that I immediately felt an overwhelming desire to do two things: to join the Orthodox Church, and to become a monk myself, ideally in this very community. But Father Sophrony's reaction to these ideas proved to be yet another surprise.

The leaders of every other church I knew had wanted me. This man, at least for the time being, did not. He already knew quite a lot about my life, both through intuition and probably from reading a short book about me, which had been published in French. When I began to speak about Orthodoxy and a possible monastic vocation, he responded firmly.

"Jesus is with you, Klaus. It is sufficient. Why do you want to 'stick a label' on your forehead? Why do you want to enter our Church? Go back home and continue on your journey with Jesus."

To begin with, this had me flabbergasted. I was speechless. This response felt like a challenge and a provocation. I felt roused to find out the motives for his "rejection". For the moment, I did return home, but my soul had been touched by an inexpressible mystery that – I hoped – would be elucidated in due course.

But Father Sophrony was adamant that my vocation was not a monastic one. I was not married at the time; there were no legal obstacles to stop me taking monastic vows. But my new teacher told me firmly: "Klaus, you are not meant to live as a monk. God has another plan for you. Go back home and continue to follow Christ, as you have done hitherto."

How did he know? The fact was that he simply knew. As I left the monastery after that first visit, my heart was pounding and I was unable to withhold my tears. It was as though Love had

Elder Sophrony – disciple of St Silouan

appeared and then quit me for good. I was crushed. I cried for hours and hours . . . no way to stop my tears. To have met such Love in person . . . it was just indescribable! It was as intense an experience as the moment when Christ Himself had spoken to me in the Cathedral of Lausanne. Tears, tears, tears. . . .

Back in Switzerland, I continued to participate in meetings, discussions, Bible studies, services, masses and liturgies. I read the Bible and many inspiring books and frequently spoke to Christian communities about my journey towards Jesus. But in my heart I felt more and more uneasy. I sensed clearly that through the work of God something was evolving. So about a year later I returned to Father Sophrony. In the preceding months, my relationship with him had seemed to deepen steadily, albeit at a distance, through my careful study of his writings. In particular, I had pored over his account of what he had learned from his own spiritual teacher, a monk called Silouan, whom the Orthodox Church has recognized as a saint. I found in these writings a depth which was completely absent in the religious writing of the Christian West. That made me all the more determined to find out why I would not be admitted to the world of Orthodoxy.

The second trip to the monastery in England was not much different. The saintly elder was full of love and also full of warnings. He told me:

"Klaus, true faith means to follow Jesus, and this signifies that you must deny yourself, yes, you must even hate yourself. It is not light food to digest – the nourishment we can offer you. You have as yet no idea what difficulties are waiting for a true Christian. Sooner or later the "old self" will return in full force and you might regret ever having set your feet on such a path. This is not the kind of spiritual food you have been used to in Switzerland so far. And indeed I may regret that I advised you to make such a difficult journey. For now, listen to me and follow your heart and Jesus – as you have done recently. That should be enough. Return, go back home to your country."

But Father Sophrony's advice to me was not purely negative. Even at this early stage, he helped me to see some fundamentally important things which I had not previously understood. Above all, he helped me to realize that there are two utterly different kinds of hierarchy and power structure. In worldly institutions, and unfortunately in some religious institutions, too, a handful of powerful and ambitious people scramble their way to the top, and they weigh down on everybody who is placed in lower positions. This is a pyramid of the ordinary kind.

But making a career in the spiritual world does not mean a step-by-step upward climb, obtaining senior positions and honours, with all the satisfaction of being important and famous. On the contrary, a spiritual journey means climbing down, taking a walk downwards into humility, so as to carry others on our shoulders. This walk downwards involves sharing the pain and fear of the people we carry – that is not something that can be done only in theory, or from a lofty distance. We can only sustain others if we ourselves are sustained by Christ.

In an earthly pyramid, as Father Sophrony told me, the people at the top exert power and literally have the world at their feet. This is combined with all manner of hidden or overt fights for prestige and influence. People in each layer are carried on the backs of the unfortunate folk underneath.

In the Kingdom of God, my teacher explained, the pyramid is turned upside down. Christ is at the apex, but that is because he has stooped so low that he is carrying the entire world on his shoulders. Christians are called to be with Christ at the tip of the pyramid, but it is an inverted pyramid. This paradox is indicated by some well-known passages in the Gospel. "Whosoever will be great among you, let him be your minister; And whosoever will be chief among you, let him be your servant." (Matt. 20:26–27).

Indeed, wherever you look in the Bible, there are calls to paradoxical humility. "Do good to them that hate you", "He that shall humble himself shall be exalted", "Love your enemies", "The last shall be first" . . . in a word, the Cross.

To elaborate this point, Father Sophrony began to speak to me of his own spiritual teacher, Saint Silouan. While my teacher was a highly educated product of the Russian intellectual class, the monk Silouan came from much more humble peasant origins in the heart of Russia. But these social distinctions made no difference at all in the monastic realm of Mount Athos, a place of perpetual prayer and spiritual battles. The very idea of spiritual warfare has been virtually forgotten in the Christian West, but as I came to realize it is fundamental to Eastern Christianity. As the Eastern Christian advances in the faith, he or she expects to encounter both angels and demons. Invisible powers will guide our steps, but there will also be negative and destructive powers which set out to prevent us from going forward. Saint Silouan experienced spiritual warfare with extraordinary intensity. After a long battle with the demons, he was blessed with a dazzling vision of Christ. He understood that the demons' greatest weapon consisted of stoking their victims' pride and thus making humility impossible. The antidote to this poison could be summed up in a great but paradoxical spiritual insight – a message from God – that came to Saint Silouan, and was repeated again and again by Father Sophrony: *"Keep your mind in hell and despair not."*

It took me quite some time to understand what this meant. Gradually, with the assistance of Father Sophrony's guidance and prayers, I became acquainted with my own pride, and I realized that pride, first among all the sins, leads us to hell. The more clearly I apprehended my own sinfulness, that part of me which logically culminates in hell, the more I longed to be free from that sinful self and its consequences. This honest and painful recognition – that in a sense, hell is our proper place – triggers repentance and that in turn opens the way for redemption. Exactly for that reason, we must not despair. The more tears of repentance we shed, the more we will be justified, vindicated by God. The world – the realm in which only worldly logic prevails – perpetually seeks to justify itself, to claim that it is without sin, and therefore it will be condemned. By seeing clearly the contours of our own sin, we open up the hope and possibility of salvation. Does this sound like masochism? No. Later, another monk – Father Zacharias, a disciple of Father Sophrony – offered an important elaboration on the idea of self-condemnation and "charismatic despair". Whatever this means, it does not refer to some neurotic psychological state. On the contrary, it calls for a very sober kind of self-understanding.

As I took in this rich spiritual lesson, I began to see why Father Sophrony was not in a hurry to receive me into the Orthodox Church. Sticking a new label on my forehead might seem attractive, but it would not have any magic or instant effect. Yet I still yearned to join my teacher's Church. Whenever I was in his presence, I felt this indescribable something, a world of mystery and love hiding behind his humour. When he laughed – and this happened often when we were together – his whole body shook and he seemed to be carried by a cloud. Who would have guessed that he had been gravely ill for many years?

At the end of my second stay at the monastery in England, he gave me a sort of parting gift, convinced that it would enrich my life.

In every human being, he told me, there is the potential to return to the image and likeness of God, in which we have been created. There was a concrete way to achieve this, he added: the use of the Jesus Prayer, which I had already heard while staying at the monastery.

This prayer, which is one of the greatest treasures of Orthodox Christian spirituality, usually consists of the simple formula: *Lord Jesus Christ, Son of God, have mercy on me, a sinner.* As Father Sophrony told me, "If you say this prayer of the heart regularly, you will see how His Presence will change you."

"Is it not dangerous to practise it all alone?" was my question. "You know that I have some experience in Eastern meditation; but that was a different kind of practice."

"No, don't worry about it", he replied, calming my doubts, "Just do it in a simple way, and avoid all breathing techniques – which *can* in fact harm the inexperienced. Just say the prayer with your lips, and then silently. You have my blessing for that."

St Silouan – teacher of Elder Sophrony

CHAPTER SIXTEEN

HAVE MERCY ON ME A SINNER

AFTER ENTRUSTING ME with this spiritual treasure, about which I understood virtually nothing at the time, he left me to go on my way. At this stage of my life I was uncertain about my own spiritual state. There were times when I felt very confident, probably too confident, and other times when I felt very much in need of help and guidance.

I had realized by now that the world-view of some of the Protestant pastors I knew was too earthly. They seemed to be rather attached to material possessions, and indeed succumbed in a rather obvious way to certain human temptations. I supposed that Father Sophrony was trying to wean me away gradually from such earthly attachments.

In my Protestant world, I had seen some spectacular examples of answers to my prayers. But I knew I had further to go. Perhaps I was destined to undergo some great trial of faith. In some ways, I might have had things too easy. After all, the Gospel says, "Blessed are they that have not seen, and yet have believed."

On the other hand, I had received certain gifts at the time of my conversion in Lausanne, and these had not been taken away. To an extent which amazed me, my life was free from fear. Of course, I would still suffer bad dreams, but even after the worst nightmare I would wake up laughing. Somehow I knew, in my sleep as well as in my waking hours, that Christ had conquered death, and therefore there was nothing to fear. This was an assurance I had received from Christ Himself: *"In My name you will be stronger."* In one nightmare, I saw a towering, ugly giant, who was swinging an enormous club, killing people and destroying houses – everyone was fleeing in panic. When this monster came near me, I simply kept my peace and ordered him to stop this evil-doing. I raised my hand in a "halt" sign and he immediately collapsed and fell to dust.

I had received so many blessings, but there were moments when I was a bit frustrated by Father Sophrony's caution. After all, I told myself, I more or less enjoyed inner peace. I had learned, or so I thought, to forgive, just as I had been forgiven by Christ. What was I still lacking, then? I believed and observed the commandments. I shared the Gospel with others. I prayed. I felt free. But was I really? So why was the elder taking things at such a slow pace? I half-knew the answer, but I couldn't help moaning to myself at times.

The whole situation became clearer when, back home in Fribourg, I started practising the Jesus Prayer, as Father Sophrony had advised me to do.

I understood my own place in the universe better, and above all, I stopped looking at things purely from my own selfish point of view. To quote an image used by Saint Paul, infant's milk became solid food, through constant effort and discipline, but most of all through divine grace. I began to look in a new way at all the earthly problems surrounding me, whether in my own immediate environment or in the wider world, as I learned about it from news reports. Before, bad news in the media used to annoy or scare me, or leave me cold. Now it felt natural simply to pray for the victims of whatever catastrophes were taking place in the world. I felt a personal relationship with those suffering people; they were my brothers and sisters, and their destiny was of real, immediate concern to me. At an earlier time, like most consumers of the news media, I had simply regarded the victims of wars or disasters in far-away places as mere statistics, which would never really make any difference to my life. I suppose that is how most people cope with a disorderly world.

The habit of praying for the suffering people of the world was inspired in part by the writings of Saint Silouan, Father Sophrony's teacher. God always assisted me when great change in my inner life was unfolding. The greater the challenges, the more powerful and palpable was His support. Through the prayers of Father Sophrony, I began to see myself through the eyes of God, and what I beheld there was not something pink or rosy. The "good" Klaus was really a sinner, indeed there were moments when I wondered whether I had the right to call myself a Christian. Father Sophrony had begun to explain to me the way in which "passions" enslave us and prevent us from receiving the Holy Spirit in our lives. I had thought that I was free of such passions, but this was far from the truth. Now I began to understand why Father Sophrony had given me such grave warnings about the dangers that lay ahead. He was a true servant of Christ and thanks to his love and prayers for me my eyes had opened. I realized that I was not free at all.

A struggle against three great enemies began at that very point: my own fallen nature, my old habits, and the demons. During my years of involvement with Eastern religions, I had undergone an intense experience of demons. In the Christian tradition, although this is often forgotten in the West, demons are understood as fallen spirits who follow Satan and try to ensnare us, using our weaknesses. In my case, there were plenty of weaknesses which the demons could try exploiting. Among these were vanity, anger, love of food, addiction to television, thoughts of revenge, lack of patience, rushing, laziness over certain tasks. Then there was the problem, which probably touches over 90 per cent of men, of sexuality. These weaknesses of mine had been unpleasant companions for many years. They were ugly to look at and hard to uproot.

It is easy to talk about taking refuge in Christ. But when you start to see and feel the heavy load of your offences against the God of Love, when you perceive your weaknesses and repeated falls from grace, then you need a friend. I had such a friend in Father Sophrony, and this was a most precious gift. I was able to speak with him at a much deeper level when we met for the third time. He gave me some powerful advice, because I was ready to receive it. I was no longer naïve enough to think that those dark inhabitants of my inner self could be overcome without super-human help. Habits are called habits, because they are patterns of behaviour which are not easily uprooted. Certain vices had been deep inside me for the last 25 years or so, and by now felt quite at home. They clearly thought they had a perfect right to remain in that comfortable place for the rest of my life.

To have any chance of changing this, I had to understand things in a new way. Every time I gave in to any bad habit, it was as if yet another wire had entwined itself with all the others, forming a thick rope that I could not break without some extraordinary help. The elder began to explain how these ropes might be broken, by helping me to understand my thought process better. He explained how thoughts come into our conscious being. Such an understanding, he said, was the basis of any attempt to deal with bad thoughts and the bad actions which followed them. He said there were five stages. First the "enemy" would plant a suggestion, then a sort of inner dialogue with this suggestion would begin. Then we give in to the suggestion, which is the point where sin arises. Then the mind is taken captive, and we fall into some sinful action. If, finally, the action is repeated many times, it turns into a passion, to which we become enslaved, and we will experience a recurring desire to commit the sin all over again.

"There are several ways to fight against bad thoughts", Father Sophrony said. "Either you take refuge in the Jesus Prayer and concentrate on His Name and presence, or you lift up your hands, stretch them towards the heavens, and ask Christ to come to rescue you." At that point, the elder placed himself next to me and showed me the movement. At that moment he looked incredibly young and vigorous.

As I came to realize, there is a place in our hearts where the Spirit of God should be enthroned. But when old habits prevail, the evil one has usurped God's position, and the tragedy is that this has happened through our own free will. Consequently, I had to declare war on these habits, in order not to remain their slave. The fortunate thing, I knew, was that whenever I truly turned to

Christ, the demons would be automatically dethroned, dissolved like harmless soap bubbles. When Our Lord said, "Resist not evil", He was telling us not to focus anxiously on evil or become obsessed with it; we should simply call upon Christ and evil would be dispelled instantly. The way to invoke Christ, as I was now learning, was to use the Jesus Prayer – while remembering that the Name of Jesus Christ is not a "talisman". We cannot call on His name without having faith.

But there is no guarantee this battle will be easy. I now understood much more clearly Christ's saying in the Gospel: "If any man will come after me, let him deny himself, and take up his cross, and follow me" (Matt. 16:24). He doesn't say, "Please follow me on a nice easy path, and sing Hallelujah." Reaching the Kingdom of God requires great force, even something akin to violence, albeit in a spiritual and not literal sense. We need not merely to understand our old selves, but to *hate* our old selves. This was something very different from practising yoga or Zen, in order to find inner "balance" and relaxation.

Christ's way was virtually the opposite. The encounter with God can be an overwhelming, even a terrifying experience. We read in the Old Testament the saying of Isaiah (6:5): "Woe is me … my eyes have seen God!" The insights that I was granted with the help of Father Sophrony could also be painful – although they were joyful at the same time. I began to see why the elder had hesitated before inviting me to taste such bitter-sweet experiences.

As I grew in self-knowledge, I asked myself, was it Satan who convicted me of sin and showed me the bitter truth about who I *really* was, or was it the work of the Holy Spirit? In one sense, Satan is the accuser; he gloats over our sins, and plants in us the idea that the situation is hopeless, irredeemable. The Holy Spirit works in the opposite way, by revealing the truth but simultaneously showing us a way out, a way to regain our freedom.

In the tragedy of Judas, we see a man who could only hear Satan's gloating, and therefore hanged himself in despair. By contrast, the repentance of Peter, who had denied Christ three times, was a moment of tears and pain, which led immediately to redemption. The same mixture of tears and hope can be seen in Christ's command to Saint Silouan: *"Keep your mind in hell and despair not."*

The grace of God and His mercy made me aware of an "abyss of evil" inside me, and hence guided me on to the path of humility. The more I learned to glimpse reality through God's spectacles, and the less attention I paid to the views and judgments of the world, the closer I came to Him. At the same time, I experienced my sins and shortcomings with ever-greater clarity. "Father, forgive us, as we forgive others. ..."

I had set out on a road which led towards repentance, self-denial, and confession. I could see that at the end of this road lay real freedom and happiness. To an increasing extent, my sights were focused on eternity. I no longer judged who was bad, good or close to God, but my only question was: How far *am I* away from Him? This threw me into His arms and made me long to benefit from the Holy Sacraments of the Church, like Confession and Communion.

What a difference from the Eastern teaching of karma and of reincarnation! Only gradually did I begin to see clearly the difference between the promise of Christ, that *"In My name you will always be stronger"*, and the cold *technique* used in meditation, which at best skilfully covers up our wrongs instead of *revealing* them.

"Through the Jesus Prayer the Holy Name of Jesus is revealed", said Father Sophrony. And in turn, through the Holy Name, uttered in faith, our sins are revealed. This had nothing in common with a mantra, mandala or any other spiritual technique like transcendental meditation or yoga, as he explained:

"The main difference lies in the fact that the Jesus Prayer is based on the revelation of the One, True and Living God. He can be experienced personally, as you can confirm yourself. Whereas practitioners of Eastern meditation try to elevate themselves towards an anonymous and impersonal "Absolute", by divesting the mind of all that is ephemeral and "relative", including their own existence. Relying on their own willpower, the practitioners want to reach a state of non-being, by dissolving the person through extinction of the "atman" (soul). In Christ, on the other hand, we find our true selves.

I once asked the elder, "Father Sophrony, are you still a sinner?"

He replied, "Of course I am, and believe me, I am the worst of all sinners." This was unbelievable for me. He then began to ask me questions about my life, not in a spirit of scolding, but as though he expected to learn something. He really gave me the impression that I was the one who could teach him something, from my rich spiritual "knowledge". His incredible humility was not a game – I could sense that. On the contrary, he was perfectly sincere. The result was that I developed ever greater trust and faith in him. He must have seen that as a result of my former experiences with gurus, clergymen and teachers, there was still a lot of hidden distrust in me. Through his wise attitude, I allowed him to take me by the hand and lead me into the realm of trusting love. And did not Christ do something similar? He came to our "human" level and emptied Himself of His divine glory – with the aim of teaching us trust and love. Father Sophrony was showing me his own version of "self-emptying", which as I now realize is known in Orthodox Christian language as "kenosis".

You should have seen Father Sophrony coming to the church to celebrate the Divine Liturgy, as the Eucharist is called in Orthodox Christianity. As he entered the church, I had the sense his feet were not touching the ground; that he was floating on air. The Liturgy itself transformed the church into heaven and you wouldn't notice time passing by . . . one hour, two hours or more. What does that mean, when you are in the presence of Christ, when you are out of time and space? This was truly holy ground. This was my true "home".

In the Protestant churches, where I had my first intimation of Our Lord, there was real love of Christ and good knowledge of the Bible. But there was something lacking in the worship. It appealed to superficial emotions. I had seen people being "slain in the Spirit" at Pentecostal services, writhing on the ground as loud music boomed around them. I came to the conclusion that this was a shallow psychological phenomenon. As I had learned more from

Father Sophrony, I began to realize that his kind of humility was something quiet and sober. It led to tears, but not to hysteria.

With all my being I felt that Orthodox Christianity was simply the "right worship" – worship worthy of Christ – and indeed, that is what the word means. (It combines the Greek words "orthos" – *straight* or *correct* – and "doxa", *glory*.) And hence I longed to participate fully in the life of the Orthodox Church. In a way, the word "Orthodox" was not particularly important to me; I simply had the sense that I had discovered the Church as Christ meant it to be. And that made me long to participate fully in the Mysteries of the Church.

I told the Orthodox priest in Geneva that I wanted to be baptized in his church. Initially he did not agree to a full baptism. In the Western world, people who convert from, say, Anglicanism or Catholicism to Orthodoxy, are usually received by a rite known as "Chrismation" or "anointing with oil". This, so to speak, complements the original baptism, by invoking the Holy Spirit. The fact was that I had been baptised a Roman Catholic when I was a three-year-old boy, and the Orthodox priest knew this.

My heart told me, however, that I needed to make an absolutely new beginning in my spiritual life. "Father", I complained to the elder, "they refuse to baptize me! They give all sorts of reasons – but I know, deep inside, that I do not merely need a Chrismation. I want to be baptized. What shall I do?"

"Are you really sure about this?"

"One hundred percent!"

"Would you like me to pray about the situation?"

"Yes, if you kindly could do that …"

"I promise. But make sure not to tell anybody that I am praying for you! You agree? And then just tell the priest next time you see him you want to be baptized. Nothing more."

I can't remember exactly what I said to the Orthodox priest in Geneva, though I certainly didn't mention Father Sophrony. But I do remember his reply: "Yes, you can be baptized next Saturday!" O my beloved and holy Father Sophrony. …

Once he had made up his mind, the priest, Père Jean, could not have been more helpful. He borrowed a large plastic vessel, normally used in wine-making, for my immersion. On the appointed day a group of perhaps 15 friends, some Orthodox and some not, drove the 140 kilometres from Fribourg to Geneva. A respected local politician and founder of Fribourg's small Orthodox community, Noël Ruffieux, agreed to be my godfather. There was a discussion over whether I should be given a new name. In the end, Père Jean ruled that I should have the name, "Nicholas", which was the same as my old name, "Klaus". I have two very powerful memories of the ceremony. One is the moment when I was asked, three times over, to renounce the devil and the powers of darkness. This took place outside the church, a modern building in the suburb of Chambésy. The baptismal candidate is supposed to indicate his renunciation by spitting – this is a kind of exorcism. Most people just make a token spitting gesture; but remembering my past involvement with demonic powers, I spat with all my might, from the very depth of my heart. I felt I was spitting in Satan's face. The second unforgettable moment came after my third immersion, when I rose from the tub, wearing my white shorts. Tears rolled down my cheeks. They were tears of unmixed joy. I had "put on Christ" and now, in every way, it was official and permanent.

The problems and dilemmas that I brought to Father Sophrony were practical as well as spiritual. One concerned an early version of the book that you now hold in your hands. A London publisher had my life-story and was amazed by it. He offered a global publishing contract. I met up with one of his employees, signed a contract and was duly paid a good amount of money, merely for my signature. Cheerfully, I calculated that – if I had read the contract correctly – I might be a millionaire within one or two years. But when I went to the monastery to discuss the matter, Father Sophrony was not at all enthusiastic. He was worried for my soul.

"So you have made a contract with the publisher?"

"Yes, Father – I signed the paper in London." I felt proud that I was about to become a famous writer. Probably I could do a lot of good with all the money I would soon see coming in.

"This will probably lead you into great danger. You are like a new-born baby, so inexperienced, you do not know about the snares

of the enemy", he continued. "I have written several books in my
life and you can trust me that I know what I'm talking about."

"But, Father, I have signed the paper and they have paid me
a rather large sum of money already – there's no way back", was
my response.

"Would you like me to take care of this situation? I mean,
would you mind if I prayed about it?"

"No, of course not, you certainly know better than me, and I
trust you. But I believe it's too late now."

His will be done! Before even a single copy had been printed,
the publisher sent me a letter which declared that they had put
the whole contract "on ice" until some later date. Bang! Such was
the power of his prayer – a miracle had happened. More than 15
years later, I re-wrote the whole story and I realized how mundane
and misleading my first script had been. I had glorified my old
adventures and built a monument to the ego of Klaus. Thank you,
dear Father, for your protecting power. Now you have the new
version in your hand and can judge for yourself whether I have
succeeded in giving all the glory and honour to Christ. I beg the
reader's pardon if I have not. By the way, the publisher in London
never wanted any money back and has ceased trading. Some people
have suggested to me that the very idea of writing about my own
life is foreign to the Orthodox spirit. All I can say is that the final
preparation and publication of this book was undertaken under
the close guidance of my spiritual father. It is my prayer that it will
lead people to Christ, and not encourage them to glorify me.

After shelving, for a while, the idea of publishing my own
memoirs, I spent a lot of time in the English monastery's bookshop.
The writings I found there were a never-ending source of life-giving
wisdom – and this was the case with many works, not only the
ones which referred to the Jesus Prayer. These books, written by
countless Church Fathers, were so rich in content and so moving
that I had the impression I would have enough spiritual food to last
me a lifetime. *These books read you*, rather than vice-versa. In fact, it
would be enough to read only one of them: they all repeat the same
point in different ways, and this has been so since the beginning

of the Christian era. They are "translations of the Gospel" into everyday life. If you manage to absorb one book and put its teaching into practice . . . you're a saint! One writer that I found especially helpful was the 20th century Serbian bishop, Nikolai Velimirovich, who has been proclaimed a saint by the Church.

In different ways, all the spiritual books I read helped me to wrestle with the sin of pride. Pride chases the Spirit of God away. Pride is demonic and creates suffering and loneliness – this I had known for 36 years – and in this monastery I found myself in a "training camp" of meekness. Humility is the only realm where the demons cannot follow you. That is what I have been taught by Father Zacharias, a member of Father Sophrony's community who remains close to me. As Father Zacharias puts it, "Humility is hell for the demons".

Once again I return to the question that I was always asked by other Christians: "Why does nothing happen when I pray?" The answer, of course, is in the Jesus Prayer. On my third visit, Father Sophrony allowed me a glimpse into an "open mystery". In what follows, I not only return to some of our discussions, but also to the writings of Father Sophrony in his book, *His Life is Mine*, because this completes what I may have forgotten from our talks. When I was taking notes during and after our meetings, the elder slapped me lovingly on my shoulder and said:

"Don't bother with writing notes now. You will forget them. But don't worry, because you will find all we have been talking about in my books."

How right he was! Actually, I don't know how, but sadly I lost all these papers, except the book with his dedication to me. So when I finished one of his books with the title, *His Life is Mine*, I was so touched that I wanted to translate it into German. I considered Germany a spiritually poor country. Because of Hitler and the aftermath of the war, all the great writers from Russia or other Orthodox countries went to France, Italy, the USA, and elsewhere. Consequently, the rich and life-giving thoughts in the books of such great authors were nowhere to be found in German. (Quite the contrary. Ironically Saint Nikolai Velimirovich ended up in the

German concentration camp of Dachau! But he survived.) Being of German origin myself and having suffered from the Germans (for example, I ended up in prison on August 13th in 1961, when they started to build the Berlin Wall, because on just that day I was on my way to Berlin), I felt a strong love for its people, whom I wanted to have access to such wonderful literature.

So I asked the elder's blessing for the translation. At first he was just smiling. He must have thought, "Poor Klaus has no idea". But after I insisted, he gave me his blessing. This blessing had the effect that I found great help in this challenging task: two people helped me to "perfect" what I had accomplished more or less "imperfectly".

A great part of the book is about the Jesus Prayer, and everything Father Sophrony taught me about it was now accessible to others. He said the following:

It is not sufficient to say the prayer with just your lips. Particularly important is the fact that you love Him Whom you are calling upon. This cannot happen by the automatic repetition of the prayer or even through thoughts. If we do not strive with all our strength to keep His commandments, we call on His Name in vain. God warns us clearly about not uttering His Name in vain (Ex. 20, 7). In pronouncing the Name of Jesus we have to be not only conscious of the presence of the living God, but also of His true wisdom. When people blame God for all the problems, wars and injustice in the world (e.g. why does God allow this?) the opposite happens; man crucifies Jesus once again, instead of crucifying himself together with all his sins, while through His forgiveness man would be freed of the remorse for which he himself is answerable. This is the drama of today. On the one hand, mankind accuses God for all the evil in the world, whilst on the other, the Christian begins his journey by getting to know God, in order to discover for himself if the blame belongs to Him or is in the heart of man.

During the short interval that is the present, which we call "our time", it is given to us to seek the road back to Paradise, from which we have been banished through Adam's sin. John the Baptist tells us how to do this: "Repent! For the Kingdom of Heaven is at hand." (Matt. 4:17). Repentance is possible only in admitting one's own weakness. And recognition of weakness is only possible when we call on the Name of Christ in the Holy Spirit. This is the umbilical cord that connects us to God, and through which we receive divine power, and without which we can do nothing. I repeat emphatically: this is not possible by any kind of meditative technique. A theology based purely on theory, without any application in practice and using the intellect instead of the heart, as far as the Name of Jesus is concerned, has always created a void in the lives of Christians. It is not enough to remember the name of Jesus, mentally or psychologically. Such a prayer is a waste of time – just as the prayers said for material gain remain "unheard."

The way out of this world's dead-end is prayer, and one kind of prayer is the "Jesus Prayer", effective only, though, when it is said in faith and through acknowledging our sins and in asking to be forgiven. Yoga and physical exercise cannot free us, as some learned people try to convince us (1 Tim. 4:8), only grace and our faith combined with endless patience. These attributes seem to have been lost in our fast-moving world. We want everything and as quickly as possible. Esotericism offers the promise of immediate success. I urge you strongly not to make such a mistake. "Beware of false prophets, who come to you in sheep's clothing, but inwardly they are ravening wolves" (Matt. 7:15). And these kinds of wolves had devoured not only myself in the past, but, since the publication of my book in various languages, I find myself confronted with the alarming drama of men and women who have fallen prey to them – both inside and outside the Church. If the general and worldwide apostasy continues at this rate, I believe the end of time is close at hand.

But let me return once more to my search through Hinduism and Buddhism. This kind of meditation allowed me to experience the "other world", and to enter into a realm beyond my understanding. It was a way of blanking out thoughts, a way of finding myself in a certain mystical state out of time and space. For a while, I believed I had found some peace regarding the constantly changing phenomena of the world and its events, and I even had the impression of touching eternity. But the living God, the God of all truth, was never present in any of those experiences, which were nothing more than veiled self-love, where we monks admired ourselves – in a veiled way – as if we were the centre of the universe. As Father Sophrony puts it: "The practitioner attains divination of self, instead of seeing God as divine. That was the very same tragedy that caused the fall of Adam. Some *one* had been changed in a subtle way, into some *thing*: through non-personal meditation, man can no longer know the personal God, and so becomes the victim of the idea that he himself is God. Once he has been blinded, by the fascinating beauty of the experiences mentioned above, man is on the road to self-destruction, believing that he can return to the same state that he was in before being born. In the Eastern religions this state is an impersonal one. Man destroys himself and becomes a nonexistent, a non-entity, whereas God performs the reverse, and calls man from non-being into being, through the great I AM."

Therefore our prayer must always be personal, face-to-face. God created us to become partakers, through grace, of His Divine Being, *without* destroying our own personal identity. This is what is meant by "immortality" and it can only be attained when we overcome the world. Unfortunately, I find the opposite, both in the world as well as among all different Christian denominations: no one struggles to overcome the world, but instead, with all their might, people, priests and pastors try to avoid asceticism, suffering and the authentic struggle against worldly influences. Self-justification makes them blind to God's plan, which lies behind these phenomena. But the message is clear: We must conquer the world in Jesus. Alienated from God, we are the conquered ones, enslaved by death. Because of this, it is a foolish mistake, no matter for what reason, to fall into the net of false teachers and prophets, and replace the wisdom of the Church with their human ideas and teachings and so rejecting Christ Himself. In this way, love for our neighbour changes to insensitivity and love of self. This leads to alienation not only of self, but also of those around you, and even of the whole of humanity, which has been created as "One" in God. The most terrifying enemy of love of neighbour is pride and it has great power. We must strive to conquer pride, because the desire for power means death to the soul. If we cannot destroy our lust for power and pride from within, then all our prayers are a profanity to the Name of the Holy One.

Humility is the only medicine against pride and lust for power, as Jesus has shown us.

If we strive with all our heart to hold the presence of God and His Word at the centre of our lives, we shall, little by little, be freed from sin, passion and negative liaisons. The true Christian prayer consists in a continuous calling on the Name of Jesus: *"Lord Jesus Christ, Son of God, have mercy upon me (a sinner), and upon Thy world."* "This prayer of the heart", as the elder always repeated, "learnt in good time, is then effective when we are on our deathbed and even when our brain is no longer fully working. In ceaseless calling on the name of Jesus Christ, we clothe our soul for the journey into eternal life. Without humility a sincere prayer is not possible. Humility shows up our true self, which is a state of alienation from God!" This state of alienation is its own hell, the place where I had lived for 36 years. However, if we accept to see our real fallen state and hence condemn ourselves, in His mercy God will justify us. If we find excuses to justify ourselves or blame others, then God will condemn us (Matt. 23:12). This is the mystery of life: the grace of prayer brings salvation and opens the door of life after death. This is the path "from head to heart".

The purpose and reason for this book is to testify to the fact that forgiveness and transformation are possible always and everywhere, no matter what the circumstances, when our hearts are moved by the love of the Father, the Son, and the Holy Spirit. The inexpressible love of God overshadows us, just as it did before the world was created. Whosoever opens his heart, into him that LOVE will enter, here and now.

Lord, Jesus Christ, Son of God, have mercy on me, a sinner.

Publications by
Mount Thabor Publishing

Saint Gregory Palamas: The Homilies (2009). The first full edition of all sixty-three extant sermons by St. Gregory.

Selections from the homilies, arranged thematically:

Mary the Mother of God: Sermons by Saint Gregory Palamas (2005).

The Saving Work of Christ: Sermons by Saint Gregory Palamas (2008).

On the Saints: Sermons by Saint Gregory Palamas (2008).

Forthcoming in 2012

The Parables of Jesus: Sermons by Saint Gregory Palamas.

Miracles of the Lord: Sermons by Saint Gregory Palamas.

Ecclesial Being: Contributions to Theological Dialogue, by Constantine B. Scouteris (2006).

The Enlargement of the Heart: "Be ye also enlarged" (2 Corinthians 6:13) in the Theology of Saint Silouan the Athonite and Elder Sophrony of Essex, 2nd Edition, with indexes, by Archimandrite Zacharias (2012).

The Hidden Man of the Heart (1 Peter 3:4): The Cultivation of the Heart in Orthodox Christian Anthropology, by Archimandrite Zacharias (2008).

Remember Thy First Love (Revelation 2:4-5): The Three Stages of the Spiritual Life in the Theology of Elder Sophrony, by Archimandrite Zacharias (2010).

Born to Hate, Reborn to Love: A Spiritual Odyssey from Head to Heart, by Klaus Kenneth (2012).